THE MULTIMO[?]

THE MULTIMODAL WRITER

Creative Writing Across Genres and Media

JOSIE BARNARD

First published 2019 by
RED GLOBE PRESS

Red Globe Press in the UK is an imprint of Springer Nature Limited, registered in England, company number 785998, of 4 Crinan Street, London, N1 9XW.

Red Globe Press® is a registered trademark in the United States, the United Kingdom, Europe and other countries.

ISBN 978–1–137–60792–8 hardback
ISBN 978–1–137–60791–1 paperback

A catalogue record for this book is available from the British Library.

A catalog record for this book is available from the Library of Congress.

For Steve, Louis and Ynys

CONTENTS

INTRODUCTION

We are in the throes of what is being called the 'fourth industrial revolution'.[1] The ability to move between different types of writing, often at speed, is increasingly essential for writers. From blogs and Wikipedia entries to Twitter and Instagram, from smartphones to tablets, e-books and online multiplayer games, genres are morphing and new technologies are emerging apace. These are exciting times. Changes in new media technologies bring new opportunities. However, the pace of change is so fast it can feel hard to keep up. It is estimated that 65 per cent of children entering primary school will go on to work in jobs that do not yet exist.[2] We must prepare for technologies that have yet to be invented. To be 'deeply literate' in the digital world means being at home in a shifting mix of words, images and sounds.[3]

How do you come to feel at home in such a shifting mix? Even a seemingly comprehensive set of new technological skills could soon be obsolete.

Creative flexibility is key. The aim here is to enable development of such creative flexibility. This book presents a model of creativity that is designed to provide a writer with the means of building writerly resilience and embracing the wealth of new and emerging writing and publishing opportunities.

The fourth industrial revolution, featuring as it does the emergence of, for example, artificial intelligence and smart systems, is arguably a more comprehensive and all-encompassing revolution than anything we have ever seen. We take its impact for granted. Even a very basic website might feature text and sound and visuals and space for users' comments. Via a few clicks on a smartphone we can access maps and podcasts and archives all over the world. Such multimodality is now an everyday reality, it is the 'experience of living'.[4] In a digital age, the need to work with different technologies and genres is par for the course for everyone. Just take the UK, the government's 2017 policy paper, *Digital Strategy* puts digitality at the centre of the country's future.[5] Within 20 years, it says, 90 per cent of all jobs will require some element of digital skill, and, an estimated 1.2 million new technical and digitally skilled people will be needed by 2022 to 'satisfy future skills needs'.[6] There is pressure on us all in today's workplace to be proficient and resourceful communicators using a range of software and platforms, able to pick up fresh technological skills near-instantaneously. Users of new media technologies must be able to, 'assimilate messages from multiple sources; manage such inputs resourcefully and swiftly; turn such inputs into one meaningful, persuasive, relevant output; and remain adaptable as new technologies emerge'.[7] This kind of speedy, savvy weaving between screens and applications and inputs and outputs is at odds with the (strangely persistent) cliché of what it is to be *a writer*.[8]

According to the cliché, *a writer* is someone who works alone, perhaps with a chewed favourite pen or a battered second-hand typewriter, most likely in a cold and icy garret, periodically hurling screwed up pages into a waste paper bin, removed and isolated. Such a state of isolation may be useful for targeted sections of time but it is not, as we move deeper into the twenty-first century, a realistic long-term aim for writers, or even necessarily desirable. To remove ourselves like that is to remove ourselves from possibilities.

We might be on the go on a train checking emails or social media posts on an iPad when, suddenly, notification of a short story competition pops up, and, we have exactly the story, it is the right length, its theme and subject fit, and it is there in cloud storage ready to be converted into the correct format and submitted immediately. Visuals present new opportunities, with emojis starting to feature in fiction not as illustrations but as part of the language used to tell the story.[9] We can, using open-source tools such as Twine, write simple interactive online stories with no need for any knowledge of computer coding at all.[10] YouTube has a thriving book reviewer community; anyone can set up a camera in their living room, kitchen or bedroom and upload a review, becoming at the click of a button a 'BookTuber'.[11] Meanwhile, 'technostress' is a recognised phenomenon and on the rise.

For creative writers, whether established or aspiring, the task of embracing multimodality – its challenges and opportunities – is key today. Yet, literature that can help is, as will be discussed, notable by its absence. This book addresses that gap.

The Multimodal Writer has been arranged so that it is possible for readers to take a non-linear route through, if preferred. Perhaps your priority is to start developing skills needed to tackle multimodality immediately via practical exercises, in which case you could jump straight to Chapter 5, start an assignment and come back to other chapters later. Alternatively, the book is designed to give, if read from start to finish, a full picture of the context that makes a new kind of creative flexibility necessary, what such creative flexibility comprises, how to develop it and how to apply it. The aim is to provide an easily readable text, one that is underpinned by extensive research and can be picked up for use in an everyday context. The personal voice adopted reflects a belief shared with scholars such as Davis and Shadle that learning is 'autobiographical and passionate'.[12] I have, over 30 years of writing fiction and non-fiction books, scripts and articles, faced the challenges addressed here. In my role as a teacher spanning 20 years, I have helped a wide range of creative writing students with a wide range of writerly aims face these challenges too. That experience informs this book throughout.

Although Friedrich Nietzsche was talking about friendship when he described it as a 'problem' worthy of a 'solution', his words apply well here.[13] The 'problem' of how the 'digital turn' affects creative writing is certainly worthy of a 'solution'. With the programme of research that underpins this book, I set out to find one. To do this, I roamed widely, on occasion crossing disciplinary boundaries. Observing that there are, of course, 'risks' attached to 'fraternizing with "other" disciplines' (perhaps even 'grave risks'), Olson suggests that *trespassing* should be viewed as a 'scientific technique', one that has particular value in a field such as literacy.[14] Similarly, Webb and Brien refer to a 'bricoleur-bowerbird' approach, whereby, in the field of Creative Writing, practice-led and traditional research methods inform each other.[15] Thus, as Webb and Brien phrase it, research and writing 'draws on modes from across the human sciences' and occurs 'through the filter of creative practice'.[16, 17] Where necessary, I have 'trespassed', applying Webb and Brien's 'bricoleur-bowerbird' approach along my journey.

Creative Writing has arrived at a stalemate in which the opponent is itself. On one hand there is fear of the challenges multimodality brings and, on the other, recognition that it is necessary to embrace multimodality wholeheartedly and immediately. *The Multimodal Writer* is an intervention intended to help break that stalemate.

First and foremost, this book is for creative writers. It is for established writers who want to embrace change. It is for students of Creative Writing and writers who are just starting out. It is also for tutors who want to help students thrive in a writing and publishing landscape that is being transformed by the digital turn (the assignments feature 'Tutor notes' so they can be used in a classroom setting). It is hoped, too, that the book will be helpful to academics working in the field of Creative Writing as a research method, an area of enquiry that, as scholars including Kroll and Harper and Peary and Hunley note, although still not yet well documented, is growing.[18, 19] However, above all this book is intended to be a practical tool. The aim is that it will help anyone who is grappling with the task of storytelling in our fast-paced twenty-first century to identify and delineate problems and find solutions.

The Multimodal Writer has at its centre one question: how can a writer optimise his or her ability to move between genres and technologies? To consider this question, the volume is grounded in theory, brings an experiential perspective and provides empirical evidence.

This introductory chapter lays out the book's rationale and aims, positions it with respect to existing Creative Writing research, sets out the methodology, and outlines the book's contents. The first matter for the rationale concerns the term 'multimodal' and how I will be using it.

Not surprisingly, given the way multimodality now permeates every aspect of our lives, the study of multimodality is widespread; its impact can be seen in areas as diverse as medical discourse, urban planning, popular music and space exploration.[20, 21] There are now large bodies of work on multimodality, most notably in the fields of Linguistics, Stylistics and Rhetoric and Composition. It is beyond the scope of this volume to provide a literature review of this research. Although there is undoubtedly room for a work that provides close analysis of how research into multimodality in these fields might be applied in the field of Creative Writing, that is not this book. However, a brief discussion of multimodality is pertinent.

At its most basic, 'multimodal' simply means many modes, or, to give *The New Oxford English Dictionary* definition of 'multimodal': 'characterised by several different modes of activity or occurrence'.[22] With the dramatic changes in new technology and new media (with the advent of the Internet, Web 2.0 technology and social media, for example), since the early 2000s, 'multimodal' as a term has gained new importance.

Historically, printed prose has been considered distinct from other media, with a book viewed as a stand-alone object (we 'talk about novels and books of poetry as *mono*graphs', observes Krauth[23]). Of course, we can continue to approach *books* in this way (as single, discrete items), and, 'print,' as Koehler puts it, 'will always be one force available to the creative writer'.[24] However, new media technologies have added new ways of producing and consuming stories. Smartphones, e-books, computers and other technologies enable users to access text, audio and moving images simultaneously. In a book, such as a novel, meaning is generally conveyed primarily via the printed *text*. On a website, by contrast, text does not stand alone, it may not even carry the main burden of meaning-making. Instead, text operates in conjunction with pictures and sound; the different elements work together to create the meaning/s that each reader takes away.

In fields such as Linguistics; Stylistics; and Rhetoric and Composition, then, 'modes' are generally considered to be channels of communication such as 'speech; still image; moving image; writing; gesture; music; 3D models; action and colour'.[25] Thus a website might feature all these modes. However, Page cautions against 'mode-blindness': 'What might count as a mode is an open-ended set, ranging across a number of systems including but not limited to language, image, colour, typography, music, voice quality, dress, gesture, spatial resources, perfume, and cuisine'.[26, 27] She cites Baldry and Thibault, who 'describe multimodality as "a multipurpose toolkit, not a single tool for a single purpose"'.[28] Bowen and Whithaus keep their definition broad by choice, because, 'it is our belief that we cannot restrict how individuals might interpret and employ multimodality as a way of thinking about designing and composing beyond written words'.[29] As Kress states, in the twenty-first century – with the exponential growth of new media technologies – 'we cannot afford to be reluctant in introducing necessary new terms', since, 'using tools that had served well to fix horse-drawn carriages becomes a problem in mending contemporary cars'.[30]

In Creative Writing, we need new tools. With this book, I have set out to provide some.

Storytelling is not just about selecting a set of words. To be fully immersed in the task of telling a story – finding the right metaphor, the right pace, the right narrative arc – is to forget everything around us. Story telling is a complex, exhilarating experience that can stimulate all our senses and ignite our very core. A piece of technology that is new to us (or a technical glitch or a power surge which crashes everything) can in an instant make us feel possessed only of ridiculously limited knowledge and inept fingers that seem perpetually to be pressing the wrong key. It can feel as if technology is coming *at* us and we are diminished. With sensations and memory and the unconscious factored in, we can feel that we are multimodal and better equipped to not merely tackle but instead embrace the challenges and opportunities that come with new media technologies, and to begin to enjoy the possibilities. This is why the term 'multimodal' is so useful in Creative Writing. If we conceive of ourselves as multimodal beings then, when we are tackling multimodal problems, we can feel we are fighting fire with fire.

Breaking from the usual use of 'multimodal', Bowen and Whithaus and Palmeri refer to 'multimodal composing'.[31, 32] To describe writing that incorporates different modes (e.g. text, images, sound), Millard and Krauth instead refer to 'multimodal writing'.[33, 34] This book, as its title suggests, gives 'multimodal writing' the central role. Like Bowen and Whithaus, I choose to keep my definition of multimodality broad, and, where necessary, I introduce new terms in order to give flexibility and dynamism to how individuals may use material presented here to develop their own unique, uniquely appropriate and sustainable creative practice.[35] Throughout, the aim is that all terminology is clear in its local context. In addition, this section provides summary definitions.

A book that has pictures as well as text, for example, can be considered a **multimodal object,** thus a Medieval illuminated manuscript is multimodal, as is a web page.[36] In this work I adopt this definition. I define a **multimodal writer** as: a professional writer who, making use of multimodal strategies, sets out to – and does – produce a body of published work that comprises different genres (e.g. fiction and non-fiction) that is disseminated through a range of media (e.g. social media, radio, print journalism and book publishing). I define a **multimodal writing practice** as: a creative approach wherein the inter-relationships between and among a writer's decisions and different media and modes contribute to the production of meaning. A multimodal writer who has adopted a multimodal writing practice works to develop a personalised model of creativity robust enough to enable improvement of productivity and/or creativity in the face of fast-paced change. Like Page, I consider what might count as a mode to be a 'fluid' and 'open-ended set', and, I recognise that 'narrative is not just a means of artistic expression but a fundamental endowment' in which 'the role of sensory modes remains vital'.[37] Thus this book argues that to work effectively in a twenty-first century writing and publishing landscape characterised by multimodality, a writer must acknowledge and learn how to deploy an *internal* multimodality – that is, all the mental work (conscious and unconscious) a writer does before operationalising any medium. The channels of communication that work together are, in this context, primarily internal channels – intellectual enquiry, moods, sensations, for example – which are brought to work together by a co-ordinating unconscious capacity which I conceptualise as the 'inner auteur'.

Gibbons observes, 'One of the strongest criticisms of existing approaches to multimodality is the lack of empirical testing behind them.'[38] Gibbons, Bateman and Page point to the need for models in multimodality studies that are, as Page phrases it, 'systematic', 'replicable' and 'flexible enough to embrace the rich diversity of all that multimodality encompasses'.[39, 40, 41] The aim here is to provide such a model for creative writers.

This book shows how, by harnessing an internal multimodality (and, in doing so, establishing a multimodal writing practice), a writer can build a personalised model of creativity suitable for the twenty-first century writing and publishing landscape. The aim is that this personalised model of creativity will enable a systematic and ongoing transfer of skills (or, 'remediation of practice') that will ensure the development of a practice robust enough to effectively and productively negotiate challenges and embrace opportunities as they arise. (For further discussion of *The Multimodal Writer*'s model of creativity and its component parts, see Chapter 4.)

There is some resistance in the field of Creative Writing to engaging wholeheartedly with the digital turn. There are writers, of course, who delight in new media technologies. However, others do not.

Considering the challenge of upgrading from a typewriter to a computer in 1990 and then, later, starting to use the Internet, the novelist Deborah Moggach writes: 'Our bond with our tools is a profound and secret one; if we venture into the new technology, will we somehow lose our voice?'[42] Kim Wilkins describes how the pressure on practising writers to build and maintain author platforms – which might include websites, Facebook, Twitter, Instagram and Pinterest – combined with the addictive nature of social media can undermine creativity and productivity.[43] In an article titled 'Shutting out a world of digital distraction', Carl Wilkinson notes that writers including Zadie Smith, Nick Hornby and Dave Eggers have all used computer applications 'configured to increase productivity by blocking access to the internet' having apparently 'taken to heart a comment made in 2010 by Jonathan Franzen, who famously wrote portions of *The Corrections* wearing a blindfold and earplugs to reduce disruptions: "It's doubtful that anyone with an internet connection at his workplace is writing good fiction"'.[44]

In the Creative Writing classroom too, a sense that writers can *either* embrace digitality *or* write 'good fiction' continues to hold sway. 'In spite of calls for more digital engagement and the fact that students are arriving on campus with digitally connected skills,' observes Taylor Suchy, 'creative writing classrooms are generally "low tech and quaintly humanistic"'.[45] Such resistance is not unique to Creative Writing. Surveys of academics across a range of disciplines show a deep wariness and even outright dislike of the idea of embedding technology and/or social media in teaching delivery.[46] Comments suggest that the sheer breadth of options – Twitter, Facebook, Prezi and more – induces a strong feeling of what could be termed 'innovation fatigue'. Fears that social media may be 'a distractor to pedagogy' continue to be widespread.[47]

Consequently, there remains, as Sheppard observed a decade ago, a 'lack of resources bridging practice and theory' to support multimodal writing practice.[48] This lack is especially acute in the pedagogy of Creative Writing. A number of creative writing scholars have noted the gap: 'Creative writing has been hesitant to join other writing disciplines, such as rhetoric and composition and professional writing, that have recognized the importance of digital influences,' say Dean Clark, Hergenrader and Trent.[49] They remark that despite the recent growth in Creative Writing scholarship, 'very few works deal with the profound impact digital technology has on our discipline'.[50] 'There has been much discussion about the implications of digital technologies for reading and publishing via new platforms such as tablet computers and e-book readers,' say Millard and Munt, adding that 'By contrast, there has been relatively little discussion about shifts in writing *practices* as a result of these technologies and processes.'[51] Krauth says 'one set of concerns … remains largely unaddressed: the ways in which creative writing, or creative writing studies, engages with, understands, responds to, and thrives in an age of digital writing'.[52] Yet, the Quality Assurance Agency *Subject Benchmark Statement* for Creative Writing in higher education states: 'In a rapidly changing technological environment in which employment opportunities exist, it is important that students have the opportunity to work and experiment in writing for new and still emerging media.'[53]

In short, then, as Dean Clark puts it, 'Creative writing instruction needs to change.'[54] But, change is difficult, and, as indicated, literature that addresses the question of how to effect such change has been notable by its absence.

Outside the pedagogy of Creative Writing, there is a range of work that addresses how to teach and create multimodal assignments, most notably in the field of Rhetoric and Composition. Works such as those by Selfe (2007), Wysocki et al. (2004), Lutkewitte (2014) and Davis and Shadle (2007) consider how to theorise, teach and mark multimodal compositions. Straddling the fields of Composition Studies and Creative Writing, Koehler's *Composition, Creative Writing Studies, and the Digital Humanities* (2017) points to the urgency with which the pedagogy of Creative Writing needs to step into the twenty-first century and engage fully and enthusiastically with the digital turn. In their collection *Creative writing pedagogies for the twenty-first century* (2015) – which builds on work done in Rhetoric and Composition by transferring pedagogical models developed there into the field of Creative Writing – Peary and Hunley point to the need in Creative Writing for a 'new tier of nuanced pedagogies' that are not merely 'tried on' from other disciplines.[55] There has for many years been what many see as an over-reliance on the workshop method resulting in a need for, as Micheline Wandor puts it, a 'genuinely radical overhaul of CW teaching methods'.[56, 57] Such an overhaul has started. In the field of Creative Writing, there is now a small but growing body of work that considers how practitioners can begin to tackle some of the challenges presented by a writing and publishing landscape characterised by multimodality. Krauth's *Creative Writing and the Radical: Teaching and Learning the Fiction of the Future* (2016) examines how experimental writers from the past – such as Laurence Sterne, Apollinaire and the Dadaists – have, in effect, been 'rehearsing' the possibilities of multimodal writing for over a century. As well as presenting a 'history of radical change in creative writing processes', Krauth aims to 'initiate new ideas about the teaching and learning of creative writing in the current climate'[58]; with this in view, Krauth provides some practical examples from history that writers can follow and adapt for contemporary use (e.g. Dada 'cut-ups', which foreground collage and curating in the process of creating narratives[59]). Works such as Smith's (2005) *The Writing Experiment: Strategies for Innovative Creative Writing*, which provides classroom assignments with a bias towards 'experimental approaches', features suggestions for ways of embedding new media technologies in pedagogical projects.[60] Dean Clark et al.'s (2015) collection *Creative Writing in the Digital Age: Theory, practice and pedagogy* also makes important strides in addressing the impact of multimodality on creative writing. As well as theoretical chapters by authors including Harper, Koehler (2015), and Amato and Fleisher, Dean Clark et al.'s book features practical chapters with suggestions for assignments, including by, for example, Clancy, Scheg and Brown Jr. on using digital storytelling platforms, social media and computer code in the Creative Writing classroom.

However, the works cited above tend to focus on producing discrete multimodal compositions (how to make a single website, for example). Yet, multimodality requires writers to shift between types of writing. From a writer's perspective, this is perhaps its key and most challenging characteristic. Even within a single website, it may be necessary for the person creating it to write in a number of different genres and use a range of technologies (perhaps embedding a vlog and a podcast alongside a blog, for example). Further, if an author is creating such a website (complete with vlog, podcast and blog) as part of the job of building an author platform to promote his or her work, then the material on the website is just one section of the bigger picture of the job of being a writer. That is, while creating the website, he or she may also be writing a proposal for a screenplay and/or working to get to grips with an unexpected and unwanted software upgrade; as well as posting every few hours on social media, he or she may be completing a full length novel.

In summary, then, a key problem for writers in the digital age is the need to move, often at speed, between different genres and technologies. The works cited above highlight the fact that a new kind of creative flexibility is necessary. None of these works set out to directly address the question of how to develop such creative flexibility even where they acknowledge the pressing nature of the question. For example, Krauth presents a 'radical' writing process as 'a constellation of particular strategies that produce ground-breaking outcomes'.[61] He does this by 'Following Deleuze and Guattari who put rhizomatic root systems on the agendas of cultural and literary studies'.[62] It is not his aim to delineate how a writer today might develop such a constellation of interconnected, 'rhizomatic' strategies; he only observes the possibility. It is, however, a driving aim of the current volume.

There are many books on how to write fiction *or* screenplays *or* creative non-fiction *or* video games.[63] The question of how to move between genres and technologies remains a neglected area with only a small amount of published scholarship existent. In the field of Creative Writing, works such as those by myself (Barnard, 2015, 2016, 2017, 2019), Krauth (2014, 2015, 2016), Harper (2015) and Koehler (2017) address the fact that, in a digital age characterised by multimodality, a new kind of creative flexibility is necessary. Barnard (2017) and now this book address directly the linked questions of how to develop such creative flexibility and how to then apply it to moving between genres and technologies.

Having set out the rationale and aims and positioned myself with respect to existing creative writing research, I will now turn to the methodology. As noted, the book is grounded in theory, brings an experiential perspective and provides empirical evidence. That is, in keeping with a book that considers how to tackle a complex and dynamic writing and publishing landscape, I have pursued a number of avenues of investigation.

One of these was to look at my own experience of moving between different types of writing for different modes of dissemination.[64] My practice is characterised by an occupational eclecticism. Thus the auto-practitioner study uses three decades' practice and output as a prism through which to view the early stage development of a sample multi-modal writing practice (see Chapter 2).

I also looked to other writers' experiences of moving between genres and technologies, in order to gather together a range of tactics and see where crossovers lay. I interviewed eight writers of international standing who each have 19 years or more experience of multimodal writing practice: Simon Armitage, Robert Coover, Jim Crace, Juliet Gardiner, Charlie Higson, Rhianna Pratchett, Kate Pullinger and Michèle Roberts. The writers interviewed represent a wide range of types of movement between different types of writing for different platforms. The study set out to obtain a range of honest, reflective observations. Some inter-viewees had extensive experience of new media technologies, others did not. Because no one technology or set of technologies is central to the development of multimodal writing practice, the writers' responses were significant in their indications of how technologies that are new to an individual are approached and how creative flexibility can be sustained (see Chapter 3).

For the assignments – as well as drawing on my own years' teach-ing experience – I was informed by the work of scholars including Kress, Yancey and Harper, who delineate some of the skills writers need to nego-tiate the twenty-first century writing and publishing landscape.[65, 66, 67] Kress, Yancey and Harper all highlight the need to teach adaptability and, as Kress phrases it, 'reflective risk-taking and exploration of the unknown'.[68] They point to the need to enable the ability to creatively transform templates and they write of the need to help develop skills associated with becoming 'members of a writing public' who engage in real-time discourse via 'non-linear and connective' new media technolo-gies that blur the boundaries between professional and personal life.[69, 70] Additionally, each assignment was trialled with Creative Writing students (undergraduate and postgraduate), with student feedback gained for each trial (see Chapter 5).

Thus, the auto-practitioner study, author interviews and in-class trials were used in combination to help identify the key resources (internal and external) and skills needed for an effective multimodal writing practice. Using these findings, a model of creativity was then developed and trialled as a class assignment itself, to test whether it can be used as a template to help a writer identify the appropriate resources, develop the set of necessary skills and then orchestrate those components parts effectively in order to enable him or her to work productively and creatively as a multimodal writer. (For further detail of the methodology, see Appendix III.)

Having sketched the methodology, I will turn now to the arrangement of the book's chapters, which are intended to work together for the creative writing practitioner. The aim is that reflection on theory will inform reassessment of and alterations to creative practice.

Chapter 1 outlines the twenty-first century writing and publishing context that makes a new kind of creative flexibility necessary. It considers how developments such as the Internet, Web 2.0 technology and social media are affecting not only how we write but also how we read and even the nature of creativity. Chapter 2 addresses a key issue that arises from this endemic volatility: it is simply not possible for a writer to be permanently abreast of all the technological changes; he or she must find ways of reusing existing creative resources (i.e. 'remediating' his or her practice). To consider how a writer might do this, Chapter 2 presents an auto-practitioner study (as indicated above), providing an experiential perspective.

Chapter 3, by contrast, sets out to provide more broad-based insights. Each writer's experience of moving between different types of writing and technologies is, of course, unique. Through author interviews, this chapter considers whether, within the vast range of individual responses to the experience of moving between genres and technologies, there are patterns and commonalities that can be observed.

A number of scholars have, as noted, pointed to the need for models that are, as Page phrases it, 'systematic', 'replicable' and 'flexible enough to embrace the rich diversity of all that multimodality encompasses'.[71] Chapter 4 delineates such a model for use in the field of Creative Writing. It shows how writers draw on a mix of internal and external writerly resources and utilise a range of writerly personas in order to move between different types of writing. It proposes that, to orchestrate the huge number of possible permutations, a writer utilise an 'inner auteur' to identify which resources and personas, in what combination, will be optimally effective for particular moves between different types of writing. Thus, the model of creativity is designed to account for the fact that decisions about moves between types of writing must factor in the need for a writer to continue effectively with each separate type of writing *and* maintain an authorial voice that is at once appropriate for each separate genre and recognisable as the author's own, unique, authentic voice.

Chapter 5 contains a set of assignments designed to support the development of a multimodal writing practice and enable construction of a personalised model of creativity that is complex and robust enough to enable effective negotiation of the twenty-first century writing and publishing landscape. Areas identified as key to the development of a robust multimodal writing practice have specific assignments allocated to them. For example, the assignment titled 'Talking it over' is designed to develop skills in real-time discourse, 'Picture this' is designed to develop skills in transforming templates, 'I "♥" looking' is designed to develop skills in deploying visuals and 'Story mash-up' is designed to develop skills in non-linear storytelling. Although readers may choose to apply new media technologies, neither complex equipment nor specialist technological knowledge are required for any of the assignments. Jenkins et al., Leahy and Dechow, Pittaway and others suggest that new media technologies be embedded with *play* as a guiding principle. The intention is that all the assignments embrace this principle.[72, 73, 74]

Rounding up this introduction, then: *The Multimodal Writer* sets out to both provide theoretical background and serve as a practical tool to help writers face challenges and embrace opportunities robustly, effectively – and with pleasure. Enjoy!

1 TWENTY-FIRST CENTURY WRITING AND PUBLISHING: A WIDER CONTEXT

Writing and publishing have arrived at a new juncture. We can expect the unexpected on a regular basis. Novice writers who start publishing on fanfiction sites might attract the interest of mainstream publishers and become bestsellers overnight, with oft-cited examples of writers who have made such stratospheric leaps including E. L. James and Anna Todd, whose *Fifty Shades of Grey* and *After* became international bestsellers.[1, 2] Rupi Kaur – one of 'a burgeoning group of young "Instapoets"'[3] – gained a huge fanbase on Instagram and went on to sell 1.4 million copies of her first book, *Milk and Honey* while still in her early twenties.[4] Established writers have direct access via the Internet to existing and new readers worldwide. On Twitter, Joyce Carol Oates, Salman Rushdie, Margaret Atwood and Stephen King have 193,000, 1.2 million, 1.9 million and 5.2 million followers respectively. Authors with traditional portfolios can embed more experimental work simply by making it available online. To accompany the publication of his book *The Last London*, for example, Iain Sinclair released extracts from his collaborative sound and music CD on Soundcloud via his website.[5, 6] Online additions like these can be actioned with a few clicks of a computer mouse. Media technologies mean that a novelist could have uploaded, published and begun promoting via social media a new eBook – and made sales – within a matter of hours, or even minutes.

The pace of change in the twenty-first century publishing world is fast.

Publishing, then

A state of change is not unique to the twenty-first century, of course.

When Johann Gutenberg invented the printing press in the fifteenth century, he revolutionised how text can be disseminated.[7] After a long period of prohibitively expensive, hand-crafted hardback books, the invention of the steam press in 1814 made mass paperback printing possible.[8] The rapid spread of literacy following the 1870 Education Act brought a huge new readership and new wave of book sales.[9]

Yet, despite such changes, from the eighteenth century till the start of the twenty-first century, the basic mainstream publishing model remained essentially the same, with publishers as gatekeepers.[10] Whether independently or via literary agents, authors submitted their manuscripts to publishing houses (such as Collins, Gollancz, Penguin and Random House) and commissioning editors chose which manuscripts to accept for publication. In this traditional publishing value chain, 'publishing activities such as editorial, marketing and design are all performed by the single entity of the publisher'.[11] Thus the traditional mainstream publishing model can be summed up simply as: 'AUTHOR → PUBLISHER → READER'.[12] It is a model that gives the publisher a very tightly controlling position.

Exclusion from mainstream publishing did not necessarily stop dissemination of writers' works. In nineteenth century England, for example, one politically radical publisher decided to evade the government's tax on paper by printing on calico.[13] In Soviet Russia, to avoid censorship, multiple copies of subversive texts were typed out and circulated secretly to readers who themselves typed out more copies in order to distribute the subversive text still further.[14]

However, these are examples of radical self-publishing; they were exceptions to the mainstream publishing rule. By contrast, in the twenty-first century, 'The traditional value chain,' note Squires and Murray, 'is being disrupted and disintermediated at every stage'.[15]

We are in the throes of a revolution as dramatic as Gutenberg's.

Publishing, now

'A democratisation has occurred. A different hierarchy is now formed by writer, publisher, book production, and reader,' says Krauth.[16] 'On the internet, everyone's an author, every scrap of prose a publication,' notes Baron.[17] From the hypertext novels of the 1980s to locative narratives of the 1990s to twenty-first century transmedia storytelling and technologically 'augmented' traditional books, or, 'a-books', new ways of producing work continue to emerge.[18, 19] There are a whole host of storytelling platforms, apps, resources and tools that can help you make anything from interactive videos to augmented reality games and artificial intelligence

(AI) chatbots.[20] The 'Internet of Things', whereby 'Wireless technologies, microcontrollers, services and the Internet' converge, means information exchanges can take place between, for example, lamps, smartphones and items of clothing.[21] It is possible, using easily available prototyping tools, to turn workaday household items into scriptable 'actors' and create an interactive installation.

The possibilities for storytellers are endless. Changes continue to crash in and cause new changes. There are too many to enumerate. However, two well-established changes can be picked out as particularly significant in the world of writing and publishing: the Internet and Web 2.0 technology.

The Internet globalised communication, thereby fundamentally undermining mainstream publishers' roles as gatekeepers. Authors no longer need the approval of an established literary agent or editor, they can simply publish work themselves, globally.[22] 'The old problem of getting books into people's hands has disappeared – if it's published on the appropriate platform, it's already there'.[23]

With communication globalised, the advent of Web 2.0 technology enabled online interaction, thereby further altering the role of traditional publishers.[24] Web 2.0 – the technology that makes social media possible – means that, instead of messages simply going out (as in the traditional publishing model), users can comment on those messages or demonstrate approval with actions such as clicking 'Like' on Facebook or retweeting on Twitter. Thus Web 2.0 technology enables writers to build reputations dynamically via online author platforms.

Peer-to-peer recommendations have always carried more weight than, for example, an advert in a newspaper.[25] On social media platforms such as Wattpad, on which writers publish their work, peer-to-peer approval is core to the infrastructure. Writers work as part of a community, clicking the icon that indicates they are 'following' other writers and responding to their stories (with clicked 'votes', for example) as well as producing their own. Scholars such as Davies stress the significance of Wattpad's structure as a *social network of connections* that may appear informal but, critically, provide individuals with opportunities to increase their status within the network.[26] 'Every follow and read of every chapter of every story is logged and the total displayed on the user's profile', says Davies.[27] Reciprocity means that 'reads and votes can expand exponentially into the millions'.[28]

Until relatively recently, the consensus was, as Philip Roth puts it, that 'writers should remain in the shadows'.[29] The consensus has changed.

Miranda Hart gained extensive advance publicity for her second book, *Peggy and Me* (2016) – a story about her pet dog – through initiatives including starting a Twitter account for her dog and inviting potential readers to 'share stories about their pets ... using the Twitter tag #AndMe'.[30, 31] International bestseller Paulo Coelho has spoken about how his novel *Adultery* (2014a) was inspired by interactions on social media with readers.[32] In 2013, Neil Gaiman worked collaboratively with his readers via social media to create twelve linked stories: 'So the plan is,' he said, 'I'm going to write them, but they're going to be absolutely inspired and illustrated by you'.[33] Gaiman posted twelve questions on Twitter and in direct response to the answers received, he wrote *A Calendar of Tales*.[34]

These examples make clear that social media is not necessarily just about self-promotion for writers, not by any means. The 'feedback loops' between writer and reader have become highly complex. Some have sped up. A reader need not write out a letter of praise or criticism longhand and post it to the author via 'snail mail' via the author's publisher anymore, he or she can post thoughts about the work direct to the author on social media. Meantime, writers who are researching new books often send out requests to readers via social media for information and writers such as Gaiman and Hart (above) involve readers directly in new projects.

As well as affecting how work is disseminated and promoted, then, changes that have arrived with the twenty-first century have affected the very nature of what it is to be a writer and reader and even the nature of creativity.

Writing, reading and creativity

Some aspects of the publishing world that are important for writers are under threat. One is the author-editor relationship.

It is exciting, of course, that a 'democratisation' has occurred. 'Unsolicited' author manuscripts are known collectively in the publishing trade as 'slush piles'. 'Slush piles' can be big, it can take companies' employees a long time to work through them. If a writer can simply self-publish, his or her main feeling might be of elation that an impediment has been surmounted. The whole process speeds up and a sense of agency is regained. However, it is not just every scrap of *grammatically correct* prose that becomes a publication on the Internet. The 'send' or 'publish' buttons work just as well whether a piece has typos or not. There are other issues at stake here too. Sometimes, when at work on a substantial project such as a novel or full length screenplay, writers need a 'critical friend' to help see both where major rewrites are needed and how to approach revisions. Sometimes, it is the author's literary agent who acts as a 'critical friend', giving overview editorial comments on the manuscript; traditionally, the role is taken by the publisher's editor.

Bruce Chatwin's work *In Patagonia* has been described as 'probably the most influential travel book written since the war'.[35] Chatwin's editor was Susannah Clapp. Describing their work on *In Patagonia* as 'a completely collaborative process', Clapp recalled: 'we spent a summer going through the manuscript, sometimes each with a manuscript on our knees, sometimes looking at one manuscript, reading out every line. Bruce would pace around and I would query something, he would dispute it or not dispute it ... What he would do is, go home, look at what we'd considered, come back' – and the detailed, lengthy discussions (about sentence structures, turns of phrase, particular adjectives) would continue.[36] In the most productive author-editor relationship, observes Betsy Lerner in *An Editor's Advice to Writers*, the editor is 'like a good dance partner who neither leads nor follows but anticipates'; supporting and cajoling by turn, a good editor helps the writer negotiate the 'gift' of writing, which can also feel like a 'whip'.[37, 38]

Alternatively, *time* can take on the role of 'critical friend', and prove surprisingly effective. Writers often talk of putting a draft piece of writing 'in a drawer' for a while in order to gain a critical eye on his or her own work. It depends from writer to writer. A week, month or year might be the period needed to enable a writer to see the work's faults. Whatever time span works best, to identify and action solutions, the writer must be able to go back to a draft ready and able to dissect – and herein lies another problem.

New media technologies have highlighted the need for self-editing skills. Yet, they undermine the close reading skills that support self-editing skills.

As Hayles observes, new media technologies mean that, more and more, we practice hyper reading.[39] Readers are considered to be so time-poor that online magazines now often put the estimated reading time at the top of an article (e.g. '6 min read', '5 min read'). The optimum length of a block of text is often guided by the size of a screen; many social media platforms give *character* rather than *word* limits (e.g. Twitter and Pinterest with 280 and 500 character limits respectively). We skim, we fragment, we jump between small, often disparate blocks of text. While welcoming hyper reading, Hayles stresses that the deep attention that is needed for close reading is a 'precious social achievement', and it is in crisis.[40] As Francine Prose notes, to learn their craft, writers must engage in extensive, critical reading 'putting every word on trial', 'pondering each deceptively minor decision'.[41]

It is not only editing and close reading skills that are under pressure in the new online publishing environment. It has become easy for writers to research, write, interact with readers and other writers and even publish without leaving their desk, so much so that writers could begin to retreat from the real world. Live events could seem redundant. Now that everything is so easily to hand online, why go to the bother and/or expense of travelling to a literary festival?

It might seem surprising that the popularity of literary festivals has increased. YouTube and TED Talks alone provide more content than it would be possible for one person to watch in several lifetimes. Literary festivals got off to a relatively slow start in the UK – the Cheltenham Literature Festival (one of the oldest) did not open its doors until 1949 – but then, from the 1990s on, the number of literary festivals grew 'exponentially'.[42] By 2008, there were enough to warrant a website titled simply 'Literary Festivals UK', which says there are now over 350 literary festivals in the UK.[43] The Edinburgh Book Festival opened in 1983 with 30 events; in 2016, the 'Ed Book Fest', as it is affectionately known, hosted some 700 events.[44] Meeting authors and hearing them read in person has gained new potency in the twenty-first century. The authors' 'real presence' – their mingling and chat – gives readers, says Meehan, the 'impression of a special kind of intertextual and even inter-authorial buzz, as [readers] move steadily through the narrative of the festival'.[45] Publishers also love literary festivals. They hope that author appearances will translate into sales. Indeed, some authors feel they are being commodified, with Alexander McCall Smith talking to Channel 4's Matthew Cain of an increased pressure on writers to *perform*: 'I think what has happened is the publishing industry has become a bit more like the entertainment industry in general, where there is this expectation that you go out there and meet people and have an impact.'[46, 47] Such events can be stressful too. If you are 'trolled' on social media, you can block the troll. At a live event, any comments have to be faced and responded to immediately, in person, in the flesh.

In an era in which remote digital communications can make us feel alienated and isolated, live interactions are perhaps more important than ever for authors.[48] Aside from the desire to make sales, it can be hard to pinpoint the value for authors of attending literary festivals. Author and festival-goer Caro Llewellyn suggests that a vibrant literary festival scene is 'an important and happy sign of the intellectual and moral health of the nation'.[49] Being part of a sign of intellectual and moral health is reward in itself. At live events, body language can be read. On a sofa or on a blanket on the grass with a cup of tea or glass of wine, conversations can take unexpected turns, surprising information and fruitful ideas can emerge. Referring to some of the many literary festivals up and down the country from Budleigh Salterton in Devon to Berwick-upon-Tweed in Northumberland, author and literary critic Erica Wagner talks of loving the fact that each festival has its own distinct 'vibe'.[50] A 'vibe' that is contributed to by the smell of the grass, half-heard laughter and murmured chat resulting from hearing a romance novelist followed by a historian is not something that can be accessed via a wireless connection. Tempting as it may be to save the train or bus fare, writers should, as writer and Creative Writing academic Jonathan Taylor notes, continue to, 'Go to events. Talk to readers and writers. Perform [their] work out loud to audiences.'[51]

Just as being in a live environment interacting with other writers and readers can be helpful, so too can the feel of a favourite pen. Of course, writers can and do continue to use biros and typewriters. Indeed, as this book will show, choosing to use 'old' technology can be an important choice that aids creativity.

However, hard copy index cards may be brilliant when an author is trying to plot out a story, and he or she can experiment moving bits of plot about on the floor, but when it comes to hammering through the final draft with a deadline looming, a computer's cut and paste function is invaluable. Even if a writer chooses to eschew new technology while creating a narrative, the moment the story arrives at the publishing house, it will become part of a workflow that involves digitalisation.[52]

Technology has always been something writers must contend with. Denis Baron points out that a pencil is a technology.[53] However, previously, when the pace of technological change relating to writing was relatively slow, writers could – and did – become fiercely attached to particular tools (a gold-nibbed pen, or a particular weight of watermarked paper, for example). Such tools can become central to a writer's creativity, hence novelist Deborah Moggach's description of a writer's bond with his or her tools as 'profound', 'secret' and so precious that his or her authorial voice could depend on it.[54] Increasingly, tools cannot be relied on to last. Hyptertext novels were hailed in the 1990s as an exciting new means of storytelling, then faded almost completely from fashion.[55] New digital media and the associated rapid-fire change – featuring what can seem like perpetual updates of hardware and software – undermines the chance of growing attached to particular tools and practices.

Grappling with new tools, then – learning what tools can do (and discovering their limitations) – has become an integral part of the experience of reading and writing. So, too, has working with multiple platforms. How we read has changed.

'[T]he traditional reading path for writing', says Krauth, 'is linear, chronological, and causative, while that for images is spatial, juxtapositional, and comparative.[56] In multimodal productions, these reading paths intertwine with each other, and vary each other's shapes and effects'. Reading – for example on websites – is now often 'non-linear'. Two readers may enter and leave the same website at completely different points and take completely different journeys along the way.

Some video games allow players to become active producers of game-related content.[57] Previously associated perhaps primarily with the games industry, such user interactivity is spreading. In Charlie Brooker's *Black Mirror* television series, a 'gamechanging' episode titled 'Bandersnatch' allows viewers to interact with the narrative, making choices that result in different story outcomes.[58] No longer passive consumers, readers and viewers are often 'prosumers', buying and reviewing books on Amazon, for example, writing their own entries on Wikipedia as well as reading those of others.[59]

Declaring that diversity is 'your best friend', Wendig says, 'There are too many ways and means nowadays to choose just one method of storytelling.'[60] When we create multimodal publications, we have access to an infinite combination of possibilities. A range of modes can be operated by one multi-skilled person near-simultaneously. Via a single interface, he or she can question at a range of points whether to use speech, music or a video clip, for example, to tell part of a story: 'Multimodal texts,' notes Lauer, 'are characterized by the mixed logics brought together through the combination of modes (such as images, text, color etc)'.[61] Visuals cannot be ignored by writers, says Takolander.[62] Gifs and photographs can all easily be incorporated into narratives. Use of emojis in journalism is predicted to increase.[63] Xu Bing's *Book from the Ground* tells the story of one day in an office worker's life entirely in the symbols, icons, and logos of modern life, including emojis.[64] Novelist David Mitchell's experiment with Twitter fiction, '@I_Bombadil', featured tweets that are 'rife with caps, emojis, photos, links to YouTube videos, hashtags and so forth'.[65] That's on one hand. On the other hand, as well as pointing to the opportunities for including visuals that social media provides, Mitchell's Twitter fiction points to the constraints of the platform. Twitter has a strict character count. For a story such as Jennnifer Egan's serialised Twitter story 'Black Box', each tweet is written so that, as well as being part of a longer story, each tweet can stand alone.[66] This constraint cannot fail to affect the writing style. The means of delivery has taken on a newly central role, notes Yancey, and, 'what a shift in the means of delivery does is bring invention and arrangement into a new relationship with each other.'[67] As users access websites, download PDFs and upload photographs, cutting and pasting links and refashioning their own and others' text, 'selection and text-making as *bricolage* becomes the signifier of a contemporary notion of creativity', notes Kress.[68]

For new and established writers alike, the kind of movement that is now a routine requirement for writers (between tools; between modes of dissemination) does not, as indicated, come without cost. The work needed to maintain online author platforms – posting new pictures on Pinterest, updating events information, for example – can 'lead to distraction, anxiety, self-blame and stasis: all of these are the enemy of resilient writing', notes Kim Wilkins.[69] Nicholas Carr describes the Internet as 'an interruption system. It seizes our attention only to scramble it.'[70]

By January 2011, less than a year after her decision to self-publish her novels, Amanda Hocking was selling 100,000 copies of her books a month and had arrived on the Kindle bestseller list; by 2012 she was 'dealing with technical glitches on Kindle, creating her own book covers, editing her own copy, writing a blog, going on Twitter and Facebook to spread the word, responding to emails and tweets from her army of readers' and, 'burned out by the stress of solo publishing', she signed a deal with mainstream publishers, St Martin's Press in the US and Pan Macmillan in the UK.[71] It is of note that when Hocking concluded that she was 'burned out' by the stress of these demands – of Kindle, of social media – she was still only 27.

As well as embracing diversity in terms of platforms, many writers are starting to pay close attention to areas that were traditionally the preserve of literary agents – such as copyright details agreed on contracts – thinking ahead to a time when they might want to self-publish. In this new writing and publishing landscape, there is just too much to do and know.

It is not surprising if technostress has come to the fore. Equipment becomes faulty and software redundant with a frequency that can make it seem we are always dealing with one 'techno crisis' or another.

The notion of 'digital natives' (that is, the idea that all young people are automatically at ease with all new media technologies simply because they have grown up in a digital world) does not help either. In fact, the idea of digital natives is now widely accepted to be a myth. Certainly, says Letter, there are 'power users' and 'digital addicts', but research has shown that many young people's use of technology is actually 'passive, solitary, sporadic and unspectacular', which is perhaps only to be expected.[72] At any age, we might seek a 'comfort zone' when it comes to new media technologies. Yet, the myth of the digital native has stuck quite stubbornly, and, its negative effect is two-pronged. The myth can make younger users of new media technologies embarrassed to admit it if a lack of proficiency is revealed. Defensiveness can result, and, consequently, the myth can actually inhibit learning.[73] Meanwhile, the myth can make more inexperienced and/or nervous users of new media technologies feel that everyone else knows how to do whatever it is they are struggling with and that they must be deficient for not being able to work it out more easily.

One important reality that applies to everyone ('power users' and nervous users alike) is this: the pace of change as regards writing technologies is so fast that it is not possible for anyone to be expert at everything for all times. There will always be a point at which a new technology is new to a writer and so may present difficulties.

To recap briefly, then, changes that have been heralded in with the digital age that affect writers and writing practice include threats to skills in self-editing and close reading. There have been additions, some that we already take for granted, such as non-linear reading patterns, others that are actively unhelpful, such as technostress and the myth of the digital native. Some aspects of Creative Writing that previously felt clearly delineated may now seem blurry, even perplexing.

Voice

'Voice' has long held an important place in the craft of Creative Writing.[74] Creative Writing textbooks reiterate time and again the 'requirement' that each author finds an 'authentic' voice for long-form work such as novels.[75] All well and good, but, to support long-form work, as noted, it is now widely expected that authors should post on author platforms that feature, for example, Facebook, Twitter and Pinterest accounts, and here too, his or her voice should be 'authentic'. We tend to think that being 'authentic' on social media should come naturally. According to the Oxford Dictionary, the word 'authentic' just means 'of undisputed origin; genuine'. Therefore, if an author is posting as him or herself, the post should automatically be 'authentic'. However, we also tend to think that we can each have just one 'authentic' voice. If that's true, then it is not possible to write a novel *and* post on social media and be 'authentic' on both. It can start to feel that instead of expressing a natural subjectivity, 'voice' becomes a 'technology'.[76] Then, 'voice' becomes something to wield, it can feel cold and calculating.

Thinking of 'voice' as a 'technology' can invite technostress in. If one's voice is a technology, and technology is unnerving, then one's own voice could be as much to be feared as the thought of learning html coding or how to create a wireframe. Furthermore, on many social media platforms, it is necessary to go live and public at the outset. This can also provoke anxiety. Any faux pas or snub will immediately be out there for everyone to see.

Once the leap has been made and a comment posted by a writer, that is not the end of it. The reception of social media posts too may be imbued with doubt and suspicion. Issues that 'shake people the most about forming relationships online center on identity. When people's bodies aren't visible, will they lie about who they are? Can they be known? Can they be trusted?' observes Nancy Baym.[77] Even for seasoned users of social media, the idea of starting to post on a new platform (or a platform that is familiar but is now being approached in a new way) can be fraught.

Situations that are *fraught* and/or in which we feel *wary* tend to undermine. As researchers for the Carnegie Trust UK note in their 2017 report *Not Without Me: A digital world for all?*, for anyone setting out to improve their online skills, the job of gaining confidence is key.[78] Confidence is amorphous. It draws on, and results from, an infinite number of interconnected factors that may be external and/or internal, in the present and/or from the past.

Questions around how to build the confidence needed to boost and develop engagement with and sure-footedness in the online world are addressed throughout this book and tackled directly with a number of the assignments (see, for example, 'Me, myself, I' in Chapter 5). For more detailed discussion of my 'authentic' online voice pedagogical pilot, see Barnard, 2019. To sum up here, an important first step is simply to problematise and reflect critically on two key widely held assumptions: the myth of the 'digital native' (see above) and the notion of 'individual genius'.[79]

The idea that a writer must be a single unified self is not new.[80] It is often associated with the Romantic tradition and can be tracked back to the first century BC when Philodemus suggested that the 'goodness' of a poem stemmed from the 'individuality' contributed by the poet.[81, 82] Charles Dickens is one author who is generally viewed as an 'individual genius'. Yet, Dickens was hugely sociable. He collaborated regularly including with fellow author Wilkie Collins, he ran the magazine *Household Words*, he conducted notoriously busy and far-reaching speaking tours.[83]

The understanding that, actually, we comprise a range of selves also has a long history. 'Identity scholars such as Goffman (1959) have long argued that the self plays multiple roles in everyday life and cannot be understood adequately as a single unified identity', notes Baym.[84] The multiple selves we have to negotiate may well have become more complex with the advent of social media. Elwell suggests that with our Facebook, Blogspot, Tumblr and Flickr posts we are each constructing a 'transmediated' narrative of the self that is so complex and interactive that it becomes 'an artistic project' and 'browsable story world'.[85] However, if, in fact, we have always comprised multiple selves, then the task of presenting a range of interlinked voices is not new.

As part of everyday interactions, without even thinking much about it (let alone worrying), everyone 'code-switches'. That is, if we are talking to an acquaintance in a formal setting as opposed to a sibling, for example, we automatically alter intonation and vocabulary subtly but distinctly to suit the situation. To take Dickens as an example again: as biographer Peter Ackroyd notes, Dickens 'varied his conversation to suit the taste and the mood of his interlocutor'.[86] If someone code-switches, it does not mean he or she is untrustworthy or duplicitous. It is just the normal, polite thing to do.

Similarly, different environments have always had different codes and conventions to get to grips with. On Twitter, for example, one way of getting to know the codes and conventions and easing in to the environment is to start by retweeting others' tweets.

It might seem odd, but, as I have shown, retweeting others' posts can help with the job of gaining confidence and beginning to establish a user's own 'authentic' voice.[87] The retweeter does not 'lazily' press the retweet button, he or she carefully selects 'in order to indicate engagement with a particular community of practice'.[88] That is, retweets represent discernment. Retweets are also, in the prosumer tradition, production as well as consumption. They are conversational interventions and as such can be considered part of the retweeter's creative labour.[89, 90] A retweet can both support a strategy for engagement and be a creative output in itself, part of a creative practice that must in a digital age embrace *bricolage*.

So, the digital turn is affecting how we approach the concept of 'voice' in Creative Writing. It is also affecting concepts of genre.

Genre

At base, 'The word "genre" derives, through French, from Latin *genera* (pl.), where it simply means "kinds" or "types"'.[91] As Cobley notes, 'Every consumer of narratives has a rough idea of what "genre" means: a short-hand textual classification, determining whether a particular fiction is expected to conform to previous experiences of texts on the part of the consumer.'[92] In the context of reading and writing, then, the term serves a helpful practical function. As Bowen and Whithaus phrase it, 'naming a text as belonging to a particular genre helps situate that text within an interpretative framework'.[93] If we read 'Once upon a time', for example, we know we are likely to be reading a fairytale. Thus, the term 'genre' can be used to distinguish between textual patterns (patterns associated with romance novels as opposed to crime writing or science fiction, for example). Alternatively, a genre can be a form of enunciation, such as a blog.

> Love sonnets, absurdist drama, shopping lists and disaster movies are all genres of text. By extension, we can also talk about genres of everything from chats over coffee to job interviews, and pizza packaging to shopping malls. The main thing is there should be some basic similarity of form and function in the kinds of cultural product or activity, notwithstanding all the differences there inevitably are between one item and another.[94]
>
> (Pope)

'Genre', then, can be summed up as 'an "idea" or "expectation" har-boured by readers'.[95]

However, we have had centuries to become familiar with the Classical idea of what constitutes a comedy as opposed to tragedy, for example. Even a relatively new genre such as Steampunk has been around for over two decades.[96] New digital multimedia and networked environments bring a new pace. 'Never before have the technologies of writing contributed so quickly to the generation of new genres,' notes Yancey.[97]

Take creative non-fiction, for example. 'creative non-fiction' is a term which is commonly used to denote within the broader category of 'non-fiction' (which includes manuals) works which employ techniques such as characterisation, extended descriptive passages, imagery, unreliable narrators and plot twists which are more usually associated with fiction. The term came into wide use in the 1990s, pioneered most notably by Lee Gutkind (in books such as *Creative Non-fiction: Writing and Selling the Literature of Reality* [1997]). The origins of creative non-fiction are often traced back to the 1970s when Tom Wolfe used the term 'new journalism' to describe non-fiction that is 'as "absorbing" and "gripping" as the novel and the short story'; Truman Capote's *In Cold Blood* (1966) is an oft-cited early example of 'new journalism'.[98] Alternatively, the origins of creative non-fiction can be traced back to 1913 when novelist Djuna Barnes started writing articles for the *Brooklyn Eagle* for which she coined the term 'stunt journalism'[99] (Barnes underwent force-feeding herself, for example, so that she could write with more detail and empathy about British suffragettes' use of hunger striking as a political weapon.[100]).

Within the broader genre of creative non-fiction, there are subgenres, such as travel writing and food writing. However, the advent of social media represents a challenge to the accepted parameters of creative non-fiction. As Koehler notes, 'texts and tweets often, whether we want to admit it or not, have similar aspirations as a short story: they aim to connect'.[101] Social media posts can be viewed as mere 'status updates', or, they can be placed 'in a lineage that is shared with memoirs'.[102]

As Adsit notes, 'Of course there are important differences between posting online and formally publishing creative non-fiction.'[103] Yet, a social media post may be seen by hundreds or tens of thousands of people, gaining validation in the form of 'likes'. According to Baverstock's definition, self-publishing means taking 'personal responsibility for the management and production of your content'.[104] Combining Adsit and Baverstock's points, then, social media posts, when their construction has been carefully considered, can be viewed not only as creative non-fiction but as examples of self-published creative non-fiction.

If functions of a social media platform change, such practicalities can – very quickly – affect the development of the genre/s of writing emerging from that platform. For example, in 2014 Twitter experimented with the 'retweet' function, allowing users to add comments to others' tweets when they 'quoted' them and, in 2017, Twitter trialled expansion of the character-limit of a tweet from 140 to 280 characters.[105, 106] Thus more *bricolage* and more relaxed sentence structures are now characteristics of the overarching genre of tweets.

In keeping with Snapchat's reputation for Snaps that self-delete after 24 hours, episodes of the platform's 2018 webseries, 'Snap Originals', were designed for daily release and to be easy to watch via mobile phones while on the move, with some episodes' running times just five minutes long.[107, 108]

Genres and subgenres are, in new digital multimedia and networked environments, dynamic: 'genre and multimodality can be understood as cross-fertilizing influences that shape the development of written documents'.[109] Those starting to work with storytelling on brand new platforms may find they have to invent the genre as they go.

Writers have always had to be adaptable, balancing lengthy struggles developing a plot line, for example, with the need to earn a living.[110] Franz Kafka, who is widely considered one of the most important writers of the twentieth century, famously worked as an official at the Worker's Accident Insurance Institute in Prague, fitting writing into his spare time.[111] Sir Arthur Conan Doyle, one of the world's most renowned short story writers, was a practising 'Opthalmic Surgeon'.[112] International bestseller Kurt Vonnegut's range of 'day jobs' included a stint in public relations at General Electric and a period as a car dealer.[113] The challenges have changed, certainly, but the need for writers to face a tumultuous world is not new.

We are living in what can be termed a 'postdigital' (or, 'post-digital') era, in which, far from being past or anywhere near defunct, digitalism is so accepted as central to the production, dissemination and promotion of text as to be taken for granted.[114, 115]

Skills in *bricolage* must be developed. As new hardware and software emerges and communities of practice drive change, bold experimentation is necessary. As well as coming with costs and challenges, new media technologies 'produce and support opportunities for human interaction and interconnection, well beyond the local or regional geography of direct physical contact, at a pace of experience and level of convenience never before accomplished'.[116]

Moving between genres and technologies – quickly, confidently, regularly – is part of the daily job of being a writer. Having outlined in this chapter the broader context and pointed to some of the key changes in the twenty-first century writing and publishing landscape, Chapters 2–5 are designed to provide a toolkit that will enable development of the creative flexibility necessary to flourish in our postdigital era.

2 NEGOTIATING THE STARTING BLOCK: AUTO-PRACTITIONER STUDY

It is simply not possible to stay permanently up to date with all relevant technological developments, there will always be something new. To negotiate the demands that come (thick and fast) in a twenty-first century characterised by a high turnover of new media technologies, a writer can 'remediate' his or her own practice: that is, instead of rejecting experiences of 'old' media as redundant, writers can productively mobilise prior creative experiences and transfer skills gained previously into new digital multimedia and networked environments. As new challenges and opportunities arise, a writer who remediates his or her own practice 'looks to existing skills and prior experience and adapts or applies them in new contexts as part of a process of, in effect, collaborating with him or herself'.[1] To consider how a writer might do this, I conducted an auto-practitioner study.

From the outset, my practice has been characterised by an occupational eclecticism requiring 'shifts in writing practices', as Millard and Munt phrase it.[2] My range of outputs includes novels and creative non-fiction, print journalism and radio scripts.[3] Thus this chapter uses three decades' practice and output as a prism through which to view a sample writer's development of remediation of practice. As Christa Wolf notes, 'the whole preceeding period' of a writer's life dating back to infancy feeds his or her writing.[4] The main focus of this chapter is on early stage development of a creative practice that involves shifts between genres and technologies. The early experience considered is, of course, particular to me. As will be seen, it featured the Yorkshire landscape, cutting on the bias and magnetic tape. Each person's existing skills and prior experience will be different. The aim here is to use my experience to provide close focus consideration of how metacognitive processes can work to effect movements between genres and technologies. There is no one-size-fits-all piece of training that will equip everyone. The intention is that this reflective view of a sample practitioner's learning curve will help provoke thoughts and ideas regarding how others can pursue their own, personalised learning curves.

I remember 'the' moment when I decided to be 'a writer'. It happened in 1990 in a kitchen in a flat in London's Brixton. The moment looked something like this:

> In a rented flat in a 1930s block in Brixton, I was sitting in the kitchen with a cup of coffee in my hand. With its mint wall cupboards and wood draining board, the room had the feel of an ocean liner. The coffee percolator and milk pan stood erect and sturdy on the stove.
>
> I was looking at job options. So the formica-topped table was covered with a mix of paperwork: newspapers, job adverts ringed in red; application letters. And in the other room was a draft of a story I'd been writing.
>
> I was also considering starting my own business because that way, I reasoned, I could work hard, insanely hard maybe, for some years, and that would buy me time off later, in which to write. My pen was poised over an as yet umarked newspaper jobs page. My gaze, drifting, caught on a froth of milk that had spilled over the top and stalled, cooked, a little way down the side of the pan. The thought surfaced suddenly and fully in the kitchen that day: I wanted to be a writer and, if I waited, it might never happen.
>
> That was that. I had decided I was going to be a writer and start immediately.

It is a memory that is, in its neatness, reassuring. It confirms an idea that I had been going in one direction, which was wrong; I had a moment of realisation, and thenceforth I was moving in a new, correct direction.

When I looked at the memory afresh, I saw that I identified different pivotal moments from my past depending: how I defined being 'a writer'; if I differentiated between being 'a writer' and being 'a multimodal writer'; if I took into account subconscious decisions to become 'a writer/multimodal writer' or only conscious, clearly articulated decisions.

Thus, a key first question is, simply: what is 'a writer'?

What is 'a writer'?

The idea of it is steeped in cliché, cliché that foregrounds solitude and monomodal production.

Virginia Woolf's 1929 essay *A Room of One's Own* helped fix an image of the perfect writing state as solitary and wholly free of interruptions.[5] Works such as Cyril Connolly's 1949 *Enemies of Promise* reinforced this image.[6]

Getting published by a mainstream publisher involves contracts, negotiations, decisions about typefaces and jacket covers. When people decide that they want to become writers, they are not often taking account of such logistics. Perhaps more importantly, as Woolf points out in her essay, to have a room of one's own in which to be free to write, one needs money; Connolly's enemies of promise famously include commissions to do paid work and the 'pram in the hallway', that is, real life. Bernard Lahire has written about the tension that exists for most writers between the need to earn a living and interact with friends and family, and the desire to get on with writing.[7] Lahire notes that the difficulties inherent in this 'double life' are 'an absolutely central fact of literary life'.[8] That is, the idea in the popular imagination of what it is to be 'a writer', is largely (if not wholly) unattainable.

When I was a child growing up in the Yorkshire countryside, my idea of 'a writer' fitted the cliché. I conceived of a 'proper writer' as someone who was a solitary full-time novelist, and this was my aspiration. When I wrote down stories in notepads, in keeping with the cliché, I was alone. Sometimes I would write in bed under the covers by the light of a torch, or at the kitchen table (if everyone was out), all in keeping with the cliché.

However, through my childhood, two other places were significant.

Bookshelves

When I was a child, at home, in the living room, a set of custom-built bookshelves spanned an entire wall, side-to-side, floor to ceiling. Here I could find a large proportion of the English classics (works by the Brontës, George Eliot and Thomas Hardy, for example); there were poets (Percy Bysshe Shelley, Emily Dickinson); the collection took me to America (William Faulkner), France (Gustave Flaubert), Spain (Miguel de Cervantes), South America (Gabriel Garcia Marquez) and beyond. From the age of about seven through the rest of my school life, I spent a lot of time in front of those bookshelves. That is, I read voraciously, which is not unusual. As Francine Prose says, 'most, maybe all' writers as they learn their craft engage in extensive, critical reading.[9] Two other aspects of my recollections of these bookshelves are pertinent.

Reading the author notes on the books' blurbs and in the introductions gave a feeling of interaction, perhaps even collaboration. And, it was not only the books' text that counted, it was also the associated physical sensations. Often barefoot, I would sink my toes into the carpet as I surveyed the options on the bookcase and then, once I had chosen my book, I would relish the feel of the chair against my arm, the headrest against my cheek as I began to read. I felt visceral pleasure. A sense of focus that was almost tangible encased me.

Digital technologies cast spells and have 'magical qualities'; they can feel hard to get hold of.[10] Hayles highlights the importance of 'focusing on the dynamics entwining body and machine together' so, too, do Angel and Gibbs, who speak of the value of writing and reading involving 'an animism and dynamism that re-engage the movement and gestures of the body … rendering these processes explicitly performative'.[11, 12] 'If we can feel we have physically got hold of new media technologies, then we can feel that we are performing them rather than being performed by them'.[13]

My early experiences of reading involved the kind of physicality Hayles and Angel and Gibbs refer to. This was to prove useful in the context of developing a multimodal writing practice in two ways. Later, I could recall this childhood visceral pleasure and draw on it, working to recreate a feeling of animism and dynamism (of getting hold of something) if struggling with some new software application or piece of technology. In addition, I came to recognise visceral pleasure as a useful marker. It was not only triggered by *reading* stories.

Landscape

We lived outside a small village, up a hill. The second place from childhood that holds significance for me in the context of developing a multimodal writing practice lay about a mile or so above our house.

I regularly jumped a couple of drystone walls and ran up beyond a silver birch wood into a spread of moorland to Troll Bridge, a bridge over a rut in the landscape. I would sit underneath (in with gnarled roots, peaty ground, the smell of heather) and compose stories. Here I was alone, but did not take a notepad or pen. I wrote the stories down later. Under Troll Bridge, I invented.

That is, with my trips to the moor, I managed to split myself. I left the more ordered, rational side of myself at home. If I had consciously considered trying to become a writer while standing in front of the wall of bookshelves, I would have been too daunted to try to dream up my own story. Away from the shelves, in a landscape I loved, I was freed to be inexpert and play with narratives.

Hayles observes that we feel uncomfortable about acknowledging the unconscious as a key driving force in decision-making, since to do so downplays 'human agency'.[14] Particularly when we are embarking on, or shifting between, aspects of creative practice that are new to us and/ or daunting, human agency can prove an impediment. Natalie Goldberg speaks of the value of 'flashes' of thought that are 'unencumbered by ego, by that mechanism in us that tries to be in control'.[15]

The visceral pleasure I experienced when reading and inventing is akin to gut instinct. It kept taking me in unexpected directions.

What is 'a multimodal writer'?

Chopping and stitching

From the age of about ten, with a tenacity that was akin to the tenacity with which I read and made up stories, I pursued baking and sewing. I considered myself a tomboy (I made forts with hay bales; I played target practice with an air rifle, shooting tin cans off fence posts). So, this was surprising. Yet, visceral pleasure kept me moving between sewing, baking and storytelling, weaving between them, enjoying the transitions.

Writers talking about writing often quote Thomas Edison's famous line, 'Genius is one percent inspiration, ninety-nine percent perspiration'.[16] The initial, thrilling germ of an idea is only a tiny part of the process. The craft must be learned.

Elizabeth Bowen wrote in a letter to Graham Greene:

> I don't see ... that we as writers differ in the practical sense – or can rightly be expected to be differentiated – from any other freelance makers and putters on the market of luxury, or "special" goods. Had I not been a writer I should probably have struck out in designing belts, jewellery, handbags or lampshades or something of that sort.[17]

I drafted stories in an intense, focused state; I felt blinkered, down a tunnel. By contrast, when I was baking and sewing, both when faced with errors (e.g. rolling pastry out on newsprint; sewing straight over an armhole), and in my attempts to find solutions, I could be clear-sighted and pragmatic. I wanted to be able to apply that clear-sighted pragmatism to my story-writing.

Metacognitive processes were at work. From the cookbooks and sewing patterns, I was learning techniques and applying them as instructed. I was also experimenting with transferring techniques between different, apparently unconnected activities and technologies. Making a piece of clothing involves cutting up pieces of fabric and arranging them to make a whole that fits a planned design. When working to edit a story, I experimented with, literally, cutting up a draft with scissors, rearranging passages until they formed a more effective narrative.

Furthermore, the shifts between the bookshelves, Troll Bridge, drafting, sewing and baking were not random. I chose to move between locations in particular orders so that the nature and/or stage of each creative activity could support the others. That is, the act of physically laying out pieces of fabric with tracing paper pattern attached (when I was thinking about structuring) might come after a session under Troll Bridge (when I had done some unstructured inventing) and before I sat down at my desk, straight-backed, pen and paper in hand, to edit and redraft a story. Under Troll Bridge, I had been making up free-flowing stories. They did not have to make sense. My decisions to take up baking and sewing coincided with early attempts to write stories that had a clear and recognisable structure.

Not to forget, I am talking about childhood hobbies here, I was having fun. Yet, within that context, I was also learning how different ways of scheduling activities could impact both the chances of the activities supporting each other and the quality of the end results.

Further, in investigating how to ruche and hem fabric and how to make a roux and test when jam has reached setting point, I was gathering experience of finding and applying a craft's rules. Later, when I was thinking about plotting full novels, I read essays such as Bowen's 'Notes on writing a novel' and E. M. Forster's 'The Plot' as a way of assembling a strategy.[18, 19]

Of course, in sewing, cutting on the bias is cutting on the bias, there is no room for interpretation. There is difference of opinion regarding plot. '[T]o pot with the plot,' says Forster, 'break it up, boil it down. Let there be those "formidable erosions of contour" of which Neitzsche speaks.[20] All that is pre-arranged is false'. Jorge Luis Borges writes, 'tradition, conventions, "the rules," are not an obligation'; of 'those formulations that people call "an aesthetics"', Borges notes, 'they vary from author to author'.[21] Yet, in a sense, this *is* a 'rule'.

Eudora Welty says, 'Writers must learn to trust themselves'.[22] Goldberg too stresses the importance of writers learning to trust themselves.[23] I was still a child, my baking and sewing efforts were stumbling, I could not be considered 'expert' at anything much at all, it was certainly much too early to 'trust' myself as a writer. However, I was beginning to build a trust more broadly in my creative process. I allowed myself to split into different personas, to enable first (in a tunnelled state of mind) drafts to emerge, and then (accessing a more pragmatic part of myself) editing to take place. I had identified visceral pleasure as a resource. If I felt inexpert in one arena, I trusted feelings of visceral pleasure to lead me to activities I might otherwise have marginalised or glossed over that would enable me to learn skills that could be transferred.

Code-switching

Throughout my childhood, I continued taking in stories in whatever form I could find them. At school, I loved English Literature, of course. Since I considered myself agnostic, it felt surprising, but I kept a particular focus on Religious Studies (RS). Visceral pleasure was playing its part. I can remember every detail of the RS classroom, the Victorian cupboards rising in the corner, the brutal modern lines of the architecture of the rest of the room, the teacher's suits, which looked as though they were made of fawn flock wallpaper.

Our focus in RS was the Old Testament. As well as enjoying the narrative drive and twists of the stories, I was interested in how different they felt in structure, voice and delivery to those we were reading for O'Level English Literature. For example, repetition, which is generally considered something to avoid in storytelling, is a characteristic of Bible stories.[24] I was entranced by the uncompromising sweep of the tales, by the lists, the excess. My interest was caught, too, by the question of authorship, by the fact that the Bible was huge and treated as a single entity despite the fact that it was written by many different people with recognisably different styles.[25] I became interested in how, while observing particular genre conventions, a writer could express individuality and maintain an identifiable voice.

Genre is a key consideration in the twenty-first century. Driven by new media technologies, as noted, new genres are emerging apace, from email to blogs to Snapchat.[26] Writers must become serially familiar with new genres as they emerge. Further, in moving between genres, writers must 'code-switch', adapting language so that it is appropriate for different genres while retaining a distinct, overarching identity.

In RS, I was paying close attention to questions around how to simultaneously stay clearly within a genre and retain an identifiable voice.

Reel-to-reel

Some years later, with school and a literature degree behind me, my writerly aspirations still fitted the cliché: solitude, typewriter, attic. Yet, visceral pleasure continued to take me in periodically unexpected directions, including, at the age of 21, into radio.

As I have discussed (Barnard, 2017), a commission to co-produce an experimental BBC Radio series, *The Friday Buzz* could have seemed at odds with the cliché of being 'a writer'.[27] *The Friday Buzz* was to be a weekly magazine programme comprising half a dozen features each week. That is: it was radio not print; it was primarily non-fiction and news-based. Instead of writing novels in solitude at a desk, the job would require me to move between a range of locations and work with interviewees, technicians, a co-producer and an executive producer while researching, recording and cutting material to strict weekly deadlines.

Nevertheless, in producing each feature, I would be producing a narrative. The features would serve in effect as chapters within each week's programme, and each programme would also need an overarching narrative drive. I approached the BBC Radio commission with the aim of gaining new skills in the craft of storytelling which I could transfer.

The technologies were distinct, of course. I would have to train myself up in recording audio and editing magnetic tape. Initially, I viewed the time and effort this training would take as collateral damage.

The moment I stepped into the BBC studio for the first time, my view changed. As I stared at the recording equipment – which comprised a vast reel-to-reel recording machine, known in the trade as a 'Uher' (the name of a main manufacturer) plus microphone plus headphones plus leads – I could see immediately that it would have a fundamental impact on both how my narratives were composed and the subjects and content of the resulting stories. Writers' tools are, traditionally, quite discrete. With a pen or typewriter it is possible to produce an entire manuscript. With a few strokes of a pen or taps on a keyboard, a writer can take the reader from Torquay to Timbuktu. Today, radio production can be similarly discrete (a whole radio programme can easily be made using a laptop). However, my BBC commission was won in 1985. It was clear just from looking at the recording equipment that its sheer bulk would restrict where and how far I travelled to find my stories (a Uher alone weighs about 3.5 kg, even a short bus journey becomes an endeavour when carrying a Uher). The editing equipment was similarly unwieldy. The editing trolley was the size of a small desk. It bore two reels, each the size of a dinner plate, with the magnetic tape onto which the sound had been recorded winding from one reel to the other. Edits were marked on the brown magnetic tape with white pencil. Unwanted lengths of sound were cut out with a razor blade. Then the bits of sound that had been selected to form the story were pieced back together with yellow sticky tape in the desired sequence to form the feature.

It all seems highly old-fashioned now (reels, razors, yellow sticky tape). What counts in this context is that the radio equipment was new *to me*.

Time was short. I had to both learn how to use the analogue radio equipment and reconsider what I knew about storytelling in the light of the restrictions that came with the equipment. I had to – swiftly and effectively – find a way of remediating my creative practice.

For editing, I drew on childhood experiences of cutting up and piecing together sections of fabric. I drew, too, on the Russian filmmaker Sergei Eisenstein's theory of montage, or, 'assembly', whereby experiments juxtaposing the same blocks of moving image in different orders produced radically different stories.[28] In the BBC Radio editing suite, after the first set of interviews had been completed, faced with lengths and lengths and lengths of magnetic tape and the task of reordering these strips of sound, I stuck strips of magnetic tape with yellow sticky tape to the walls and draped them over chairs as I worked to make editorial decisions regarding how to reassemble them. Experiences of sewing and my interest in Eisenstein's montage techniques, then, directly helped my work splicing strips of sound back together to form a story.

For the task of recording the material, prior experience of working my way through a manual when learning to use a sewing machine helped in quite a straightforward way with the practicalities of getting to grips with a Uher. When it came to selecting interviewees and devising questions, I thought back to the living room bookshelves. In a novel, all dialogue is under the control of the author. When recording a radio feature featuring interviewees, the producer has much less control over what is said. When planning and conducting interviews for *The Friday Buzz*, I was informed by both the collaborative feel I recalled from standing in front of the living room bookshelves (with different author's voices emerging and receding) and craft elements of novels I had read. I drew in particular on my reading as a teenager of William Faulkner's *As I Lay Dying* and

The Sound and the Fury, when I had been struck by the fact that the narratives both seemed unplanned, almost shambolic, yet in both novels, different characters' experiences and voices are pieced together to form coherent, compelling narratives.[29, 30]

Far from being collateral damage, the experience of a significantly different set of technologies (Uhers, magnetic tape, mixing desks) was providing a fresh writerly perspective and adding an unanticipated story-telling skillset. That is, as well as remediating practice in order to make the radio features, I was gaining skills and experience that could in turn be remediated later.

At one point, I cut all the 'hmms' and 'ahhs' out of a radio interview. Instead of sounding especially authoritative, the piece sounded stilted. Naturalistic dialogue tends to *need* hesitation and/or the odd stumble. This early experience of interviewing for radio affected how I approached writing dialogue for fiction later.

While I was out and about conducting the interviews, the constraints of the medium led me to notice details I might otherwise have missed. Radio producers must, for example, listen for buzzing striplights (and either switch them off or relocate accordingly), since, if inadvertently recorded, the light's buzzing in the background will sound like a technical fault. Similarly, the need for 'actuality' (sounds to contextualise, illustrate and enliven the spoken words, or, 'recorded material that isn't speech'[31]) might give the sound of a stiletto on concrete or the boiling of a kettle fresh significance. The sound of someone opening a packet of biscuits could serve as a beginning and a clip of a door slamming as the end of a feature. It is very easy for writers to focus primarily on sight. Making audio recordings engaged more of my senses more fully.

Multimodal writing practice involves being able to relatively quickly and accurately assess and delineate the particular codes, conventions and constraints of a new medium. It involves, too, being able to identify (again, quite quickly) what prior experience can be remediated. My experience of radio, then, helped with both these aspects.

A blank page

In 1990, in Brixton – in the flat with mint-coloured cupboards and the feel of an ocean liner – I made the decision to write a novel and submit it to a publishing house. Immediately I was terrified. I felt inexpert, I *was* inexpert: I had never published a first novel before.

It is not only first novelists who experience fear of the blank page. As Amos Oz presents it in *The Story Begins*, for experienced and new novelists alike: 'A blank page is actually a whitewashed wall with no door and no window. Beginning to tell a story is like making a pass at a total stranger.'[32]

Various possessions I had brought to the Brixton flat included a well-thumbed copy of Irma Rombauer's *The Joy of Cooking* and my Singer sewing machine.[33] I also had in a small box room, on a desk, an electric typewriter.

Remediating remediation

I replaced walks in the Yorkshire landscape with walks round Brixton's Brockwell Park, using pauses on benches amongst roses and climbing plants in the walled garden to allow new story sections to emerge. Work at Jonathan Cape publishing house as a blurb writer helped develop a range of skills including editing to deadline, fast. Freelance contributions to Fourth Estate's *Reader's Companion to the Twentieth Century Novel* and *The Reader's Companion to Twentieth Century Writers* further developed my editing skills, so too my experience of dissecting work in a range of genres.[34, 35] However, the blurbs and Fourth Estate pieces were non-fiction. It was a different matter applying editing skills to my fiction. Strategically positioned trips for cups of coffee in a small café in Brixton's covered market – where I had chats with other regulars and the owner – gave me both distance from the novel I was writing and a sense of external audience so that, back at my desk later, I could trim and reshape sections of text more effectively.

When my first novel *Poker Face* was nearly finished, I gained a commission to write a travel book, so for a (very intense) period I was writing both at once.[36, 37] Bruce Chatwin drew on his experience as a journalist for works of creative non-fiction.[38] Creative non-fiction famously draws on techniques more usually associated with fiction. As well as applying fiction techniques to non-fiction in my practice, I experimented to see what tools and techniques could be taken the other way, from non-fiction to fiction. In addition to helping me see the value of stumbles and hesitations in making dialogue feel naturalistic, earlier radio work recording and cutting interviews had helped me see that repetition in conversation can be symptomatic of strong feeling; I peppered repetition tactically in my fiction.

My non-fiction work also affected my approach to creative research. I applied versions of novelist and journalist Djuna Barnes's 'stunt journalism', building in field trips for my fiction as well as for my journalism. I didn't necessarily go far for such trips (to a Yorkshire field for my novel *Poker Face*; to shops, theatres and markets in London's Soho for my novel *The Pleasure Dome*, for example), but nor did I just pop down to these places.[39, 40] I ring-fenced the time, I took notebooks in which I wrote extensively, making sure to take account of how all my senses were affected, considering smells and sounds, and mood as well. I developed a system of coding and filing my notebooks so that one piece of research could go on to inform a number of different projects. For example, when I went behind the scenes in theatres for *The Pleasure Dome* to research the crossover of intimacy and business in dressing room interactions, I could see that there was more material here. The idea had not crystallised as a book proposal yet, but I was starting to think about friendship. I coded the notebooks accordingly, and so a research trip to a theatre in 1998 also informed the 2011 *The Book of Friendship*. The coding also enabled serendipity to play a part. When I was asked to produce a BBC Radio 4 programme about a group of Norwegian World War II resistance fighters known as 'The Heroes of Telemark', these same notebooks from 1998 also informed thinking about and research for the 2003 radio programme on the group and a newspaper feature.[41,42]

When working on scripts, for meetings where drafts were discussed, then too I remediated a range of earlier practices and experiences. Script writers talk of the need to 'survive' script note meetings. Feedback might come from a range of interested parties (director, producer, funder); opinions may differ, with one person thinking a passage particularly good and another considering that same passage problematic. For such meetings, I drew on my experience of blurb writing, when blurbs were taken for approval round lists of people including the author and editor and representatives from design, production and marketing departments. I thought back to the differing views on plot held by Bowen, Forster and Borges and how I'd factored them into the process of redrafting my first novel. I used my knowledge of the value of *time* in gaining perspective and so made good use of the writer's 'drawer', where I'd leave drafts – complete with others' comments in the margins – for a night, week or month as necessary.

Busy times periodically forced rethinks of creative practice. I found it's not just that I *can* if necessary read quite heavily theoretical chapters and articles as I travel. Trips on the London Underground – precisely for their contained noise and bustle (the rattle of tube train wheels, the thrum of commuters) – can help me find a particularly sharp concentration. I started scheduling different types of reading for times on a commute as opposed to a long train journey, in an armchair as opposed to a deck chair.

Work running and supervising live events such as *The Urban Programme* and the *North London Literary Festival* – with talks, events and screenings scheduled over a number of days – helped me think about storytelling as something that can be non-linear, with a festival allowing visitors to enter and leave events at different points as they move through the 'narrative' of the festival.[43, 44, 45] In the oral tradition of storytelling (a tradition to which the digital age has in so many ways returned us[46, 47]), interruptions and asides are part of the narrative. Work on this book has similarly felt like a discussion – a vibrant, multilayered, extended, intense discussion – with many different elements. Individuals, groups and institutions have all played parts, so too quantities of texts from my bookshelves and the British Library's alongside my own past and practice, author interviews (see Chapter 3), and work with students that informed development of the assignments (see Chapter 5), for example.[48]

Since that time in Brixton in 1990 – in the flat with the feel of an ocean liner – equipment I've used when making radio programmes changed from Uhers to DAT machines to Marantzs. My electric typewriter has been replaced several times over (by an Amstrad, a PC, several Macs). I have worked my way through a range of makes of smartphone. I have added a tablet to my list of equipment.

The idea that a writer's creativity is tied to particular tools and writing habits is, as I have discussed, a potent cultural concept:

> Dickens was a man of strict writing habits throughout his life. He could not start until particular objects were arranged on his desk; 'He used a goose-quill pen with blue (or occasionally black) ink. He wrote on blue-grey slips of paper, eight and three quarter inches by seven and one quarter inches' (Ackroyd, 1990, p. 562).
>
> In the film *Goosebumps* (Letterman, 2015), a writer's characters have come to life and are wreaking havoc. To save the town, the writer (children's novelist R. L. Stine, played by Jack Black), must write all the rampaging characters safely back into a manuscript. 'I need that Smith Corona!' declares the writer. 'Every story I've ever written has been on that typewriter!' – and the Smith Corona is carried round for the rest of the film, a happy resolution dependent on it. Indeed, the film's happy ending is marked by the sound of a typewriter key hitting a final full stop and paper being pulled out.[49]

In this postdigital age, we have to balance a natural desire for familiarity with the fact that in order to stay 'connected' we must upgrade regularly and embrace new tools and software. Creative flexibility is key.

The above account – with its focus on the Yorkshire landscape, sewing, magnetic tape and a London park's walled garden – is a snapshot. Inevitably, it only touches on a very small selection of the range of skills and experiences that have been remediated, in what combination, to what end.

For someone else, it may be recollections of collaborating on a school play, music lessons when only painful sounds emerged from a violin or unexpected proficiency on the hockey pitch that suggest tactics that could be remediated in a new creative context. As indicated, remediated skills and experiences will themselves in turn be remediated in different combinations, and, there is no getting around the fact that remediation is only part of the battle.

Cynthia Ozick notes, 'a redemptive literature, a literature that interprets and decodes the world, beaten out for the sake of humanity, must wrestle with its own body, with its own flesh and blood, with its own life'.[50] It is part of the job. Writers have to wrestle. There will always be a new starting block to negotiate. The hope is that the reflections provided in this chapter will help when the kind of wrestling Ozick describes must also take account of technical glitches, social media distractions and pieces of equipment that have yet to be invented.

3 PARADIGMATIC ASPECTS: AUTHOR INTERVIEWS

Each writer's experience of moving between different kinds of writing and technologies is, of course, unique. In 1680's England, Aphra Behn moved into the then risqué new genre of long-form prose simply because there was no money in writing plays anymore.[1, 2] Two centuries later, Mark Twain leapt at the opportunity to use the 'new contraption called a "type-machine"' (i.e. a typewriter), proudly claiming that he was 'the first person in the world to apply the type-machine to literature'.[3] Some writers hate such changes, others love them.

Yet, within that vast range of responses to the experience of moving between genres and tools, are there patterns that can be observed? Are there particular approaches that can make the experience of moving between types of writing and technologies more effective and enjoyable?

This chapter explores whether paradigmatic aspects of multimodal writing practice can be identified. It does so by presenting findings from interviews with a selection of writers who all have longstanding experience of multimodal writing practice. The study set out to obtain a range of honest, reflective observations. Thus, each interviewee's responses are highly personal. The intention is that the reader can, similarly, make personal judgements on the extracts presented here and see what elements might inform the development of his or her own multimodal writing practice. Some interviewees had extensive experience of new media technologies, others did not. No one technology or set of technologies is central to the development of multimodal writing practice. Rather, what is significant in the development of effective and sustainable multimodal writing practice is how technologies that are *new to an individual* are approached.

The writers interviewed represent a wide range of types of movements between different types of writing for different platforms. To give very brief summaries of the genres and platforms the interviewees have experience of moving between:

- Simon Armitage: poetry, film scripts, libretti;

- Robert Coover: traditional and experimental storytelling forms, including hypertext and 'edge-notched' cards;

- Jim Crace: novels, radio plays, features for magazines and newspapers;
- Juliet Gardiner: history, memoir, book reviews;
- Charlie Higson: television and radio comedy and drama, young adult fiction;
- Rhianna Pratchett: video games, comics, games reviews, short stories;
- Kate Pullinger: literary fiction, digital fiction;
- Michèle Roberts: literary fiction, food reviews, poetry.

(For further information on the writers interviewed, please see Appendix IV: Note on interviewees.)

This chapter is structured to reflect common themes and issues that emerged during the interviews. The intention is that the interviews will provide, as well as sample tactics, a thought-provoking dialogue on the subject of multimodal writing practice.

A dialogue

I think when you are really writing, you've opened up, you're not anymore separate from the universe, you're also part of a universe within which there is language. It's very much an unconscious imaginary space where you're not yourself, I'm not Michèle anymore, I'm just gone. That's the state in which I write and in which new sentences can come to me and that's really, really important to me as a truth about writing. So what I'm moving between is for me the sort of daily ego - the self with a name and a passport and a bank account – and this much more oceanic feeling which is about moving inside language and the imagination.

(Michèle Roberts).

One common theme through the interviews was the importance of periodically entering a state that allows the world to recede and a single writing project to take full possession. Michèle Roberts' description (above) of being fully immersed in a single writing project makes clear why moving between different types of writing can be difficult. Not surprisingly, some widely differing methods emerged. As will be seen, Robert Coover and Kate Pullinger find metaphor helpful; Jim Crace talks of 'pumping the adrenalin'; Charlie Higson, Juliet Gardiner and Rhianna Pratchett schedule tasks tactically; Simon Armitage highlights the value of 'thinking time'. However, one thing was striking. Perhaps precisely because the experience of being immersed in a single writing project can, as Roberts puts it, be 'oceanic', it is often quite everyday things that help writers move between projects and technologies, such as taking a break for a cup of tea, or, picking up a pen.

Tools

In an era when devices and software can quickly become obsolete, fierce attachment to particular tools could seem dangerous. Yet, such attachments can be used strategically to aid moves between types of writing. For example, take Simon Armitage's experience of pens:

> Finding a biro that has the right amount of drag and flow is incredibly important to me. I've got a couple of pens and they are the cheapest, most rubbishy sort of free hotel pens, but as soon as I put them against the paper, the quality of that contact I've recognised straight away has been in concert with the way I want to write.
>
> (Simon Armitage)

The act of, quite simply, starting to use a different tool can help a writer get into a different writing mindset. First, though, it is necessary to gain understanding of what exactly it is about one tool as opposed to another that proves helpful. During our conversation, Armitage periodically mimed the different actions of typing at a computer as opposed to writing with a pen as he considered the impact of different tools and accompanying actions on his engagement with different genres:

> I've often thought of poetry as a plastic art. I'm actually moulding and manipulating shapes on a piece of paper. The letters themselves are carved. There is a relationship between the speed of thought and the act of creating the letter shape. I don't know whether that's just a generational thing – because I grew up doing it that way, that's the way I feel comfortable – but it wouldn't seem right to me to sit down to write a poem with *this* action [typing]. This seems a very different action to this action [writing with a pen]. Yes, typing is like playing a

> piano, with the fingers moving like *this* I associate it with the creation of prose. But one-handed, right-handed, the carving and the shaping of letters on the page like *this* has a very comfortable proximity for me with the poems.
>
> (ibid.)

> Despite the fact that I type everything else, I handwrite my 'To Do' list, I don't know why, because my handwriting is awful. There's something nice about writing with a pen, with a *nice* pen.
>
> (Rhianna Pratchett)

'Affect' (or, the ability to affect and be affected) cropped up again and again.[4] The senses can be extremely useful in shifting between types of writing. Kate Pullinger referred to her laptop as seeming, physically, like 'an extension' of herself. Simon Armitage spoke of the importance of having the right kind of keyboard: 'I like those keys that slightly bounce back, they look chunky'.

Computers have, of course, transformed creative practice. Their affordances are many and varied. The cut and paste option featured repeatedly through the interviews as highly valuable. Moving between writing a novel and a poem is likely to require a shift of mindset; the same is true of moving between an earlier and later draft. For a number of writers, it seemed just the existence of the cut and paste option could prove freeing when it came to shifting between drafts, or starting first drafts.

> I write in a very chaotic, organic, scatter-gun way to begin with, always with the idea that I will sort this out later. And that sorting out later is perfectly possible with word processing.
>
> (Simon Armitage)

> I doubt very much if I would have become the kind of novelist I am if there wasn't a technology which enabled me to move prose around. I'm such an intense editor that moving stuff around is three-quarters of what I do. After the undercoat, it's all about this: month-in, month-out, moving stuff around, shifting stuff, changing, holding, hovering.
>
> (Jim Crace)

> I still need to print out a hard copy but obviously, once you've printed out your hard copy and think, 'No, that paragraph is not sequential', you can then go back and you don't have to get out the scissors, sticky tape and Tipp-Ex™.
>
> (Juliet Gardiner)

If a range of different work is being done on a single device, different affordances of that device can be used to help a writer shift between genres.

Icons can help trigger different writing moods. Just the act of clicking on the work email icon might automatically trigger a brisker writing tone. Clicking open a social media icon may bring a more informal writing tone. Similarly, opening a different piece of software – Final Draft or Microsoft Word, for example – can be a useful way of getting into a different writing mood:

> I certainly think it's useful for me that if I'm writing a script I'll be using Final Draft and if I'm writing a book I'll be using Microsoft Word. So, yes, you are changing the process and moving between different ways of using your computer.
>
> (Charlie Higson)

> If I'm writing in Final Draft, I'm writing a film or TV script. Final Draft isn't usually used in games because you can't annotate. Games companies tend to prefer Word. So I know if I'm working in Word and it looks like a screenplay I'm writing a game.
>
> (Rhianna Pratchett)

Within a single project, it might be necessary to shift between quite significantly different types of writing, and, again, software can prove helpful here:

> The requirements for a big AAA (which is a big blockbuster action game) are very different from the requirements for an Indie game or a role playing game. For a film screenplay you know the average screenplay is going to be between 90 and 120 pages and you have a rough structure for it in Final Draft. There's nothing like that for games. There are usually quite a few different types of script involved in a game, so there might be a cinematic script for something like *Tombraider* (2013), which might be about 70 pages or so, and then there'll be a script for all the AI dialogue, so that's barks, which are short lines of dialogue, and that would probably be in Excel or something like that. And then there would be level dialogue, which would probably be another Excel document, and then you'd have notes and letters and artefacts text, and that might be in a Word document or another Excel document.[5] So you have different layers of narrative, which all have their

own scripts. That's *Tombraider*. With other projects, they do them in different styles, so they might have made their own bespoke software to make the dialogue flow, particularly if it's a branching narrative, for example, ink – which was used to make *80 Days* (2014) – which is very popular.

(ibid.)

A shift between genres can be enabled by an act as simple clicking on an icon, then, or, just picking up a pen.

Panning out to take a slightly wider view of the desk: other artefacts a writer gathers around him or her can play roles as well. Jim Crace speaks of the 'huge difference between the organisation of your desk when you are writing fiction and when you are writing journalism', since, with journalism, research must be done, so 'you start off with your desk loaded':

You've got several notebooks, you've got your quotes, you've got that book which explains some background to you, you've got some newspapers articles. You've got the finished product you know that you're heading for. As you proceed, the desk gets tidier. When you're finished and it's all over, you put that last dot and the desk is empty because you've used everything that you wanted to use, or you decided you don't need that anyway, it goes in the bin. When you are writing fiction it's exactly the opposite. You sit down and you've got a vague idea in your head, there is no one to talk to, there is no one to gather information from, there are no resources to go and collect, the only resource is you. You start off – and I know this because I'm writing a novel at the moment – you start off with an empty desk and as you proceed you start to get more and more clutter. So there is a strange physical difference. And it's scary, because there is something reassuring about picking the bits off the head of the daisy that you know you've got to write, gradually getting neater and neater and doing away with it. There's something scary about the clutter increasing.

(Jim Crace)

The nice thing about the table is it's a desk and it's a dining table. It's not distinct, so the tools are also dinner, glasses of wine, cups of tea, cups of coffee.

(Michèle Roberts)

If a writer wants to secure the mood for writing a novel as opposed to a work report, for example, a cup of coffee positioned on a coaster beside the keyboard – the coffee's smell, its taste – might be just what is needed.

Panning out further, considering the space around the desk, the atmosphere of the room that a writer works in can be arranged to aid shifts between types of writing. *Noise* cropped up regularly during the interviews:

> I like a lot of stuff going on. I guess I like to control the stuff going on, that's the important bit. I can have the TV on mute or pause or just have images going on in the background.
>
> (Rhianna Pratchett)

> I've developed a working process which helps to give me the right energy and rhythm to the day. I never used to listen to music when I was writing because I found it too distracting. But I worked out that if I listen to the same music every day, then I could enjoy listening to music and it wouldn't be a distraction, it would be part of the shape of the day. So when I start a new project now, I start a playlist on Spotify which I will add to constantly. So that means every time I sit down to work on a project, I can click on that playlist and it will play the music that's associated with that. It's mostly classical, film music and stuff like that. When I was writing [*Young*] *James Bond* there was a lot of John Barry James Bond music in there. So if I am switching between projects, I can switch to a different Spotify play list.
>
> (Charlie Higson)

As well as the practical tools on the desk – the pens, pencils, erasers, notepads; the computer, the iPad – bookshelves can be an enormous help. *Form* was referred to by a number of the writers I spoke to as a particularly useful tool:

> Really, moving between the different types of writing is just learning the different forms and the different techniques, which actually can be learnt quite quickly.
>
> (ibid.)

> One way of jumping between forms I've found that usually works is to go and read some of that form. So, if I'd been writing poetry and I need to write some prose in the afternoon, or a review, or I need to be getting on with an

essay, I'd go and pull a book of the form off the bookshelf, read a couple of paragraphs, and then something clicks in, you sort of think: 'Oh yes, that's what this stuff is,' and then you're back on it. I guess it's a form of imitation you're talking about, you have to go back and look at the model that you're imitating.

(Simon Armitage)

However, a novelist who wants to start work on a screenplay or a poet who wants to start work on an essay can look at innumerable examples of screenplays and essays, there are plenty to choose from, so it is easy to find an example. What if a writer is trying to get into the right frame of mind for a work that is highly experimental? What if technology being utilised is so new that there is no existing form to look at?

Moving into a genre or technology that is entirely new can be the most difficult move of all. When the creative realm entered has no predecessors, metaphor can help. During our interview, Robert Coover spoke of how Melville's *Moby Dick* has informed his creative process:

It's basically a simple story about chasing down a whale, but for Melville, the whale was everything. In his case, the central metaphor provided him a constraint of sorts. The hunt was itself a narrative action that needed to follow a limited trajectory to make the work beautiful. Sooner or later, Ahab had to meet the whale. Melville has always been a great inspiration for me, and not only *Moby Dick*, though it was from that book that I learned the virtue of intransigence. You don't let go of something because you're tired of it or because it's too difficult.

You have to chase that whale to the end of the line.

(Robert Coover)

When Kate Pullinger was commissioned by German start-up Oolipo to write a piece of fiction for smart phones, *Jelly Bone*, as part of the process of re-configuring fiction for hand-held portable devices, Pullinger says it was necessary for writer and publisher to experiment to find the right language to talk about the writing process:[6]

So when we first started talking, they were trying to come up with a metaphor for describing what is on the screen in terms of *what is the text*. In a book, you have the page. So what do you have when you are reading a story on the phone? They initially started with the idea of a 'slice' and they set a maximum word limit for the slice at 90 words, which is how I ended up writing on an Excel spreadsheet, as a way of using the cells in the spreadsheet to create these distinct discrete slices of text which can be anywhere from just a couple of words long to 90 words long. I wrote two episodes on these spreadsheets. But then their thinking moved on and for a while they moved from 'slices' to thinking about 'threads' and how a story has a main thread and it might have ancillary threads and then they moved again to where we are now which is really just thinking about 'screens', which is a simpler way of approaching it, for me a more fruitful way of approaching it, less restrictive. And I think that's been one of the difficult things for them, they never wanted writers to be restricted by the platform or the technology. It's a complex process of finding the right metaphors to talk about it.

(Kate Pullinger)

Tracking back briefly, then, pens, software, curated ambience and metaphor can all be used to aid moves between genres and technologies.
So, too, can location.

Location

I *think* in cafes, yes. I might make jottings in cafes but I don't ever work there. I very much like going away to write with a friend who also writes, so we write all morning and then maybe go and have a coffee and maybe have a little drive and then work again in the afternoons. We are at the moment doing that in Suffolk. I find that's very good. I like Suffolk because it's flat and I love flat (I love deserts), and it also has huge open skies and I find that very inspirational.

(Juliet Gardiner)

I've noticed that more and more I'm very comfortable writing poems in fairly distracting environments – cafes, trains; I feel as if I'm very good at creating enough calm and solitude within quite a busy environment.

(Simon Armitage)

If a writer knows that a particular part of the creative process or a particular type of writing is likely to flourish in one location as opposed to another, he or she can use locations to help shift between different writing projects.

Rhianna Pratchett says she often reserves particular types of writing for journeys, knowing that being on a train or plane, for example, will help her shift into the right mindset:

> Yes, I've written quite a lot of comics on planes. You get to watch movies, people bring you food. That's my perfect writing environment. Trains are quite good as well. But I do particularly like planes, I will assign writing times to plane journeys. Hotel rooms, I like hotel rooms a lot. That always makes me feel like a Stephen King character, and there's the people bringing me food element. So if I go somewhere for work I'll make sure I leave some writing time, even if it's just catching up on emails.
>
> (Rhianna Pratchett)

It was striking through the interviews that when considering the experience of moving between writing projects, as well as on long-haul train and plane journeys, value was placed on interim activities, for example, a short car journey, or a quick walk to a corner shop to pick up some milk. Such short trips can enable the finishing up of one part of a creative project and the start of a different project:

> I walk a lot, and of course I've read Dickens's beautiful essays, such as *Night Walks*, and I've written about being a *flâneur*. As a writer I walk in the city a great deal on my own, often at night, and it helps enormously with getting into a state of semi-trance when ideas can come up. It's incredibly useful. Swimming is the same, it's like meditating, you're just kind of letting all these thoughts flow through you and out of you and you're living absolutely in the moment.
>
> (Michèle Roberts)

> I think most writers will say that most of their actual writing in terms of coming up with ideas is not done when they're at the desk. It's when you're in the bath, or going for a walk or when you're away somewhere.
>
> (Charlie Higson)

If it's something not much bigger than a poem, you can be working on it even when you're driving the car and I'm sure that's what I'm doing a lot of the time, I'm working on the poems when I'm actually out and about.

(Simon Armitage)

Places with *waiting* involved can prove surprisingly valuable. Robert Coover's description of working in London's British Library presents the periods when he was waiting for books to arrive as useful for triggering new projects and facilitating moves between projects:

For example, when I was working on *The Public Burning* (1977) in the British Library, there was always a period of time in the morning when I had to wait for books to be brought from the stacks to my assigned desk by trolley. In those days, nothing was digitised and even the card catalogues were wretchedly incomplete. Most of the books were catalogued on scissored strips of paper pasted in rough alphabetical order onto poly-protected black scrapbook sheets in large loose-leaf binders, and I found them entertaining as texts in themselves.

On one occasion, while waiting for the trolley of books, I found pages of instructions to masters and mistresses on how to educate their servants, and began a little narrative about a master and his maid. The British Library was just off Tottenham Court Road in those days, and the main business on that street was not electronics, as it is now, but sex shops full of, among much else, old Victorian pornographic writings, including nineteenth century spanking stories. So I was actually researching two very different stories at the same time, an American political story about Nixon and the execution of the Rosenbergs in 1953, and what eventually became *Spanking the Maid* (1982), triggered by that idle early morning reading while waiting for the British Library book trolleys. I have no idea how one project affected the other, but I was working as you might think hypertext would work.

(Robert Coover)

The simple act of going out to a café, then, can help. Just a quick jaunt round the block can be enough to shake off one writing style and inhabit another.

It became clear during the interviews too that the value of moves within the home should not be underestimated. A small walk between floors or even just between rooms can be helpful. Bed cropped up several times:

> When I'm writing poetry I very often write it in bed because I have to write it on paper – that's A4 sheets of white paper with a black pen in my hand – and because I can only write a poem starting from the top and moving through it, it means it might have 50 drafts. So bed is great because you can sit there propped up on pillows and have all the sheets of paper around you. That's really brilliant for writing poetry, I've never been able to write poetry any other way.
>
> (Michèle Roberts)

> If I'm doing heavy lifting writing, I'll put myself in a comfortable environment. I like sitting on the bed, which I call my winter office. I'll position everything around me, so I've got the phone nearby in case anyone calls, and I've got one of those little wheelie desks that you see in hospitals, I have a version of that. It's black and two bits of the desk tilt and you have your mouse there and your laptop there so you can sit on the bed, and I've got an arm so I can have the iPad up there, and it becomes a little station. And I'll have a cup of tea there. There's usually a cat with me. I tend to do longer form stuff in bed so, for example, if I'm writing scenes and things like that, the comfortableness of the environment helps. If I'm working on a screenplay, I'm more likely to do that in bed. If I'm answering questions for an interview, I'm more likely to do it sitting in my office. So I think the bed – the comfortable environment – is used for heavy lifting writing, for long-form writing.
>
> (Rhianna Pratchett)

> In the last year and a half I've started doing this early morning writing in bed which I've found enormously comforting. Yes, I've never written in bed before but there's something about preserving that post-sleep state of mind. So I get up, have breakfast, see everybody off, everybody in the household is

> usually gone by 7.30, and then I'll get back into bed to write for a few hours. I have an office at the end of my garden and I do write in there as well, only that's slightly more formalised.
>
> (Kate Pullinger)

A return to bed with a cup of tea, a shower, a walk: such apparently incidental activities can prove very helpful in shifting between different writing activities.

So, too, can seeing different types of writing set out on a schedule.

Schedule

A simple but effective way of forcing shifts between genres and/or technologies is to schedule them in:

> In my diary, if I've got a lot on, I'll divide up days: 'This is what you're doing on this day, you're writing this or that.' If it's a big project, I'll try and put 2 or 3 days together, rather than breaking it up.
>
> (Rhianna Pratchett)

Through the interviews, *deadlines* were repeatedly presented as helpful in forcing shifts between types of writing:

> [I]t's very useful to have a deadline and say, 'OK, I've got to do this by then, and this by then.' It means I can then plan the work in advance and think, 'Yes, I have got time to do this, if something else comes in, I could say I'm interested in that but I can't start it until I've got this thing out of the way and that would take me up to such and such a date.' So, yes, I do find deadlines very useful.
>
> (Charlie Higson)

> With the food writing [reviews for the *New Statesman*], I think the deadline was probably something like a Friday lunchtime, so Friday morning might be spent writing the food columns simply because – and this goes back to my days as student – I always hit the deadline, very late, but I always, always hit it. I'm never late for deadlines. I do love them.
>
> (Michèle Roberts)

> I imported some of the habits and protocols I learned as a journalist, because there is absolutely no arguing with copy deadlines. You have to give yourself copy dates because they're imposed on you if you're in journalism but they're not imposed on you if you're in the world of fiction. If you are a feature journalist as I was in the 1970s and 1980s, your area of focus changes every few weeks. So every few weeks you're on a new story that you're researching in depth, but the one thing that's certain is that your piece is earmarked for Issue 39. The copy date is that date and you cannot miss that date.
>
> (Jim Crace)

> I trained as a journalist, so I have a healthy respect for deadlines. It's very rare for me to miss a deadline.
>
> (Rhianna Pratchett)

The deadline for a novel or a feature-length script could be a year away, or more.

It can seem essential for a big creative project such as a novel to dedicate large blocks of time to it, and this may be true for sections of the work (completing a first draft, a discrete chapter or a final edit, for example). Yet, it became clear through the interviews that scheduling in different types of writing along the way can help sustain creativity for the length of time it takes to complete a novel. For many writers, moving between projects is an essential part of the creative process:

> Certainly I think, if I'd just been writing long novels, I would slowly have gone bonkers because it is a very solitary thing. When you are immersed in a book you don't want to have anything to do with anyone else particularly, and it's constantly on your mind and you're living in it. I think also you run out of steam. You're going to run out of energy if you keep doing that, unless you're going out and refreshing yourself, doing other things and having other experiences and opening your mind up.
>
> (Charlie Higson)

Monthly or weekly schedules can be given shape by imposed deadlines. For daily scheduling in particular, self-knowledge plays an important part. Just as gaining an understanding of which tools best suit which genres can help shifts (from a pen for libretti to a computer for prose, for example), so too can gaining an understanding of which part of the day suits which type of writing (perhaps the morning is best for writing a novel, the afternoon for journalism). Then, if shifts between types of writing are necessary, a writer can schedule tasks through the day accordingly:

> When I'm writing and trying to meet a deadline I will use the first part of the day to write. So I'm a morning person in that way. When things are going the way I want them to go I will start writing at 7.30 a.m. and keep going until I sort of run out of steam, which will be anything between 10 and 11 a.m. usually, and then I will move on to do other kinds of writing work that require different kinds of concentration.
>
> (Kate Pullinger)

> I don't tend to read in the morning because I am always writing, but I'll read quite relaxing things at certain moments, like perhaps over lunch if I'm eating a sandwich I might read a thriller or something. The afternoon is a bit of a dead time for writing so I might use that for reading books I'm judging for a literary competition or look at students' work.
>
> (Michèle Roberts)

> I've started to recognise more recently that I do my best writing in the afternoon. I feel much quicker, more alert, especially if I'm writing prose, lectures or non-fiction. It seems to come more quickly and easily in the afternoon, which has made me wonder sometimes why I've bothered in the morning because I can sit there for 2 to 3 hours. In the morning, it's very slow. It feels like hard work.
>
> (Simon Armitage)

> My most productive time is late afternoon through into the early evening. So often it might be that in the morning I do something I have to because of the deadline. That's more like work, I suppose. And then in the afternoon, that's the stuff that I would enjoy more.
>
> (Charlie Higson)

> [When scheduling] I will ensure that there's a natural break period between different types of writing. So I might, you know, answer an interview in the morning then go and do something else for a bit, maybe some chores. With the

creative writing it's more likely to be the afternoon into the evening. I'm not a morning person or a night owl, I'm somewhere around dusk. I'm a kind of badger writer, that's where it falls for me. I don't stay up hugely late (though I can do if the muse is with me). I'm more a late afternoon and dusk writer.

(Rhianna Pratchett)

However, it became clear through the interviews that strict scheduling does not work for all types of writing. It is quite possible for a deadline to be necessary for one type of writing but no use, or even damaging, for another. For example, Rhianna Pratchett talks about dividing up days in her diary for her commissioned work but, for writing that does not have a deadline attached, 'I try and impose more deadlines on myself, but I find that I'm then not as good at keeping to them'. At that point:

I almost have to lull myself into writing, you know, 'Ah look, you're watching some TV or you're talking to someone,' and then you get into the writing and you realise you've been writing for hours and you haven't been watching TV.

(ibid.)

I guess sentimentally, or subconsciously, I'm only contracted to myself to write the poems but nearly everything else I do has a deadline written down on a piece of paper. The poems have always felt like stolen time, either time stolen from my employees in the past (on stationery stolen from my employers). And I think when I gave up full-time work – which was as a probation officer – to become a full-time poet, whatever that involves, I probably imagined that I would be writing poetry most of the time. But I think, the way it's turned out, I now steal time from other projects to write my poems.

(Simon Armitage)

Anything that feels urgent – and that's a visceral physical feeling – will come first, so, for example, when my mother began dying there was an absolute need to write poetry about it and that took precedence over everything else. It wasn't just, you know, me as a conscious intellectual human being saying, 'I have decided to put these poems first', it was a feeling of absolute inner compulsion: 'These poems demand to be written so I'm going to make the time to write them.' I can't honestly remember whether I was working on a novel or not at the time but I put other work to second place. So it's a mixture of deadlines that occur, as it were, in the world, like a BBC radio commission to write a short story. I have to get it to the deadline. The deadline magically helps me find what the story is going to be about, compose it, write it, send it in; similarly with the journalism. With the novel the deadline is completely self-imposed because I don't tend to work to publishers' deadlines. My publisher knows that I do my own thing, I suppose. They just let me just get on with it so I go tootling along writing the novel knowing it's urgent to me but it isn't to anyone else.

(Michèle Roberts)

Sometimes moving *away* from a project is helpful:

You know I probably play computer games several hours a day when I'm supposed to be working. But I find that's quite useful because you are switching your brain off and not constantly going down the same grooves of trying to work.

(Charlie Higson)

That period of letting something sit somewhere, in the back of my head as well as on the hard drive, that for me has always been a useful thing, that business of allowing something to percolate. My novel *The Mistress of Nothing* (2009) took me 12 years to write and there was a lot of percolation involved in that. That's too extreme, I don't want to repeat that. But percolation is part of what I find useful about switching back and forth between different forms – it can mean I can leave something while working on something else and then go back to it and vice versa.

(Kate Pullinger)

Having a clear idea of whether morning, afternoon or dusk is better, then, or, knowing which project needs 'percolation' and which needs a period of 'lulling' could prove key when scheduling moves between different types of writing. Yet, whether 'percolation' or 'lulling' is useful (and if so, when) is a highly personal matter.

Through the interviews, a common thread was the importance for a writer of gaining a good understanding of his or her individual working habits. Knowing that retreating to bed with a laptop for a day will mean a scene gets finished or that a quick break for a computer game will help your novel, for example, could play a significant part in developing a writing practice that incorporates efficient and productive shifts between genres and technologies. In order to ensure that his or her time, equipment and workspaces are used to facilitate smooth and effective transitions, it can be critical for a writer to develop nuanced writerly self-knowledge. However, writerly self-knowledge is introspective, solitary. The term 'self-knowledge' suggests that *certainty* is possible.

Collaboration – which is increasingly essential in our postdigital age - tends to bring with it a whole host of uncertainties.

Collaboration

Collaboration (messy, exciting and unpredictable; desired or necessary) has been brought to the fore by new media technologies. It may come in the form of a partnership with a web designer for the creation of a web novel or game; it may come in the form of more casual sets of interactions with friends and strangers via social media. Social media, in particular, can be difficult for writers whose creative practice depends on ring-fencing blocks of time that are free of interruptions. While for some writers such interactions are enjoyable and stimulating, for others, they are irritating distractions which can, at worst, destroy creativity.

Take 'expectation' out of the equation and social media can look very different. It can provide a useful break, enabling shifts:

> I do love the way if you choose to use social media rather than find you are forced to, you can enjoy it. So I use a very, very simple form of social media called texting. I absolutely adore texting because it's like prose poems and it's kind of witty and it's un-anxious. It doesn't have to be urgent.
>
> (Michèle Roberts)

> I started on Twitter because my publisher said I should as a form of self-promotion. In the end I am not sure I see Twitter as a form of promotion. I found that I enjoyed it and I think it is actually a very useful tool for writers for several reasons. One is, traditionally as a writer – in the olden days – you would have very, very little contact with the people who are reading your books. That's changed hugely in the last 20 years, firstly with the rise of the literary festival, and also with social

media, which means you can have direct contact. Obviously there were letters before, but social media's much quicker and easier and you get a sense of what people are getting out of your book. So it is a useful interface with your readers and it can be encouraging for you. You think, 'Oh, I've given these people pleasure'.

(Charlie Higson)

Through the interviews, ideas of *audience* recurred as important. Charlie Higson stressed, 'I can't write in a void. I've got to have some sense of who I am writing for'. Just as *form* was referred to by a number of the authors interviewed as aiding shifts between types of writing, so too was focusing on who will read the work once it is finished:

So, you think, 'I am writing for this type of person now and therefore I need to write in this way', or whatever. You know, if I am writing kids' books I've got to keep bearing in mind the kids I am writing for, so then it's very useful going out and doing schools events and talking to kids of the age groups that are reading the books and reminding myself, 'OK, that is who these books are for'. And again with TV, it's watching a lot of other stuff on TV and getting an idea of what's there and what the audiences are.

(ibid.)

I like doing literary festivals. I find that is stimulating. You meet different people, you have to think differently. You have to think, 'How long is this talk going to be?' If it's going to be 40 minutes, you've got to give a few jokes, keep the audience with me.

(Juliet Gardiner)

Publishers' editors were cited by a number of the interviewees as particularly helpful in provoking or aiding shifts between creative projects:

I've nearly always got a structure of life that means there is another novel to write at some point, that does seem to be a sort of backbone. Maybe it's in between novels or slightly lying alongside, I'll write poetry. When I'm commissioned to, and that is very crucial, I'll listen to a publisher who says, 'At this point why don't you write a memoir or why don't you do a book of essays'. It doesn't just come from me, it's about being in the publishing world and having to listen to a publisher. It's collaborating with our publishers.

(Michèle Roberts)

You might actually be focusing your attention on an executive producer or someone like that, and you're thinking, 'Well they are the main critical gate-keeper I've got to get past.'

(Charlie Higson)

One thing is striking in Higson's comment: the executive producer is not needed in person, just the *thought* of an executive producer. Merely the thought of an external figure can bring a more clear-eyed view of what is needed for a new piece of work. The key collaborations for a writer when shifting between different types of writing can be *internal* collaborations:

Margaret Atwood once said that she thought that prose and poetry come out of different hemispheres of the brain. I don't think she'd done any scientific study, she was probably talking metaphorically – unless she was talking to the right brain, left brain stuff. I understand that a little bit just in that, if I'm writing prose I am thinking usually fairly logically and rationally and using language predominantly as information, whereas I think when I'm writing poetry I'm trying to get into the other side of the brain for more of that spatial awareness stuff and the sensual responses, and that does feel to be quite a thick membrane or a hard petition for me between those two parts of the mind.

(Simon Armitage)

When Juliet Gardiner – whose focus previously had been on writing history – moved into writing memoir, she found that she had to tap into different aspects of herself:

If I am writing subjectively, as I am at the moment, I think I am a slightly different personality than if I'm writing objectively. I'm more careful if I'm writing objectively, less careful if I'm writing a memoir because I feel, it's me, so I can do what I like with it. For memoir, you're mining facts, and you're also mining your own memory. It is a very different proposition. Previously, I've always kept myself out, I've never used the word 'I' because as a historian you are supposed to be describing and analysing historical facts – though of course no one can ever be objective – historians tend to say it depends where you stand what you see and write. A memoir is very different. I found I wrote it very quickly. I found it was a tremendously enjoyable process. It's not just a memoir, it's a memoir that is interwoven with history. I've made myself my own archive, my own resource. I've had to rethink how I write.

(Juliet Gardiner)

I think many artists feel that for any worthwhile art you are making, you're going into the unknown. You're making something completely new, and perhaps it's then the bogies from the past come. The panic at the beginning of any new writing project becomes in my imagination figures from the past who beat me round the head and tell me I can't do it. So there might be a mother figure, you know, not a real mother obviously just an imaginary one, or a nun with a whip in her hand or a line of male critics who don't read women's writing and don't like it. That's how my imagination works. It works through voices but also very much in a figurative way. And the only thing that you can do with these figures of judgement and criticism – which I think do go back to very early childhood, probably – is make friends with them. So you either dance a tango with them imaginatively or you put them into your writing. So all the villains in my writing have often been drawn from the ranks of those inner figures who oppress me with their criticism.

(Michèle Roberts)

For Rhianna Pratchett, moving between different types of writing is like stepping between vehicles:

The screenplays are more the big, black American muscle cars, maybe Chryslers or Mustangs, that kind of thing, cruising along Route 66, that's how it feels to me. Games writing is more rally driving, there are a lot more twists and turns, it's a lot less sedate because you have less time to splash around in the writer's pond, I know I'm mixing metaphors here, but it's much more frantic. You're writing the story and designing the game whereas with screenplays you just get to be a writer, there's no one disturbing you telling you how the writing has to be because of the gameplay or whatever. Those would be the main car differences.

(Rhianna Pratchett)

I've been happy as I got older to recognise that there isn't just one Simon Armitage who feels the same thing all the time. I think it's more about a change of moods, that I just have different moods rather than feeling as if I'm a different personality and I don't know how and why those moods come about.

(Simon Armitage)

When I was writing newspaper articles I was being puritanical: the truth is what matters, don't exaggerate, tell the truth, be of service to your readers, try and change the hearts of men and women because of what they read. But when I am writing fiction, there is nothing puritanical about me at all. Then I become impatient and mischievous. Those are the two sides of my personality, mischievousness on one side and puritanical on the other. They don't ever come together.

(Jim Crace)

The way Jim Crace presents it, his mischievous side involves further subdivisions.

'Where journalism is concerned,' he says, 'I was never fearful because the task was always clear', however:

When you're writing fiction, there's everything to be fearful of. But why would you move from one to the other, why would you move from a practice which is not fear-making into a practice that makes you fearful? Unless there is an extra pay-off that you get from it, it would make no sense. So the extra pay-off for me was the adrenalin. So, there was something heartless and mechanical about journalism which I respected, and I knew it was important. But there is something fearful and pumped up with adrenalin about writing fiction because there is no way that you can be certain that you are going to get out the other end.

(ibid.)

As well as 'importing' a respect for deadlines, Jim Crace transferred other habits and techniques from his time as a journalist when he started writing fiction:

> So there I was, in transition, trying to take in some of the habits that I had learnt, but it was also learning to live with the new freedom I'd found. One of the habits I'd learnt was the habit of remembering the many, many occasions when I've been given a commission to write 3,000 words and I've written 3,200 words. They've already earmarked where it's going to fit in. There's no free space, so 200 words have got to go. Now, the 200 words that have to go are your adjectives or your little flourishes at the end and the jokes, the things that you love best because they're the most personal. They're the ones to get slashed. So what I've learnt over the years is to defend my extra 200 words by freighting each sentence with a greater load. Fewer carriages, more cargo, in other words. For example, 'I came early today, after breakfast, on the morning train from my country home in Worcestershire and travelled by tube into the middle of London to queue up and wait to get a Russian visa for a trip I've planned to Moscow.' So that's a long sentence with lots of little subclauses and it makes complete sense and is perfectly OK, but a few words too long. 'Today I came from Worcestershire to London by train for my Russian visa' is a truncation but it's keeping all the essentials while making the phrasing of them denser. I've made that simple editing process sound much grander than it truly is ... except it is grand! Because, actually, whatever you do in language is what gives you a voice, and I think that in some ways what people have seen as 'my voice' is to do with the way in which my sentences are freighted.
>
> (ibid.)

For Rhianna Pratchett, the experience she uses to tackle types of writing that are new to her dates back to her schooldays:

> I think as an only child, you become very good at being dropped into situations and just having to deal with it. You have to learn to adapt quickly. I went to boarding school for 2 years, so that probably helped me deal with unfamiliar situations.
>
> (Rhianna Pratchett)

Initially I wanted to be an artist when I was about five. I failed my art O-Level with grade Z. I thought, 'Oh, well I can never go to art school, oh poor me,' so I went into my second love which is writing and, as a writer, I've always been extremely imagistic and figurative. I'm just beginning to see that I always need to be drawing as well as writing to be properly myself. So when I'm writing a novel I might just be doing doodles in private, which I don't show anybody, but I've got notebooks which are just stacked with doodles or cartoons.

(Michèle Roberts)

Generating visuals, then, even if they are only doodles, might prove helpful in accessing a different mindset. Recalling methods from the past that were used to tackle unfamiliar situations might be drawn on to aid present and future shifts between genres or technologies.

Experience of scriptwriting was cited by a number of writers as a particularly useful skill in the twenty-first century writing and publishing landscape:

I think one of the reasons I was able to make the transition to writing for digital media in the way that I have over the last 15 years is because I spent about a decade before that learning how to write for film and television. I think that was very useful when I came to start to think about writing for the Internet and indeed writing for digital media because it meant that I did have some grasp of the way that writing for screen, even when there is text on the screen, is very different from writing long-form prose. So when I am writing for digital media I always know that the text is supported by other media. It's supported by music, it's supported by design, it's supported by images or video or animation, you know, whatever else is going on in the piece, which means that the text necessarily has to do less work, it needs to be concise. It doesn't need to rely on description in the same way that long-form prose can and does.

(Kate Pullinger)

With video games, there's such a lot of different writing, it's actually quite good training for other things. There's a lot of cinematic writing in video games, and that translates quite well to film. You're also having to be quite concise with your language. You don't have the luxury of the size of a screen-play, you have to keep things as short and characterful as possible, and that can be good for writing things like comics, and for things like Twitter, because you're used to condensing things down.

(Rhianna Pratchett)

The need to keep in mind the size of the screen a story will be viewed on, or to allow for the fact that music and visuals are playing, for example, may impact writing in a digital age.

A key division when considering long-form prose as opposed to games or web novels is between so-called 'linear' and 'non-linear' writing. According to this division a traditional, hard copy novel (whereby the story starts at the beginning and page by page continues through to the end) is linear, whereas a web novel or a computer game, which might involve any number of story paths, is non-linear. Thus, it may be necessary for a writer to move between a range of platforms and genres when working on a single creative project, while also providing readers multiple entry and exit points for an overarching narrative.

It is generally assumed that writing linear stories is natural and writing non-linear stories is unnatural. Robert Coover suggests that, in fact, the reverse is true:

On the Internet, one lives in a variety of interconnected, multilinear narratives, it's the natural environment, but if you want to write a novel, with a beginning, middle and end, one contained on two or three hundred paper pages, *that's* different, it's not something that's natural, one has to learn to do that. The natural thing is this multidirectional, multimodal form of narrative.

(Robert Coover)

If you see my office it's probably a physical representation of my mind and my process. Everything is there and it's all out and it's all mixed up, tangled up with everything else. But I know where everything is and it's there when I need it. I have to trust myself that when I sit down to write, the things I need to write will be there somewhere inside the jungle of my mind.

(Charlie Higson)

Shifting about, then – between thoughts and ideas and different types of writing – may after all be the natural state, with how to harness and direct such volatility a key issue:

'I have a little website I use called "Ideas Are Us"' – that's what I say when people ask me at literary festivals or children's events where I get my ideas from. But actually, that's sort of what your brain is. It's like a website. You tick the boxes of what you are looking for and your brain looks for those things. Everything that happens to you as a writer is potentially something you can use.

I mean, for instance, when I was writing the *Young Bond* series [2005–2010], which is set in the 1930s, I was just constantly tuned in to events that happened then. Then you think, 'OK, that's something I could use to generate a plot'. Now that I'm not working on the young James Bond books I'm not really interested in the 1930s at all.

(ibid.)

I'm very keen on the fractured and the fragmentary because I think that's how things work. I don't mean that you have an awful lot of fragments and then you stick them together again. But I do think it's important to recognise that not everything is linear and there is no need to make it all linear. By making it linear you can diminish its freshness.

(Juliet Gardiner)

When I started writing I only thought that I would write poetry and that I would be very happy with that. But, one of the reasons why I branched out, and I think this is one of the reasons why other poets write in different moods as well, is that, you know, you just can't write poetry all the time but you do have the urge to write. You have the urge to work with language but that can't be poetry all the time and so it's almost automatic, or at least natural, I think, to try all the forms, things that you might be able to get on with on a daily basis.

(Simon Armitage)

I've written novels that are composed of short stories, I've written short stories that are actually tiny, tiny novels in miniature, I've written novels that have poems in them, I've written poems that are very narrative, I've now written prose pieces that have drawings with them. And, to me, that's the truth about human artistry, that there is something multilayered and multi-branched that's true. It's our culture that says you must be in a genre, or you must be pigeonholed in some way, or you're this kind of writer or that kind of writer. I have to go along with that because that's the world we all live in. But the deeper truth is that, you know, word and image are very close, and we can make beautiful artefacts that explode all these divisions and separating concepts. So the *moving between* is necessary perhaps to recapture some of that potential, you see.

(Michèle Roberts)

Looking back over the interviews, then, there are a number of straightforward, practical things that can be done to aid shifts between different genres and technologies. Computer software, writers' retreats, schedules and commissioning editors, for example, can all be deployed to good effect. The authors also described some more personal and idiosyncratic techniques. Rhianna Pratchett speaks of the need to 'lull' herself into different writing projects, Jim Crace of embodying 'puritanical' as opposed to 'mischievous' writing selves. Juliet Gardiner embraces the 'fractured' and 'fragmentary'. Charlie Higson utilises 'mental radar'. For Kate Pullinger, 'percolation' is important. The British Library's book trolleys proved inspiring for Robert Coover. Simon Armitage places high value on the particular 'drag and flow' of his pens. Michèle Roberts talks of the importance of periodically giving herself over to an 'oceanic feeling which is about moving inside language and the imagination'. A number of the writers suggest that a calculated spontaneity is needed periodically in order to stay creatively fresh. Whether they are referred to as moods, personalities or cars, for example, writers collaborate with different aspects of themselves in order to shift productively between genres and technologies.

The tools and schedules that can be planned; the idiosyncratic writerly habits that must be recognised and factored in – all this draws attention back to the importance for a writer of gaining a nuanced understanding of his or her best working practices. How to set about gaining such an understanding is the subject of Chapter 4.

4 CREATIVE WRITING AND MULTIMODALITY: ASSEMBLING A TOOLKIT, COMPONENT PARTS

This chapter presents a model of creativity designed to enable development of a personalised multimodal writing practice that will optimise creative flexibility and productivity in a fast-paced twenty-first century writing and publishing landscape. The model is for use by practitioners, students and teachers of Creative Writing.

The ability to move effectively between genres and technologies quickly is, as discussed, increasingly a basic requirement for writers in a digital age, yet there is a lack of theory and/or pedagogy to help. Bateman, Page and Gibbons are amongst those who point to the need for models addressing the challenges multimodality brings that are, as Page puts it, 'systematic', 'replicable' and 'flexible enough to embrace the rich diversity of all that multimodality encompasses'.[1, 2, 3, 4] The aim here is to provide such a model.

To do this, the auto-practitioner study, author interviews and in-class pilots of assignments (see Chapters 2, 3 and 5) were used in combination to delineate key resources (internal and external) and skills needed for a robust multimodal writing practice. The model of creativity presented here was developed using the findings, and it was then trialled as a class assignment itself, to test whether it can be used as a template to help a writer identify the appropriate resources, develop the set of necessary skills and then orchestrate those component parts effectively in order to enable him or her to work effectively and creatively as a multimodal writer.

Scoping the task

First, before detailing the component parts of the model of creativity, it may help to step back and consider the scope of what the model must take into account and address. While this model of creativity is rooted firmly in Creative Writing and is for use by creative writers, the research informing its development is, inevitably, wide ranging, drawing from fields such as book history, literary criticism, media and cultural studies, linguistics, philosophy and psychology. Page's 'rich diversity of all that multimodality encompasses' embraces everything from pen and paper to microblogging to websites to video games, for example, and to technologies that have yet to be invented. Just on the basis of these two points, it might seem unrealistic to aim to provide a model that is at once systematic and replicable and flexible enough to be used by all writers at whatever stage of their writing career – but there is more. The range of experiences individual writers bring is vast, incalculably so. The experience of writing a story is not only different between writers, it alters for each writer between situations and over time. The arrival of digital technologies has caused seismic changes, certainly; but, even if we could set digital technologies aside, we must still address the fact that writerly practices have always been highly individualistic.

Insoluble pancake

Take novelist Jonathan Coe, who in an interview with *The Guardian* newspaper spoke of his writing day lacking shape and structure: 'it is of indeterminate duration and its texture is infinitely variable'.[5] It might start in the morning or the afternoon, in a relative's flat or on a bus. 'I wish I could be more helpful and prescriptive,' said Coe, 'but in short, even after 11 novels, and three decades of published writing, the process remains deeply mysterious to me.' He quotes Flann O'Brien's fictional character, Policeman MacCruiskeen to explain just how impossible it is to pin down details of his creative practice: 'It is nearly an insoluble pancake.'

However, Coe's description of his own particular 'insoluble pancake' features a number of commonalities. For example, like Simon Armitage and Rhianna Pratchett (see Chapter 3), Coe finds writing in 'noisy' locations such as trains, productive. Like Michèle Roberts and Jim Crace (see Chapter 3), the place where he works features a lot of significant *stuff* (in Coe's case including hundreds of vinyl records 'which I never play but can't bear to be parted from'). 'Caffeine' also plays an important part for Coe, so too the presence or absence at different times of people. Though Coe does not have a single writing day that could be viewed as a template, his use of trains, *stuff* and locations, for example, represent aspects of writing practice that can be seen in other writers' creative practice.

It can be easy to focus on the technologies that are coming *at* us. We may be frustrated with the ways they alter how we write or the training that's needed to master them. Switching the focus around, Coe's *Guardian* interview sheds interesting light on the cliché of the writer as essentially monomodal (working in isolation with one genre and one technology at a time). Coe's description of his creative practice suggests that, actually, he has drawn on an internal multimodality from the outset.

Robert Coover and Charlie Higson (see Chapter 3) too suggest that writers are, in fact, inherently multimodal. Indeed, in *Remixing Composition: A History Multimodal Writing Pedagogy*, Palmeri says that we have to train our minds *out* of multimodal thinking in order to construct stories for traditional page-based delivery.[6] Describing the process of writing conventional hard copy text as 'an act of translation from the multimodal mind to the alphabetic page', Palmeri cites process researchers Flower and Hayes: 'Trying to capture the movement of a deer on ice in language is clearly a kind of translation.' Such acts of 'translation' are effortful and complex, they may involve excitement and struggle.[7] The feel of a biro as opposed to a fountain pen, or the view out of the window as we write can impact the words we choose and the tone that we adopt, so too the mood we bring. Even before new media technologies are involved, then, to enable movement 'from the multimodal world of the mind (where images, words, and kinaesthetic sensations mingle) to the alphabetic space of the page (where conventionally only words appear)', Palmeri observes, multimodal thinking is required.[8] Thus, the task of developing a multimodal practice comes to be a case not of constructing something new but, instead, of reclaiming something that is accessible to us already but has been suppressed.

The kind of multimodal thinking Palmeri outlines – with sensations positioned centrally – is evident in innumerable writers' accounts of creative process. Eudora Welty presents, as key to her development as a writer, childhood experiences that engaged her senses, from the sound of the 'mission-style oak grandfather clock' striking in the hall to the smell of books in her hands to the physiological experience of reciting the alphabet.[9, 10, 11, 12] The Soviet writer Mikhail Bulgakov also notes the importance of the senses: 'One of my characteristics is that I need to listen to music. In fact I could say that I worship good music. It's very conducive to creative work'.[13] In Ernest Hemingway's description of the process of writing a story in a Parisian café,[14] 'good Martinique rum', the room's atmosphere, the people, the experience of sharpening his pencil ('the shavings curling into the saucer under my drink'[15]) all play parts.

As Page notes, 'The relationship between materiality and multimo-dality draws attention to the physical work involved in narrative process-ing, both in the use of tools and technology, and also by the human body and its sensory organs.'[16] In Chapter 3, Simon Armitage talks of needing a pen with 'the right amount of drag and flow' when he is writing poetry. Juliet Gardiner says she still prints out a hard copy as part of the editing process. Rhianna Pratchett says she has to handwrite her 'To Do' lists.

Palmeri says it is 'important to note that digital technologies are not necessarily required for a robust multimodal writing pedagogy'.[17] This book phrases the point more strongly. It is not just that 'old' technol-ogies *can* be part of a robust multimodal writing pedagogy. Rather, it is the inclusion of 'old' technologies that makes a multimodal writing pedagogy robust. 'Digital skills development starts offline and "offline" continues to be an important delivery method', note Wilson and Grant in their report for the Carnegie Trust UK, *Not Without Me: A digi-tal world for all?*[18] Strategic re-engagement with familiar technologies can play a highly constructive part in developing a multimodal writing practice.

There will always be a point at which a new technology becomes old. As Baron says, pencils were once new technology; a computer (or tablet or smartphone) could be framed as just 'a better pencil'.[19] Walter Ong notes that in Ancient Greece, for Plato, *writing* was 'an external, alien technology, as many people today think of the computer'.[20] One reason it is important to keep a rolling engagement with technologies that are new, quite new and old to us is: we will never arrive at a place where all the technologies we use are fixed and all invention of new technologies is finished. Learning a set of discrete, current technical skills could poten-tially be problematic in the long term, since, if those particular technical skills become obsolete, the job of learning new technologies will have to start all over again.

Furthermore, new technologies are often modelled on old technolo-gies. On computer document's toolbars, for example, scissor icons are used to indicate cutting tools. So, returning to old technologies can sometimes help directly with the process of getting to grips with new technologies. As Bolter and Grusin describe it in their seminal text *Remediation*, new visual media are not departures from or breaks with earlier media but rather, new media *refashion* (or, 'remediate') existing media (e.g. paint-ing 'refashions' photography which is in turn 'refashioned' by film; the early internet 'refashioned' print and then, through Web 2.0, went on to refashion the moving image).[21] Cranny-Francis, in considering how users read and understand multimedia texts, argues that rather than *erasing* evidence of mediation, as Bolter and Grusin suggest, users often play with what they know of earlier media, 'mobilis[ing] their understandings of these earlier encounters in their readings of multimedia texts'.[22] Thus, as has been explored in Chapter 2, instead of rejecting experiences of 'old' media as redundant, writers can productively mobilise prior creative experiences. He or she can 'remediate practice', transferring existing skills into new digital multimedia and networked environments. Looking back to past moments enables us to better 'understand the contemporary dynamics of "new media"', says Palmeri.[23] 'Perhaps our most valuable yardstick,' notes Hayles, 'is our own experience'.[24]

Keeping old technology in multimodal writing practice is important for another reason too: technologies that are familiar to us already can help make us feel comfortable. Use of pen and paper generally dates back to childhood (to home, to school), their inclusion can feel grounding. The 'soft graininess' and 'kinetic activity' of turning a page can be reassuring.[25] Something as simple as taking hold of a pencil can help users regain a sense of agency and see that there is not a rigid set of rules beyond their control; rather, they have choice.

Alongside music, memory played an important part for Bulgakov: 'The image of a lamp with a green shade is a very important image for me. It derives from my childhood impressions of the image of my father, writing at a desk'.[26]

In Chapter 3, Michèle Roberts talks of how a love of drawing that dates back to childhood continues to inform her creative process. Jim Crace talks of 'importing' habits from work as a journalist to work as a novelist. Kate Pullinger talks of how a period writing for film and television helped her make the transition to writing for digital media.

Coe calls his an 'insoluble pancake', and there is no doubt that each individual's writerly process is complicated and multifaceted. However, to develop a multimodal writing practice is to take account of that complexity, to acknowledge and welcome it. For Hemingway, when he was in the Parisian café, with his internal and external writerly resources – rum, rain, pencil shavings; imagination, emotional responses – working in harmony, 'The story was writing itself and I was having a hard time keeping up with it.'[27]

However, Hemingway's comment could make it seem that he was not in control of his story, and, it is not uncommon to hear statements like this. Writers often speak of 'becoming a different person' when in the throes of creating.

Dorothea Brande says that writers comprise three personalities: 'a prosaic, everyday practical person' who is 'intelligently critical, detached, tolerant'; an 'artist-self' who 'may then be as sensitive, enthusiastic and partisan as you like'; and a third personality endowed with 'flashes of insight, the penetrating intuitions, the imagination which combines and transmutes ordinary experience into "the illusion of a higher reality"'.[28, 29, 30] In her essay *Harnessed to the Harpy*, Fay Weldon refers to 'subdividing' herself into personalities, of 'splitting-offs' including of 'L and M, N and R, I called them, all more or less delinquent', with two main writerly personalities, 'A' (the one who writes the first draft) and 'B' (who edits), who she presents as fighting productively.[31] Noting the 'persistent drag' of habits that have to be struggled away from, Gertrude Stein suggests, 'You always have in your writing the resistance outside of you and inside of you, a shadow upon you, and the thing which you must express.'[32] The writer Lynn Tillman describes writers as 'shifty subjects who may from time to time be many things'.[33]

Many scholars have written about how new media technologies are impacting our sense of self. Bolter and Grusin suggest that individuals working in digital multimedia and networked environments require a new 'definition of self whose key quality is not so much "being immersed" as "being interrelated or connected".[34] The hypermediated self is a network of affiliations, which are constantly shifting'. Rotman says 'the I/me-unit is dissolving, the one who says or who writes "I" … is no longer a singular, integrated whole, but multiple: a plurality of distributed I-effects, I-roles, I-functions, and I "presences"'.[35] Elwell argues that in the twenty-first century, when 'the line between life online and life offline has become blurred in an existential equivalence of the digital and the analog', self-identity occupies 'the liminal space between the virtual and the real, reveal[ing] a transmediated self constituted as a browsable story-world that is integrated, dispersed, episodic, and interactive'.[36]

Certainly, new media technologies have brought to the fore both the existence of a range of internal selves and the benefit of not just acknowledging but, rather, embracing such internal multiplicity. However, the observations of Brande, Weldon, Stein and Tillman above make clear that such internal multiplicity is and always has been part and parcel of being writer. Deleuze and Guattari suggest that we should think of ourselves as rhizomes, with bits of ourselves breaking away and coming back to form new associations – 'any point of a rhizome can be connected to any other, and must be'.[37] This can, they suggest, give rise to a wealth of possibilities: 'An assemblage is precisely this increase in the dimensions of a multiplicity that necessarily changes in nature as it expands its connections'.[38] If, as M.M. Bakhtin suggests, a creative imagination *must* interact with different parts of itself – if writers need to gain awareness of 'this concrete outsidedness of me myself' – then, clearly, stepping back to watch those rapidly changing interactions with oneself in order to develop methods of harnessing and directing them is going to be of great benefit.[39, 40]

In the twenty-first century, there are many stages and types of writing involving a seemingly ever-widening range of technologies. There are many states of mind that help those different stages, types, tools and movements between them.

In Chapter 3, Simon Armitage talks of attaching different writerly *moods* to different types of writing. Rhianna Pratchett thinks of different aspects of her writerly self as being like different types of cars. Michèle Roberts finds it important to befriend her different writerly personalities.

Yet, it is one thing to recognise such internal multiplicity. How do we then negotiate it?

Self-trust

Eudora Welty said in one of her last interviews, 'Writing is such an internal, interior thing that it can hardly be reached by you, much less by another person. I can't tell you how to write ... Writers must learn to trust themselves.'[41] Coe, too, highlights the importance of a writer learning to trust him or herself: 'In any case, the books come at their own pace. They will allow themselves to be written when they're ready, and not before, and learning to recognize when that moment has arrived is my key to time management'.[42]

As Coe notes, he has had 11 novels and three decades of published writing during which to 'learn to recognize when that moment has arrived'. An idea that self-trust is pivotal may not be particularly welcome if a writer is just starting out, or if he or she has arrived at a crisis point involving writer's block, for example.

Yet, the self-trust referred to by Welty and Coe may not necessarily be as strange and elusive as their comments suggest. Brande refers to 'flashes of insight' and 'penetrating intuitions'; others talk of 'gut instinct' or 'inspiration'.[43] A danger of such terms is that they can suggest that key points in the creative process are ones over which the writer has no control. For this reason, rather than 'self-trust', 'flashes of insight', 'gut instinct' or 'inspiration', Melrose talks of 'expert intuition'.[44]

Cokely and Feltz note, 'research shows that the intuitions of verifiable *expert performers* tend to be highly accurate, well calibrated, and powerful'; 'To a great extent, the superior judgement and decision making of expert performers follows from differences in their *intuitions*, which can be refined and deliberated on as needed during the decision making.'[45] Describing how this works in the context of creative practice, Melrose says expert intuition allows '"something" (in the making) to "feel right", on the basis of which "new possibilities" can be acted upon'.[46]

For Michèle Roberts (see Chapter 3) as for a great many writers, a key aim is to write something completely new each time. As Amos Oz notes in *The Story Begins*, deciding on those first words and then setting them down is hard, at whatever stage of his or her career a writer may be.[47] Whether it is a first, fifth or eleventh novel, each time *any* writer embarks on a new creative project, the challenges faced can feel overwhelming. In a rapid-fire digital landscape, every writer can feel inexpert on a regular basis. 'Gut instinct' or a 'flash of insight' might steer a writer suddenly and unexpectedly to an apparently unconnected type or moment of previous creative practice. Thus, 'self-trust' – or, 'expert intuition' – can play a key role in facilitating the kinds of risks that enable the start and pursuit to completion of new creative projects.

Yet, this still leaves the question of how to negotiate our internal multiplicity, a task that could seem yet more daunting now that an additional element – expert intuition – has been added.

Despite extensive bodies of research in fields including philosophy, psychology and neuroscience and development of a great number of concepts and theories (such as theories of Affect, the Extended Mind and Embodied Cognition), we still do not know how the interactions between the material world, the body, the senses and the mind work together to create meaning and reason as we move through our lives and work. However, we know two things that are of particular relevance here.

On one hand, we prefer to think that we have full, conscious control of our actions and decisions. We don't generally like to admit it if the *un*conscious plays an important role, since, as Hayles notes in *How We Think*, to do so downplays 'human agency'.[48]

On the other hand, we know full well that consciousness is not some kind of perfect and infallible machine whereby a pristine mind contained neatly in a skull makes all our decisions in a discrete, wholly rational manner. If you have a flaming row just before you leave the house, the commute and work day that follow are likely to be quite different from a day on which breakfast is delicious and early morning conversation heartwarming. If the day is very rainy or very sunny, that has an impact on how we behave. Interactions with technologies can, as Marshall McLuhan phrased it back in 1962, bring 'trauma and tension to every living person. Our most ordinary and conventional attitudes seem suddenly twisted into gargoyles and grotesques', and, if those are our responses when we encounter technologies, any writing or storytelling that follows cannot fail to be affected.[49] When it comes to creative practice, we know that the unconscious can help build stumbling blocks such as technostress; we also know that the unconscious can play a key and highly effective role.

We may not yet (indeed, may never) understand all the biology, psychology and/or neuroscience of it. Developments such as Artificial Intelligence and Virtual Reality will lead to new findings and take research into the mind/body relationship in new directions (then new technological developments and discoveries will force new rethinks). As Hayles notes, scientific 'truths' of one generation have the 'unsettling tendency' 'to be overturned or reversed in the next, especially in fields as rapidly developing as brain science and the science of consciousness'.[50] Meanwhile, every day, with our 'mashup minds' working at the 'productive interface of brain, body, and social and material world', as Andy Clark frames it, '"messy" but powerful solutions are reliably found'.[51]

If we give the unconscious the right conditions, it can do a lot of the creative work for us (ideas and solutions often come to us at apparently humdrum moments: while we are on a bus, having a shower, on the bus, making a meal). Like it or not, we rely on the unconscious to help us – swiftly, decisively – move between different creative projects in optimum ways at optimum moments.

A writer's creative practice may indeed look like a 'nearly insoluble pancake'. However, component parts can be identified.

Noting that our total capacity for absorbing information from the world around us is 200,000 times as high as the capacity of consciousness, Hayles describes the unconscious as 'a perceptive capacity that catches the abundant overflow too varied, rich and deep to make it through the bottle neck of attention'.[52, 53] Considering how we are each 'co-present, heterogeneously connected to ourselves … always in the process of becoming multiple and parallel', Rotman calls the kind of co-ordinating unconscious activity which Hayles refers to a 'para-self'.[54] Hurley outlines a 'sub-personal' level of cognition which consists of a 'tangle of multiple feedback loops of varying orbits'.[55] Requiring a single term, I refer to an 'inner auteur'.

In the study of the cinema, auteur status is generally attached to a director whose creative vision – regardless of variables such as cast, crew, finances – stamps its mark on his or her *oeuvre*. In the context of multimodal writing practice, the 'inner auteur' is an internal equivalent.

The inner auteur as I conceptualise it is less clearly delineated than the writerly personas and more pervasive, a lurking presence (a kind of ghostly puppetmaster) that captures and acts on expert intuition, subtly, invisibly directing the available internal and external writerly resources, selecting, rejecting, adjusting. Through all this change and movement, the inner auteur – our co-ordinating unconscious capacity – helps ensure that the author's own, unique, authentic voice remains both intact and an overarching, unifying presence.

Thus the unconscious gives us both expert intuition (flashes of insight and ideas) and, in the form of an inner auteur, the means of co-ordinating our writerly resources. In developing a multimodal writing practice, the aim is to provide conditions in which expert intuition and the inner auteur can thrive.

To recap briefly, writers are inherently multimodal in their approach. It is not so much a question of learning something new, rather, we can reappropriate ways of working that are natural to us already. Thus, the task of formulating a model to account for changes in writing practices resulting from the arrival of digital technologies may turn out to be less difficult (and more enjoyable) than expected.

The model presented here is not intended to be a hard and fast set of rules. It is to be used and altered and developed over time. Each person's multimodal writing practice will be different. The model is intended to help practitioners in the task of discovering and refining the strengths, details and parameters of his or her own unique multimodal writing practice.

Model of creativity

In summary, then, the model of creativity presented here can be used to enable a writer to delineate, assess and develop his or her individual multimodal approach and so effectively and productively negotiate a twenty-first century writing and publishing landscape characterised by technological change.

As discussed, in order to move between different types of writing, writers draw on a mix of internal and external writerly resources (e.g. sensations, writing tools, locations), and, to draw on these writerly resources, many writers utilise a range of writerly personas (e.g. a more dogged persona may be needed to pursue the last leg of a novel, a more gregarious persona to engage with social media). A key resource is a writer's own prior creative practice, which a writer can remediate. Thus, as new challenges and opportunities arise, a practitioner adapts existing skills and prior experience and applies them in new contexts in order to meet challenges and embrace opportunities presented in digital multimedia and networked environments. To orchestrate the wealth of possibilities, a writer's inner auteur captures expert intuition and other writerly resources and personas, identifying which, and in what combination, will be optimally effective for particular moves between different types of creative projects.

Thus the model of creativity comprises: Writerly Resources; Writerly Personas; Expert Intuition; Inner Auteur; Creative Projects.

Writerly Resources. Each practitioner has a set of writerly resources. Exactly what his or her set is made up of is unique to each practitioner and so may vary between practitioners, perhaps significantly. The set of writerly resources comprises internal resources (such as sensations, moods, reflection, prior creative experiences) and external resources (such as tools, locations, deadlines, audience). Which resources play the most vigorous parts, and how, varies between practitioners. Sensations may be especially important (e.g. the feel of a particular pen), or deadlines might be particularly effective motivators. For each practitioner, as new media technologies and new creative projects arrive, what is and what is not considered a particularly important writerly resource and how each helps a practitioner move between genres and technologies may change over time.

Writerly Personas. Different aspects of the writing process require different aspects of our being and personality to come to the fore. These aspects may be thought of as, for example, moods, selves or personas; in the model of creativity, they are referred to as 'writerly personas'. Identifying which writerly personas are most likely to be helpful for different elements of *a single creative project* is likely to be relatively straightforward. As noted, Weldon idenfities 'A' (who writes the first draft) and 'B' (who edits);[56] similarly, Brande identifies a 'practical' and an 'artist-self'.[57] However, identifying which writerly personas are best placed (and in what combination) to help a practitioner *move* between different types of writing can require more attention (the most helpful persona may be one that gently lulls a practitioner between projects; alternatively, a more commanding persona might be required). Just as there may be commonalities but there can be no one definitive set of writerly resources for all writers, the range, quantity and nature of writerly personas is likely to differ between practitioners.

Expert Intuition. The kind of sudden conviction that arrives in a flash (telling a practitioner that a particular plot twist is right, for example, or that a new character called Clementina must be removed from the novel and put in the screenplay, or that previous experience of learning to skateboard aged 12 will help with a particularly challenging piece of new technology) may seem random, may appear risky. A practitioner must have the self-trust necessary to move ahead firmly and confidently with prospective solutions, which may well be highly experimental. Such flashes of conviction, which could even seem illogical but which a practitioner trusts and acts on, are termed here 'expert intuition'.

Inner Auteur. A flash of lightning cannot operate in a vacuum. It needs the right conditions before it can hit a tree and – apparently miraculously – split it. Similarly, a solution that may appear to arrive out of the blue has had the conditions for its arrival set up already. The 'inner auteur' is able to identify that a flash of expert intuition has arrived, conditions are right and it should be acted on. It is not merely an additional writerly persona. A writer may be aware of different writerly personas and step into them consciously. Rather, the inner auteur (a kind of internal auterist film director or ghostly diagnosing GP or puppetmaster) represents our co-ordinating unconscious capacity. As I conceive it, the inner auteur can with inconceivable rapidity alight on, assess and/or absorb an apparently disparate range of sensations and events, selecting from and orchestrating in optimal combinations the writerly resources and writerly personas to enable the practitioner to pursue and move between creative projects.

Creative Projects. The creative projects that a writer moves between might be a novel on the one hand (spanning months or years) with social media posts (such as blogs or tweets) as small, regular creative projects. The range of creative projects being worked on at any one time may include, for example, a film script and a creative non-fiction book or a linked set of Instagram posts and a game narrative, poems or reviews. The nature and number of creative projects will vary not only between practitioners but also over time.

To conclude this chapter, then, the model of creativity presented here is not (and cannot be) definitive. It is a template to work with and build on and customise.

The task of starting to build your own is the first of the set of assignments in Chapter 5 which are designed to support the development of a multimodal writing practice and enable construction of a personalised model of creativity (Figure 4.1).

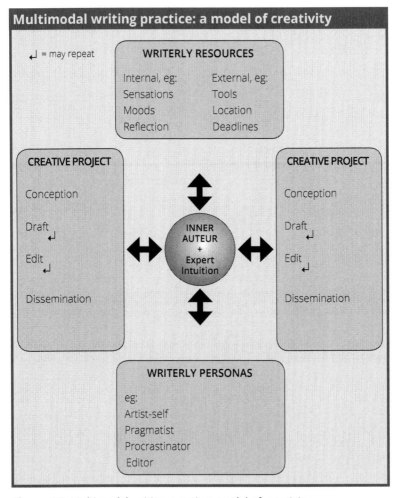

Figure 4.1 Multimodal writing practice: model of creativity

5 DEVELOPING A MULTIMODAL WRITING PRACTICE: ASSIGNMENTS

This chapter contains assignments designed to support the development of a personalised multimodal writing practice.

The assignments are for use by students of Creative Writing and practitioners. They can also be used by tutors of Creative Writing in a classroom setting. Every assignment featured is tried and tested and designed to be taken straight into an individual's practice or the classroom without too much preparation, if any.[1,2] In keeping with the structure of the book, the assignments have been arranged with the intention that, if followed from first to last, they will help build – in an optimally beneficial order – skills that support the development of a robust multimodal writing practice. Alternatively, the assignments can be dipped in and out of.

Before getting down to the details of the assignments, a few overarching practicalities. As discussed in Chapter 4, it is not necessary to introduce a wide range of new media technologies to your practice immediately. To do so will not result in a more robust multimodal writing practice.[3] Indeed, Wilson and Grant stress that 'Digital skills development starts offline' and that offline learning methods continue to be important as online skills are developed and built.[4] Thus, the assignments have been written so that they can be begun in a quite 'low tech' fashion.

You may *want* to introduce digital technologies promptly – you may be keen to use video immediately, for example – in which case, the notes at the top and/or the final step of each assignment provide suggestions regarding how. It is worth bearing in mind that on social media, if a platform is live and public, it may be helpful to start an anonymous account initially (this can free you up as you start exploring a platform's affordances and conventions more boldly).

If the idea of introducing new media technologies feels somewhat daunting, remember that you are not alone. As discussed, such wariness is widespread. So, do not feel shy of seeking help. If you are in a workplace or educational institution, for example, remember, most companies and organisations have technical departments that can provide support, the first step to getting help may well be just a quick phone call or email. If such institutional help is not available to you, the Internet features an abundance of audio, Vimeo and SoundCloud demonstrations of how to use a whole host of new media technologies, so just a quick online search can pay dividends; online 'Help' icons and 'Live Chat' options are often extremely useful. When Mark Twain decided – at the time, radically – to move from handwritten to typewritten manuscripts, this is how he approached it: 'In a Boston store window, [he] had spotted the new contraption called a "type-machine". He went inside, watched the salesman's "type-girl" demonstrate that she could bang out fifty-seven words a minute and bought one for $125'.[5] Like Twain, ask staff in shops to show you how it is done. Although, it is worth noting that once Twain had purchased the 'type-machine',

> 'Back in Hartford, he practiced typing "The boy stood on the burning deck" until he could make twelve words a minute (all in caps and with a carriage return that worked via a foot pedal), and sent typewritten letters to relatives and friends, most of them on the topic of sending typewritten letters'.[6]

Practice is often needed, and practice takes time and energy. It is worth staggering the introduction of new technologies so that you are embedding only one or two platforms that are new to you and, meanwhile, you can continue working with a raft of genres/technologies with which you are comfortable.

Perhaps above all, be prepared to experiment. As Leahy and Dechow put it, position *'Play!'* as a guiding principle.[7]

As indicated, key skills necessary for a robust multimodal writing practice were identified using the three research areas that this volume represents with the precise composition of the assignments further informed by the pedagogical need identified by scholars including Kress, Yancey and Harper.[8, 9, 10] The main skills subdivide into generic skills (flexibility, reflective risk-taking and bold exploration) and specific skills (transforming templates, real-time discourse, code-switching, collaboration, remediation, non-linear storytelling, swift editing, selecting, curating, deploying visuals).

Any timings are, of course, indicative only as each asssignment's duration will depend on participants' interests and expertise. You may want to quickly fit in an assignment during a lunch break, or develop a piece of work into something more substantial. Hence, suggestions for shorter or extended versions of each assignment are provided.

And now, with practicalities addressed, to the assignments!

Doing it!

Assignment 1: 'Getting personal'

Map your writerly resources and assess how best to deploy them (i.e. start building your own personalised model of creativity).

Skills: Flexibility | remediation, collaboration.

Individual/group: Solo exercise.

Equipment: Pen and paper/computer.

Time: One hour, or, 10 minutes a day for a week (for a shorter version, after Steps 1–2, jump straight to Step 6).

> **Practitioner note**: It may be helpful to read Chapter 4 before doing this assignment. Depending on personal preference, you can commit a solid period of time to this (an hour or more). Alternatively, you can take the approach you might with a writer's diary and spread the assignments over a week, 10 minutes a day, recording thoughts in a text, audio or video diary.

> **Tutor note**: Doing the assignment in class in a single block gives opportunity for questions and group discussion while the activity is fresh in students' minds. Alternatively, if the assignment is set as homework, students can respond to creative challenges as they occur in their daily lives (they could collate thoughts via a text, audio or video writer's diary). It may be helpful to set Chapter 4 as a reading in advance of the class; alternatively, Chapter 4 can be summed up as needed in class.

'Getting personal'

Map your writerly resources and assess how best to deploy them (i.e. start building your own personalised model of creativity).

ACTION: This is a reflective assignment designed to help you identify strategies and skills that help you move between different genres and technologies with a view to developing creative flexibility and productivity. Initially, the component parts of your creative process should be considered separately.

Step 1: Consider your current creative writing *projects* (e.g. a novel and/or Twitter and/or a screenplay). Note them down on the template provided (Figure 5. 1).

Step 2: Consider the writerly *resources* you use. Of the resources, first, list the *tools* you use for writing (e.g. pen, computer, software applications). Against each writerly tool listed, make notes about which type of creative project it is used for. For example, you might use a pen for first drafts and a computer for a final edit. Add your writerly resources to the template.

Step 3: Repeat Step 2 for your other writerly resources, external and internal (as per the template). The task of listing and making observations about the external resources is likely to be relatively straightforward. Allow a little more time for the internal resources.

Step 4: Now consider the kind of person you become for different types of writing and at different stages of the creative process. Do you have different 'writerly personas' such that, like novelist Fay Weldon, a wilder part of you comes to the fore for a first draft then makes way for a more pragmatic self who can action a clear-eyed edit?[11] List these different writerly aspects of yourself. Make notes about when and how they operate. Think, too, about the part your subconscious plays. If you have finished a short story but remain unsure whether it is ready to enter for a competition, does something playful or defiant deep inside you leap past the objecting voices to enable you to press the 'Submit' button? You might think of this as writerly 'self-trust' or 'expert intuition'. What enables or inhibits it? Note down your observations. And finally for this section of the assignment, consider how you co-ordinate all these different resources and aspects of yourself. Do you have a kind of 'inner auteur' busy selecting and directing, or, is it more helpful to think of having a sort of pre-conscious triage doctor or puppetmaster who orchestrates your selection of tools and moods as you pursue each creative project? Again, note down your observations.

Step 5: Now that you have mapped out the separate component parts of your creative process, you can begin considering: what particular combinations of writerly resources and aspects of yourself help you *move* between genres and technologies, and how do they help? Thus the moves might be, for example, between writing a chapter of a novel and a blog post, the plot of a screenplay and a tweet. What roles do tools such as deadlines play in these moves, does a bossy part of yourself have to step in, and if so when? Note down your observations. The aim here is to identify how your writerly resources can be deployed, in what combinations to best support moves between genres and technologies.

You now have a personalised model of creativity fit to tackle our twenty-first century writing and publishing landscape. You can continue adapting and updating it as you pursue your creative practice.

Step 6: Reflect on your findings.

Step 7: To extend this assignment, repeat it at a later stage in your development of a multimodal writing practice in order that – following completion of some or all of the other assignments – a new, refined document mapping writerly resources etc. can be created.

Discussion points: Areas for discussion/reflection might include: how easy or difficult was it to identify and delineate a discrete creative process; any surprises? (On completing the assignment, a student in one of my classes, said, 'I didn't even know I had a creative process, and look, there it is!'; another realised that, for her, having a green pen for 'loose thoughts' and a red pen for editing was key).

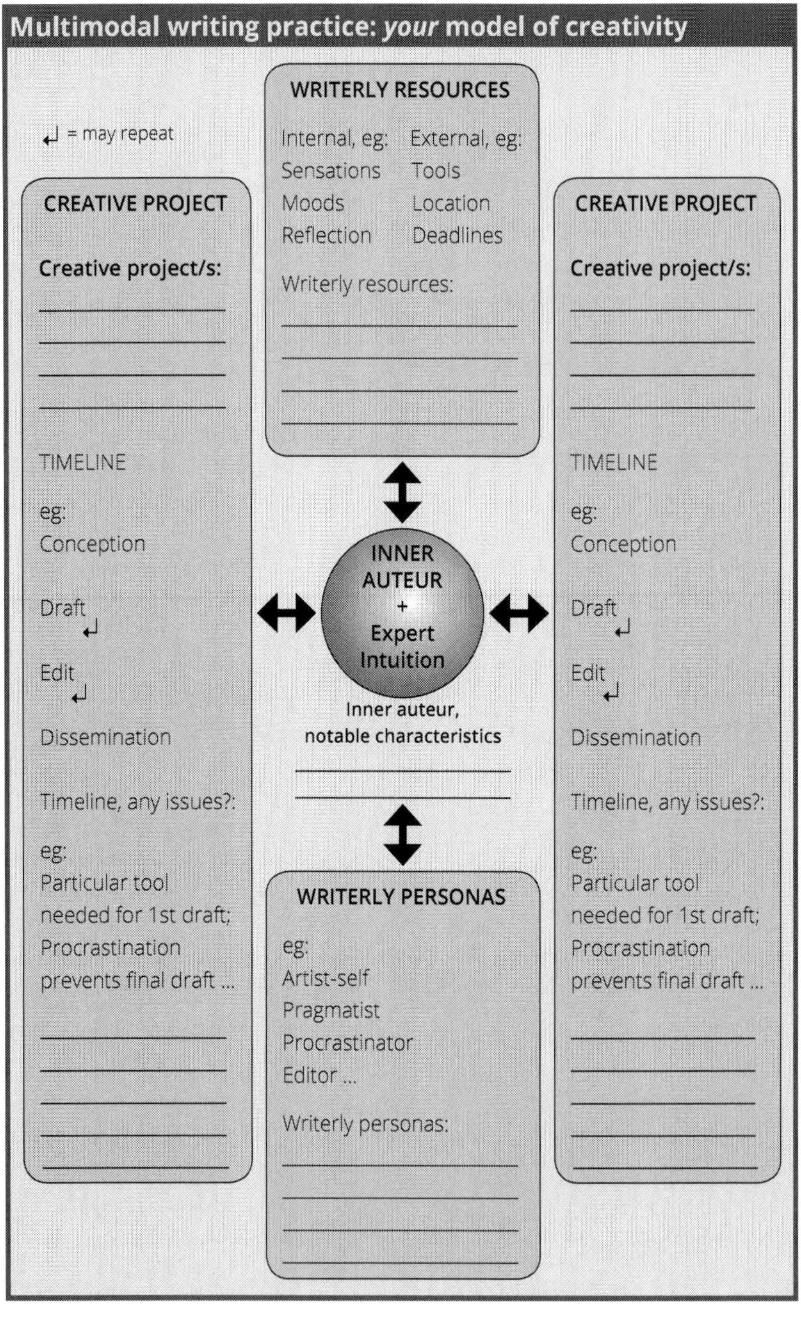

Multimodal writing practice: *your* model of creativity

↵ = may repeat

WRITERLY RESOURCES

Internal, eg: External, eg:
Sensations   Tools
Moods   Location
Reflection   Deadlines

Writerly resources:
_____
_____
_____
_____

CREATIVE PROJECT

Creative project/s:
_____
_____
_____
_____

TIMELINE

eg:
Conception

Draft
↵

Edit
↵

Dissemination

Timeline, any issues?:

eg:
Particular tool
needed for 1st draft;
Procrastination
prevents final draft ...
_____
_____
_____

INNER AUTEUR + Expert Intuition

Inner auteur,
notable characteristics
_____
_____

WRITERLY PERSONAS

eg:
Artist-self
Pragmatist
Procrastinator
Editor ...

Writerly personas:
_____
_____
_____
_____

CREATIVE PROJECT

Creative project/s:
_____
_____
_____
_____

TIMELINE

eg:
Conception

Draft
↵

Edit
↵

Dissemination

Timeline, any issues?:

eg:
Particular tool
needed for 1st draft;
Procrastination
prevents final draft ...
_____
_____
_____

Figure 5.1 Multimodal writing practice: model of creativity as assignment

Observations: This relatively straightforward assignment underpins development of a multimodal writing practice.

As discussed (see Chapter 4), the development of self-trust is identified by many writers as key to developing a sustainable creative practice. Knowledge of your own creative process can be pivotal in building self-trust. Building skills in collaborating with different internal aspects of yourself is an important aspect of developing your own creative practice and helps develop abilities in collaborating with others too. Different writerly practices in different combinations work for different writers, so it is important to both identify as many preferences, habits and creative stimulants as early on as possible and begin developing the self-reflective skills necessary to continue noticing writerly practices and habits and any new developments as they occur.

The model can periodically be tested for robustness by introducing and mapping use of a new media technology and/or genre.

Assignment 2: 'I "♥" looking'

Reassess how you 'see' storytelling.

Skills: Flexibility | curating, transforming templates, deploying visuals.

Individual/group: Solo exercise.

Equipment: Smartphone, pen and notepad; glue and scissors (optional).

Time: One hour (for a shorter version, just do Steps 2, 4, 6 and 7).

> **Practitioner note**: If you don't have or don't want to use a smartphone, this assignment can be completed using hard copy images only. Alternatively, if you have skills in InDesign and/or Photoshop, for example, after completing Steps 1–7 as outlined, apply those skills to a published version of your finished story.

> **Tutor note**: A sense of privacy is generally helpful for Step 1, so, the first step of this assignment could be set as homework, or, alternatively, students could go on individual 'field trips' with a notepad for half an hour to each find a window that captures his or her interest. Steps 2–8 can all be completed in a classroom setting. At Step 8, if students can contribute different skills (e.g. if one has experience with (InDesign and another has particularly strong photography/film skills), they could produce stories collaboratively.

'I " ♥ " looking'

Reassess how you 'see' storytelling.

ACTION: The task here is to: first look, then produce a story using images only. This two-pronged task might seem simple enough. Toni Morrison famously said, 'I'm just trying to look at something without blinking'.[12] Writing has always involved intense looking. The idea of producing a story using images alone is not new. It dates back to cave paintings. John Berger's seminal *Ways of Seeing*, famously changed our way of looking at images, undermining assumptions that pictures and images present neutral 'truths', and Berger's book was published back in 1972.[13, 14] However, images have a different place in narratives today. A significant proportion of what we see of the world is through screens and via others' photos. Acts of curation and *bricolage* have new centrality. The top 'word' of 2014 was an emoji of a love heart.[15] The basics of this assignment – to first *look* then produce a story using images – could take a very short amount of time. What counts is the application of criticality. The aim is to 'look', as Morrison puts it, 'without blinking'.

Step 1: Choose a window. Ideally, choose a window that you usually take for granted. Make sure you won't be disturbed (if necessary, you could wear headphones so that any friends or passersby assume you're listening to music and leave you be). Look out of your chosen window and write down everything about it. What are the reflections doing? What are the shapes of the view, the colours? Is there action – is it a busy street outside, or quite an industrial view? What dominates the view? What's the sky like, and how does that change as you look? What comes into the sky, what leaves it?

Windows are potent things. They're boundaries between you and the outside world. They allow you to look out, and others to look in. They're see-through, fragile sheets where interiors and exteriors collide. Keep writing everything that comes to your mind as you look through the window. See if you can capture what you feel is most important/interesting about your chosen window in two or three photographs.

Step 2: Now apply close focus to the screen of your smartphone. Initially, just look at the blank screen. What reflections does it catch, are there any chips or cracks, have fingertip patterns been traced where you swipe or tap the screen, for example?

Such screens are complex 'windows'. They can, via their photo and video functions, let others see you, but only when you choose to do this, and only in ways you curate. It can seem that others' posts are snapshots of 'real life', but of course their snapshots are curated and edited too. Think about how your emotional response to an image changes if you are given a long view as opposed to a close-up, for example. How does the juxtaposition of different objects affect your reaction? Keep writing down your observations – although, don't keep going indefinitely. Links and posts can suck you in. Set a time limit of 15 minutes or so for this part of the assignment.

Step 3: Take screenshots of a few of the images that particularly captured your interest. They might be scenes from your chosen window or images you came across during Step 2. The key thing is that they've caught your interest.

Step 4: Have a look through your emojis. Gather a few on a text or Whatsapp, for example; don't send the text or WhatsApp, the point is to assemble a few emojis that interest and/or amuse you.

Step 5: Lay out the screenshots and/or photos. It doesn't matter whether you do this metaphorically or actually. You can lay them out as thumbnails on your phone or computer. Alternatively, you might prefer to print them out and add actual scissors and glue into the equation so that you can literally start cutting and pasting. Look at your screenshots. Now look at the emojis you've gathered.

What story is suggested? You might be drawn more to the screenshots or the emojis, or, they might have intertwined in your imagination. Things can be spied through windows. People can spy through them. Perhaps a spy story will emerge, or a love story that's run through with tension and suspicion. Perhaps a few different stories are suggested, in which case, select the one that feels most rich to you.

Step 6: 'Write' your story, but, aim to 'write' it without words. It doesn't have to be long. Ideally, the arrangement of images should tell the story with no need for text interventions. If the odd text intervention is necessary, see if there is a function on your phone or computer that will allow you to impose it or embed it in the image, for example, maybe you can write directly on the image in the form of a speech bubble.

Step 7: Finally, test the effectiveness! Show your story to a friend. Get them to summarise the story they see. Does it tally with the one you intended to tell? If not, where and what are the differences and how have they come about?

Step 8: To extend the assignment, apply InDesign or Photoshop, for example, to your stories using existing technical skills or use the task of developing the stories to give focus to your development of new technical skills. Alternatively, make a film, the challenge being to make it a silent movie, i.e. no dialogue, images only!

Discussion points: Areas for discussion/reflection might include: what details – of the window, for example – were missed at first and only noticed after the process of *not blinking* for a while; did you view emojis differently (and/or spot any new ones) when considering how – rather than just serving to support a message – they might, on their own, tell a story; how easy or difficult was it to remove words from the storytelling process?

Observations: This assignment supports a number of skills that are important in the development of a multimodal writing practice, including flexibility, curating and transforming templates. We can easily slip into thinking that we must make our content fit the templates that social media platforms provide. At the outset, when setting up an account, it's not necessary to fill in every single request for personal details, we may choose to simply omit information about our location or age, for example. Once we're up and running, if elements of an apparently fixed website or social media platform layout seem limiting, we may find it is possible with a little research to make tweaks and adjustments so that the website or platform suits our purposes more effectively (one of my students decided to use a paint tool on Instagram to create an entirely new icon on Instagram, for example, to provide a gateway to content that would otherwise have been buried). This assignment is designed to help in the task of stepping back from usual ways of seeing the world so that fresh options can be identified and practitioner flexibility improved.

As discussed (see Chapters 1 and 4), there has been a tendency to assume that creativity is located in a single, 'special' individual and that this creativity arises from his or her distinctive thinking patterns alone. It is important, as Maria Takolander puts it, to consider 'both the creative practitioner's embodiment within a social or institutional network and also the affordances and constraints of creative materials'.[16] That is, the technical constraints of a medium and the social element of social media platforms both play integral parts in a practitioner's creativity. If you go on Instagram, it is necessary to have or gain both skills in photography and the ability to recognise which elements of a message or narrative can be told with images alone and which need supporting text (and, *what* supporting text). Cutting and pasting someone else's work would, traditionally, have been seen as 'stealing'. In the digital environment, 'manipulation' and 'management' of others' content is an entirely valid form of creativity.[17] More than that, as Adam Koehler notes, it forces an 'ideological examination of voice and style' and 'subjectivity' that can be extremely helpful for creative writers.[18] The simple switch to seeing curating and *bricolage* as creative can help make storytelling in a digital environment more productive and enjoyable.

Assignment 3: 'Collaborative plotting'

Plot a new novel collaboratively.

Skills: Bold exploration, reflective risk-taking | collaboration

Individual/group: Solo or group exercise.

Equipment: Smartphone, pen and paper.

Time: One hour (for a shorter version, skip Step 2 and do Step 3 more quickly).

> **Practitioner note**: You can do this assignment with one or two friends who are also working to develop a multimodal writing practice. If working with friends, you could collaborate via a Facebook group or Google doc, for example. Alternatively, if doing this assignment solo, repeat Steps 1–3 so that a range of characters, texts and places are available to you; it may help to do the assignment in a busy environment that is suggestive of collaboration (e.g. a café).

Tutor note: This activity tends to work well early on in a course, when it can serve as an icebreaker, helping students get to know each other. The first three steps should be done by students individually, Step 4 in small groups (3–5 students per group), Step 5 as a class discussion. At the end of Step 3, let the class know that if any of the information noted down is personal, students might prefer to quickly choose alternatives, since the activity is about to become a group activity. At Step 4, different genres can be assigned to different groups to gain range in the class reflection at the end.

To extend the assignment, after Step 5, the homework can be to write the opening or first chapter; in this case, even if different students develop the same plot, how their approaches differ can be a discussion point in the next session. The students' off-campus collaboration could continue via an intranet group chat, for example.

'Collaborative plotting'

Plot a new novel collaboratively.

ACTION:

Step 1: Write your own name out in full, including any middle names. Rearrange the letters to make a new name. It is not necessary to use all the letters, the aim is simply to create a new name that sounds different from your own (e.g. 'Jane Smith' could become 'Sam Jet' or 'Mrs J. N. Thame'). Ideally, make a few anagrams of your name. See which alternative name comes most quickly to life as a character, make some notes about who this character is and what he or she is like. How old are they, what is their job, for example. Are they single, married or divorced? What are their food preferences or hobbies?

Step 2: Get out your mobile phone and make a note of the third to last message that came in (it does not matter if this is a very practical text, just make a note of it).

Step 3: Think of a place, let your mind drift back to it. The place might be a cupboard from when you were a child or a sunny beach holiday, whatever it is, write it down and make a few descriptive notes (what you can hear, what you can smell, what the place looks like).

Step 4: Now, take a genre (e.g. sci-fi, romance, thriller). If possible, include *all* the characters, messages and places from Steps 1–3, using them as, respectively, dramatis personae, bits of dialogue and settings, and: plot a novel! Make sure you give your plot a beginning,

> middle and end (or, crisis, thickening, resolution). You can, if you wish, extend the assignment by adding subplots (and you can extend it still further, of course, by going on to complete the full story). Don't forget to give your novel a title.
>
> **Step 5**: Reflect on the experience of creating the plot of a novel from scratch starting with just your own name and a text message!

Discussion points: Areas for discussion/reflection might include: how quickly were characters suggested by the names alone; how did the day-to-day nature of the SMS messages contribute (perhaps they made dialogue feel real, perhaps they suggested plot twists); how did the constraint of genre help with the task of plotting?

Observations: The assignment supports a number of aspects which can be challenging but are central to a multimodal writing practice (e.g. exploration of the unknown, risk-taking, collaboration), and it does so in a framework that is generally stimulating and enjoyable. It helps make the idea of interacting with strangers in a live and public situation (a key characteristic of social media) feel less unnerving, so too the task of inventing stories for new contexts.

Assignment 4: 'Talking it over'

Finessing (and critically assessing) discourse skills needed for social media publishing.

Skills: Reflective risk-taking | real-time discourse, code-switching.

Individual/group: Solo or group exercise.

Equipment: Pen and paper; technology to enable audio recording (optional).

Time: One hour (for a shorter version, jump straight to Step 2).

> **Practitioner note**: You could find a co-conspirator to pair up with for this activity. Alternatively, imagine yourself in the shoes of a celebrity figure you admire or have long found interesting and develop an internal Q&A to complete this assignment.
>
> **Tutor note**: Steps 2 and 4 should be done in pairs, Step 3 individually, Steps 1 and 5 as a class. At Step 6, instead of audio, video can be used (as for audio, video-editing software is easily available online, for example, Adobe's Premiere Rush[19]).

'Talking it over'

Finessing (and critically assessing) discourse skills needed for social media publishing.

ACTION:

Step 1: Consider what constitutes 'good' *listening* and 'good' *questions*. The following overview thoughts can be used as a starting point.

What makes a 'good' *listener*? In an interview, a listener may be largely silent, only speaking to ask a question. Alternatively, he or she may interject repeatedly (e.g. saying, 'No way!', 'Wow', 'Gosh' and/or 'I can't believe it'). An 'active' listener is generally considered to be a listener who can see the value of the odd silence; he or she is able to engage with the silences as well as the verbal communications, thus giving space for the thinking and reflection that may be taking place while nothing is said.

What makes a 'good' *question*? Just as the way in which an interviewer listens can affect how an interview plays out, so too can the questions he or she asks. 'Closed' questions are questions which invite only 'yes'/'no' answers, whereas 'open' questions invite more expansive answers. Another approach is to use 'clean' questions. Counselling Psychologist David Grove famously devised a system of 'clean' listening, whereby the listener uses the speaker's words to make the speaker feel comfortable, echoing them back to the speaker. Thus a 'clean' question might be, 'What kind of x?', 'Whereabouts is x?', 'Is there anything else about x?'

Step 2: Think of a celebrity. The celebrity you choose could be a current or past footballer, singer, writer, for example. (If you are working in pairs, agree on a celebrity who interests both of you and continue Steps 2 and 3 together.) Think of a key issue or life event about which the celebrity is likely to feel strongly. This might be a scandalous marriage break-up, for example, or a controversial live appearance. Sketch out the main details of the celebrity's life, including this key issue/life-event.

Step 3: Make notes about the questions an interviewer could ask. Consider the best order for the questions. Is there a potentially difficult question, and if so, might that be better positioned later on, so that the interview has a chance to get warmed up first? Make sure to include a mix of 'open' and 'clean' questions (see above). Can you think of a particularly strong closing question?

Step 4: Now, if you are working in pairs, take turns being interviewer and interviewee (i.e. when you're the interviewee, you're pretending to be the celebrity you chose!). If you're doing the assignment solo, imagine the Q&A so that one voice inside you is the interviewer, another is playing the celebrity; if it feels easier, act it out, literally wearing different hats when you're interviewee/interviewer. The aim is to get a really good interview, including discussion of the celebrity's key issue/life event.

Step 5: Consider the experience of being interviewee and interviewer.

Step 6: To extend the assignment, record interviews as audio. This can be done easily on smartphones. To extend the assignment further, download and edit the interviews and turn them into podcasts. Audio editing is relatively easy to learn and can be done on a computer using free software (such as Audacity[20]).

Discussion points: Areas for discussion/reflection might include: how easy/difficult was it to ask 'open' as opposed to 'clean' questions; how did the different types of questions affect not only the answers to individual questions but also the flow of the interview as a whole? The Counselling Psychologist David Grove famously developed a system of 'clean' questions to help treat traumatised children. A potential disadvantage of 'clean questions' is that they can make the interviewee feel as if they are in a police station or on an analyst's couch and discussion can close down. Was this an issue? When does silence play a part? What about body language? What was it like to 'code-switch' out of being yourself into being an interviewee/interviewer? Was it hard, and, if so, did it continue to be as difficult throughout or did it get easier and if so, how and why? As the interviewer, what did knowledge of the interviewee's life and work contribute? For a journalist or a writer of a creative non-fiction book, any interview questions should generally be informed (i.e. research should have been done beforehand so that the interviewer can pose informed questions in response to answers during the interview); thus, when interviewing as research for a piece of long-form journalism or a book, clean questions are likely to be highly useful. On social media, by contrast, during a live discussion (which may involve strangers pitching in), it could be perfectly acceptable to ask for clarification regarding who someone is, and, clean questions would most likely look overly pared back, or even plain odd. How does context affect how you listen and respond?

Observations: This assignment supports a number of skills that help development of a multimodal writing practice. It helps deepen understanding of the dynamics involved in the to and fro of conversation in an environment that is live and public and a *version* of natural. Thus, even if no technology is involved, the assignment aids critical consideration of how to engage with social media, when a version of self must be 'performed' naturalistically and with a feel of authenticity. The activity also aids consideration of how writing for the ear differs from writing for the page. For example, repetition may be helpful. If text is only heard not read, repetition that could be irritating on the page, can be necessary to keep the listener engaged.

The assignment in its extended version, with audio editing included, may also help in a highly practical way. As noted, an author platform (which might involve websites, podcasts, videos etc.) is now widely considered an essential element in marketing a book. A podcast – of a writer reading a piece of his or her own work, for example – is, using a computer and free software, a manageable and potentially highly engaging addition to an author platform.

Assignment 5: 'Small tales'

Turn random strangers' posts into a coherent narrative.

Skills: Bold exploration | selecting, curating, non-linear storytelling.

Individual/group: Solo or group exercise.

Equipment: Tablet or computer, Wakelet account (or equivalent), Twitter account.

Time: One hour (for a shorter version, just do just Steps 1–3 or 4–7).

> **Technical note**: For this assignment, ideally, you will have access to a platform that enables you to curate social media posts. There are a number of such platforms, including Wakelet, which is widely considered to be effective.[21] The now defunct Storify, which ran 2011

to 2018, was so closely associated with social media content curation that, if Wakelet doesn't suit you, typing 'Alternatives to Storify' into a web browser should bring up a range of alternatives which you can experiment with.

For the content that is curated, other social media platforms can be used, of course, but Twitter tends to work particularly well for this assignment because it is text-based and has a small character count. At Step 5, when you start generating your own posts – anticipating the task ahead – you can post text-only tweets that are short and consequently easier to curate.

A different way of curating posts is to simply 'like' or 'bookmark' them, for example, thereby pulling posts out for separate consideration.

Practitioner note: To free yourself up to experiment, you might prefer to tweet from an anonymous account for this assignment.

Tutor note: Wakelet is not difficult to use, but if you are new to it, make sure you have done a couple of experiments before taking it into the classroom. This assignment works best if you have projection facilities and can project Wakelet at the front of the class. Ensure you make clear that the aim is to project the tweets so students can factor this in to decisions regarding whether to quickly start an anonymous account. For Step 1, if you decide the hashtag and set it as a class task for the students, this can get the activity off to a quicker start. At Step 4, again, decide the hashtag in advance (and check it is 'free'). At Step 6, pull all the students' posts onto Wakelet, viewing them on a screen at the front of the class. The task of curating the posts – deciding the order, devising text to link the posts – can then be done as a group activity with accompanying discussion.

'Small tales'

Turn random strangers' posts into a coherent narrative.

ACTION: The aim of this assignment is to collect random strangers' social media posts and turn them into a story. One way of doing this is to use hashtags in combination with Wakelet (or an equivalent 'curating' platform).[22] As if the hashtags are metal filings and Wakelet is a magnet, Wakelet allows you to pull hashtagged posts out of cyberspace. It also provides tools that enable you to then move these posts about and/or add comments. Thus, you can treat the social media posts you collect as if they are hard copy items, curating and annotating until they form a story that feels and looks whole and complete.

Step 1: First, choose an existing hashtag. It's worth experimenting with a few to see what kind of posts come up. For example, a quite general hashtag such as #onthisday is likely to bring up a wide range of thoughts on, and information about, historical events that previously took place *on this day*. Alternatively, you might prefer a more close-focus hashtag such as #flower or #Sunday. You could also check which hashtags are 'trending' in case any of these catch your fancy.

Step 2: Once you've found a hashtag that interests you, pull posts featuring that hashtag into Wakelet and start thinking about how to turn the posts into a narrative. The quality of the narrative is not the point. The point is simply to experiment, pulling in random posts and turning them into something that reads as coherent and ordered. First, just read the posts. You're looking for a basic beginning, middle and end (crisis, thickening, resolution). Is a narrative emerging of its own accord? For #onthisday, perhaps a story will start forming about a literary figure or sports hero you admire, one that charts their rise to prominence (or fall from grace), for example. Hashtags such as #flower or #Sunday might yield posts with more personal or emotional edges, giving potential for a narrative arc that takes a character from sad to happy or vice versa. Hashtags like #amwriting bring up comments on the writing process that it might be possible to turn into a chronological step-through of a writer's working day.

If you're using Wakelet, remember, you can add comments in the spaces between posts to help strengthen the narrative.

Step 3: Once your story is finished, step back from it. Maybe allow a bit of time so you can see it afresh. Reflect on the process of gathering random strangers' posts and turning them into a coherent narrative.

Step 4: For the next part of the assignment, the idea is to generate some of your own tweets. They should all be on a single topic and they should all feature the same hashtag. A key thing here is to check before you start tweeting that the hashtag you've chosen is 'free'. That is, if you type in your selected hashtag, do lots of posts by other users come up? If so, you're likely to have trouble finding your own tweets. Just adding a couple of letters or numbers to a word can be enough to make the hashtag unique to you (e.g. instead of #walking, you could make it #walking22).

Confirm which topic and hashtag you'll be using. Topics like *reading* or *walking* tend to work well because they're quite neutral and most people find they have a good amount to say about them (maybe a particularly loved or hated book or walk comes to mind, for example).

Step 5: Now, with a topic decided – and without overthinking it – start posting some tweets. Each time you must remember to include the hashtag you've devised. But as far as is possible, treat the tweets as 'free writing', that is, just write down thoughts about the topic that occur to you, let those thoughts lead to other thoughts, following the train of thought wherever it goes.[23]

Step 6: Lastly, using the hashtag you've devised, pull up your own posts and curate them into a story. Topics like *reading* or *walking* tend to provide natural beginnings and endings. As well as a particularly hated or loved book, there's likely to be a first book you remember from childhood, for example. Walks inevitably have beginnings, middles and ends. Thus a tweet about a book from childhood might serve as an opening for a collection of posts about reading, a tweet about collapsing in a chair exhausted after a long walk might serve as the closing tweet for a collection about walking.

As you did for Step 2, see if the posts suggest a narrative of their own accord. Where necessary, add comments in spaces between posts to help strengthen the narrative.

Step 7: Reflect on the process of gathering your own posts as if they were strangers' and turning them into a coherent narrative.

Step 8: To extend this assignment, write a story that is designed explicitly for a social media platform such as Twitter or Instagram, that is, a piece of original 'digital born' fiction. 'Digital born' fiction is, as Bell et al. put it, fiction that 'would lose something of its aesthetic and semiotic function if it were removed from that medium'.[24] The aim here is to ensure that you don't merely take into account the constraints of the medium but allow those constraints to inform some of the creative decisions. If the platform allows you to make gifs, for example, do some free writing/thinking regarding whether/how a gif might be part of the story.

Once you've completed your story – and not before – do some research, there are a growing number of online journals and prizes that your piece might turn out to be a good fit for. The important thing is to let the combination of your creativity and the platform's affordances – or, opportunities and limitations – be the guiding forces. See where your creativity takes you, surprise yourself!

Discussion points: Areas for discussion/reflection might include: how hard or easy was it to get to grips with Wakelet (or equivalent) and, if it was hard, were there any particular strategies that helped in the job of tackling it (did you find that you remediated any earlier creative practice in particular, for example); how hard or easy was it to write tweets intended for immediate live publication (again, if it was hard, did any particular strategies help); what were the main impacts on your story of the platform's affordances?

Observations: This assignment supports a number of skills that are important in the development of a multimodal writing practice, including bold exploration, selecting, curating and non-linear storytelling. Bold exploration is needed to gain new technological skills and enter new technological and creative spaces and mindsets. Selecting and curating are embedded aspects of the assignment. Although the end products are linear stories, the reading and writing that produce them require and develop non-linear storytelling skills. This assignment also helps in the development of structuring and editing skills and – particularly if you explore the #amwriting hashtag – understanding of market. It can prove helpful with grammar too, since the small character counts of tweets and close reading required during the writing and curation process tends to naturally draw attention to grammatical errors.[25]

There is something else important that this assignment helps with: remediation of practice *between contexts*. Use of social media for *leisure* is almost guaranteed to utilise skills in exploration, selecting, curating and non-linear storytelling, as we shift between the posts of friends and families, cutting and pasting gifs and retrieving previous posts. However, research shows that it can be hard to first see that such leisure activities involve often quite sophisticated digital skills and to then successfully transfer those skills into a work or more formal context.[26] This assignment is designed to enable identification, transfer and application of skills from a leisure context into a fast-paced, complex publishing context. As Andersen notes, serialisation, after a heyday in the eighteenth and nineteenth centuries (with the novels of writers such as Dickens appearing in serial form), has come to the fore in publishing once again, including on Twitter, where, due to the character limit, users habitually split thoughts into several tweets and post them in serial form.[27] Writers such as Jennifer Egan and David Mitchell have with stories published in serial form via Twitter – 'Black Box' and '@I_Bombadil' respectively – taken storytelling into new territory.[28, 29] New digital media and emerging formats are creating 'new literary forms, and these forms will remain in flux'.[30]

We are at an exciting nexus, genres will emerge that haven't been conceived yet; creative writers who are ready to experiment with technology can be at the vanguard of conceiving them.

Assignment 6: 'Me, myself, I'

Generating and sustaining an 'authentic' online voice.

Skills: Reflective risk-taking | real-time discourse, code-switching.

Individual/group: Solo or group exercise.

Equipment: Smartphone, tablet or computer, a Twitter account.

Time: An hour and a half (for a shorter version, just do Steps 1–6).

> **Practitioner note**: If the idea of generating an 'authentic' online self makes you at all nervous, it can be helpful to find a co-conspirator to pair up with for this activity. Alternatively, if you feel you already have an effective online author platform, you may want to jump straight to Step 7 and experiment by introducing a new element (if you're already comfortable with Facebook and Twitter, for example, you could now try Instagram).

> **Tutor note**: The main part of this assignment (Steps 1–6) takes about an hour in class, start to finish.

> It can be helpful to do Steps 1–4 as a short discussion in class, and, it is generally helpful at Step 5 to either a) allow students to sit next to friends and chat as they start tweeting or b) suggest that the students start tweeting off-campus at a live event that is relevant to their own practice or about which they feel passionate.

> To extend the assignment, at Step 7, invite the students to co-ordinate their online selves and start posting to promote a class event (such as a literary reading with an invited speaker) or a class publication (such as a collection of the group's short stories).

'Me, myself, I'

Generating and sustaining an 'authentic' online voice.

ACTION: This is a reflective assignment designed to help with the task of developing a robust online voice. Writers are now widely expected by publishers and readers to have online author platforms (which might include, for example, Facebook, Pinterest and Twitter profiles) to promote their work and engage with readers. For writers working on long-form projects such as novels, finding an 'authentic voice' has traditionally been a key aim. Yet, it is necessary on social media to 'perform' a *version* of the self, or even several versions of the self, all of which should, ideally, be 'authentic'. We tend to think that we can each have just one 'authentic' voice. If that's true, then it is not possible to write a novel *and* post on social media and be 'authentic' on both. For this assignment, the aim is to use a single platform – Twitter – to start experimenting with how to establish and sustain an 'authentic' online voice, and to then branch out, using different platforms.

Step 1: Consider what the main barriers might be to setting out to generate an 'authentic' online voice. Is the fact that Twitter is live and public an issue? Does 'technostress' affect you?

Step 2: Decide whether you are going to use an existing Twitter account or start a new Twitter account which you might choose to make anonymous (anonymity might help free you up to experiment).

Step 3: Decide what kind of writerly self you might like to present. As part of this decision-making process, do some research into writers who work in the area you're interested in. Think about what makes the authors you're researching likeable or annoying. What makes the authors seem *authentic*? Make a note of your observations.

Step 4: Have a think about your creative practice, what might help you feel more comfortable about starting to tweet, might it help to imagine that you're tweeting to someone in particular, for example? Might you find it easier to tweet in busy places such as trains or cafés, or in a place that feels appropriate to your subject, such as a bookshop? If you're sitting next to a friend when you post your first tweet for this assignment, could it help to follow and retweet each other, for example, sharing thoughts and experiences as you go? Have a think about your leisure-time use of social media, are there skills you can transfer? Make a note of your observations.

Step 5: Start tweeting an 'authentic' self!

Step 6: Consider the experience. How difficult or easy is it to be 'authentic' via Twitter? What happens if friends or strangers tweet back? Are there any particular strategies that help? Is retweeting others' tweets a helpful way of finding your feet? Make a note of your observations.

Step 7: Now you have experimented with generating one 'authentic' online self, repeat Steps 3–5 with a different social media platform. You could try one that's more image-based, such as Instagram, or a platform with a longer word count, such as Tumblr. The aim now is to ensure that you observe the conventions (or, 'netiquettes') that are particular to each platform yet establish an overarching self (or, as Elwell phrases it, a 'transmediated self'[31]) that feels coherent as you switch between platforms. Make a note of your observations.

Step 8: Write a short self-reflective piece (about 300–500 words) on the experience of setting out to generate an 'authentic' online self. This reflective piece should do two things. It should identify any style and/or content details that mark the separate outputs as all belonging to you. It should reflect on whether, when facing barriers, the same strategies that you found useful when using Twitter could be applied, or, alternatively, whether new strategies were needed.

Step 9: It's often assumed that online author platforms are just about promoting an author's work. However, more and more authors are experimenting with social media platforms in different ways, using them to archive their creative process or extend their creative practice.[32] Novelist Joanne Harris says she thinks of Twitter as her 'water cooler', a place to tweet chatty thoughts and general 'beefs' about the literary world.[33] Poet George Szirtes says he likes the 'evanescence' of the form and has tweeted tens of thousands of poems on Twitter as an extended 'experiment'.[34] So, now you've started generating an online self, experiment. Have some fun. What are the possibilities for you?

Discussion points: Areas for discussion/reflection might include: Did the idea of *intending* to be 'authentic' make you feel fake? Did the fact that Twitter is live and public make you feel vulnerable to making mistakes and/or being 'trolled'? If you experienced 'technostress' at any point, what strategies helped you overcome it? Did retweeting play a part in helping you feel comfortable, what about the 'delete' button? In fact, as Laing notes and Charlie Higson flags up in Chapter 3, it's debatable whether Twitter and/or other forms of social media help greatly with promotion.[35] Writers who post too many 'plugs' for their work can find that instead of gaining sales they lose followers. Perhaps a main reason for being on social media is actually just to participate. Might a shift in how you approach social media make a difference?

Observations: This assignment (a version of which features in Barnard, 2019) supports a number of skills that are important in the development of a multimodal writing practice, including reflective risk-taking, real-time discourse and code-switching.

The task of finding an appropriate, robust digital voice is an important aspect of confident and comfortable digital engagement. Perhaps it is even the cornerstone. The cliché of the 'digital native' (i.e. the notion that all millenials are immediately at ease with all technology) can, as noted, inhibit learning. Knowledge of social media in one context may only serve to intensify awareness of potential pitfalls. Thinking 'LOL' means 'lots of love' rather than 'laugh out loud' could make you look foolish; a full stop in the wrong place could make you look insincere or even rude.[36, 37] Use of Twitter for fun with peers may be significantly different from use between networking journalists and writers. It can be hard to transfer skills gained on social media during leisure time into a more formal context. Additionally, social media users of any age may find the idea of being 'trolled', or, abused online somewhere between off-putting and terrifying. In either case, when the task of generating an 'authentic' online self is begun, reflective risk-taking is necessary. The risks must be weighed and strategies marshalled for tackling them. When finding your feet in an online environment that's new to you, don't underestimate the value of activities such as retweeting or 'liking' other people's posts (for further discussion, see Chapter 1). Another useful strategy for engagement is the 'delete' button. It's surprisingly easy to forget that, as the person posting, you can remove a post if you're worried about it. You can just press the wastebasket icon.

If you feel there is pressure on social media to entertain others, this can feel stultifying. Perhaps the key is to find the aspect of engaging with social media that entertains *you*; Michèle Roberts (see Chapter 3) talks of loving 'the way if you choose to use social media rather than find you are forced to, you can enjoy it'. What's your route in?

Assignment 7: 'Picture this'

Use bar graphs and pie charts to help unpick a (very) short story.

Skills: Bold experimentation | transforming templates, swift editing.

Individual/group: Solo or group exercise.

Equipment: Pen, paper and the set of short stories in Appendix I; Excel or similar computer software (optional).

Time: One hour (for a shorter version, consider just one story).

> **Technical note**: Data visualisations can be produced easily and clearly using pen and paper; alternatively, Excel can be used, or, there are a wealth of free and easy-to-use software applications available online.

> **Practitioner note**: If possible, take the time to do data visualisations for all three stories to see whether/what different patterns emerge.

> **Tutor note**: If stories in addition to the stories provided in this volume are used, it is generally best to select flash fiction, to prevent the sheer length of the task becoming daunting for the students. To ensure all students can engage fully in the concluding discussion, time should be allowed at the start (Step 1) for students to read *all* stories selected for use. At Step 2, assign different short stories to different students, so findings can be compared at the end; when this is set as a class assignment, leave out Step 4, since, with different stories assigned to different students, there will be plenty of data visualisations to consider. For longer stories such as the Thomas Hardy story, Step 2 can be done in pairs, with the story split in half.

'Picture this'

Use bar graphs and pie charts to help unpick a (very) short story.

ACTION:

Step 1: Read the set of (very) short stories provided.

Step 2: Using your selected story, count the number of sentences and the number of words in each sentence, and note them down.

Step 3: Produce a data visualisation of your findings. You can draw a simple pie chart or bar graph by hand or use computer software. You might choose to assign pie slices/bar graph columns to show, for example, the proportion of sentences comprising: ten words and under; ten to twenty words; over twenty words. How you represent the data you have collected is up to you.

Step 4: Repeat Steps 2–3 with a different story, ensuring that at least two stories have been assessed using a data visualisation before moving on to Step 5.

Step 5: Compare the different data visualisations. Reflect on your findings.

Discussion points: Areas for discussion/reflection might include, did any patterns emerge (did you notice that longer as opposed to shorter sentences tend to appear at the beginning or middle or end of the stories, for example)? In places where shorter and longer sentences are alternated, did you feel this affected the pace of the story, did the story engage you as a reader in a different way as a result? Do you think the period when a story was written impacts sentence lengths? What do the pie charts/bar graphs for Thomas Hardy's Victorian and Suniti Namjoshi's twentieth century stories look like if you put them next to each other, for example?

Observations: Data visualisations are not new, of course. Neurath wrote in 1936 of their value in making the meanings of obfuscating reams of numbers clear.[38] However, data visualisations have gained new significance for writers in the twenty-first century. Big data means they are now important tools for journalists; Manovich writes of their importance to all humanities students of helping see patterns.[39] As use of data visualisations in the media increases exponentially, then, just to begin to think critically about how a data visualisation can be used to tell a story has value.

Additionally, the task of creating simple data visualisations helps develop a multimodal writing practice directly in a number of ways. It helps develop skills needed to tackle the potentially dangerous fact that the world of social media lacks the equivalent of a publisher's editor. That is, it can be tempting on social media for users to just splurge some words. Regardless of quality, anyone can press 'tweet', 'publish' or 'submit' and his or her prose is out there. More than ever before it is necessary for writers to develop self-editing skills. This assignment is particularly helpful in developing close reading and self-editing skills. In considering how a short sentence might get a story off to a brisker start and a longer sentence in the middle might alert the reader to the fact that the story is just about to take a new twist, for example, the activity helps in the identification of different component parts of storytelling templates (e.g. beginning, middle, end; crisis, thickening, resolution). Especially if using pen and paper, the task foregrounds physical sensations and so aids remediation of practice.[40] Since data visualisations might more usually be found in a maths class or a daily news article, flexibility is required to transform templates. Data visualisations can serve as a soft way of leading users to different technologies (interest piqued, keen to improve the visuals, he or she might seek out and start experimenting with new software voluntarily). In some of my classes, students began experimenting with the idea of using data visualisations to tell traditional stories (one student revealed the story of two lovers via data including their heart rates).

Assignment 8: 'Proppian analysis'

Transport a 1920's story template to twenty-first century new media technologies.

Skills: Reflective risk-taking, flexibility | transforming templates.

Individual/group: Solo or group exercise.

Equipment: Pen, paper and the set of short stories in Appendix I.

Time: One hour (for a shorter version, jump from Step 1 to Step 5).

> ***Practitioner note****:* If doing this solo, repeat Step 3 using different stories.

> ***Tutor note****:* Step 1 is a class discussion; Steps 2–3 are pursued by students individually; Step 4 can be done in pairs and/or as a class discussion.

'Proppian analysis'

Transport a 1920's story template to twenty-first century new media technologies.

ACTION:

Step 1*:* Consider the nature of a Proppian analysis, which can be summarised as follows. In the 1920s, Vladimir Propp analysed 115 Russian folktales and famously concluded that – whatever their length or subject and however many characters featured – they all shared 31 'functions'.[41, 42] To create a more manageable framework, these 31 functions can be reduced to seven: initial situation, departure, trickery, magical agent, difficult task, victory and reward.[43, 44, 45, 46, 47, 48, 49] Thus a Proppian analysis of the well-known fairytale 'Hansel and Gretel' might give the 'initial situation' as the two eponymous children rejected by their stepmother; the 'departure' is to the forest; the 'trickery' is perpetrated by the witch; the 'magical agent' is the children's own resourcefulness as they engage with the 'difficult task' of struggling with the witch; the 'victory' is the point when the witch is pushed into the oven, resulting in the 'reward' of freedom and return home.[50]

SIMPLIFIED PROPPIAN ANALYSIS:
Initial situation
Departure
Trickery
Magical agent
Difficult task
Victory
Reward

Figure 5.2 Simplified Proppian Analysis.

Step 2: Read the stories in Appendix I.

Step 3: Using the table above (Figure 5.2), do a Simplified Proppian Analysis of one of the stories you have just read. When doing this, keep in mind that different elements from the table may be represented by the same character/event in the story (the initial situation may also be the departure, for example). Similarly, the various elements of the table may come in a different order (in the story, the magical agent – the element that transforms the characters' situation – may appear early or quite late in the story). And, remember, there is no wrong answer! Think 'outside of the box', use your imagination to extrapolate.

Step 4: Consider your findings. For example, could different elements in the same story be identified as alternate magical agents/trickery/victory?

Step 5: Write a social media post that fits the simplified Proppian formula. The only requirement is that the piece is short. So, it might be a 75-word Tumblr blog, or a series of Snapchats totalling 50 words, or it might be a single Instagram annotation or tweet. You can start by adapting one of the stories you have just read (how far can you shrink the plot down while still keeping all the Proppian elements)? Once you've done that, branch out. Invent a micro-story that's suitable for the social media platform of your choice. It can be on any subject, it can be fiction or non-fiction. Just remember to keep it short.

Step 6: Reflect on the experience of doing the activity.

Step 7: To extend the assignment, repeat Steps 1–6 with different short stories and/or scenes from novels (descriptive scenes from novels by William Faulkner and Elizabeth Bowen, for example, tend to work well).

Discussion points: Areas for discussion/reflection might include: how easy or difficult was it to do a simple Proppian analysis? How easy or difficult was it to shrink a plot that fits the Proppian formula down to Snapchat-, Instagram- or tweet-sized? Did the constraints of the Proppian formula and/or the social media platform help, if so, how? How small do you think a piece of prose has to be before it is too small for a Proppian anaysis? What might a Proppian analysis look like of one of your favourite films or video games?

Observations: This assignment helps with a range of skills needed for a multimodal writing practice. Like 'Picture this', 'Proppian analysis' is particularly helpful in developing self-editing skills. Giving structure to a post can be the start of shifting a post from 'status update' to creative non-fiction.[51] There are a wide range of proposed formulas. Booker says there are just seven basic plots, Tobias puts the figure at 20.[52, 53] The idea that there is a formula for storytelling can seem reductive. However, while it may be necessary when writing a long-form story such as a *novel* to, as Cynthia Ozick describes it, 'wrestle' with the text's 'own body, with its own flesh and blood, with its own life', when they are shifting between genres and technologies, writers must often be pragmatic.[54] Whatever platform a writer is working on, good storytelling is key. It may only be a starting point, but it can be helpful when faced with a new genre and/or technology to have a template that can be adapted, and Propp's template can prove very useful.

Assignment 9: 'Story mash-up'

Develop skills in interactive storytelling using a mashed up fairytale.

Skills: Flexibility | non-linear storytelling, selecting, curating, swift editing.

Individual/group: Solo or group exercise.

Equipment: Pen and paper.

Time: An hour and a half (for a shorter version, complete Steps 1–4 and Step 9 only).

> **Practitioner note**: At Step 6, it can be helpful to test the effectiveness of the write-ups with a friend; another way of gaining objectivity is to simply put the write-ups aside for a while and come back to them with a fresh eye.

> **Tutor note**: This can be quite a challenging assignment so it is best done towards the end of an undergraduate programme of study and/or with postgraduate creative writers. Steps 1–4 should be done as a class discussion, and can be done quite quickly (in about 15 minutes). Steps 5–7 are longer activities and best done in pairs for each block (at Step 5, students work in pairs; at Step 6, each pair of students sits with another pair of students to test each others' write-ups, with one pair reading their Block A write-ups to the other pair and gaining feedback, then vice versa). Step 9 is a class discussion.

'Story mash-up'

Develop skills in interactive storytelling using a mashed up fairytale.

ACTION: Video games and websites often involve *non-linear storytelling*. That is, instead of interacting with the story in a traditional *linear* way (i.e. starting at the beginning and continuing to the end), users – in a *non-linear* reading pattern – enter and exit a narrative at different points. If *users* can play fast and loose with the order in which narrative elements are revealed, this presents a challenge for the *writer*. This assignment is designed to develop skills in non-linear storytelling. It drafts in the fairytale 'Jack and the Beanstalk' to help.[55]

BLOCK A (*snapshot* moments)	BLOCK B (*existential* moments)
1. Door slams	1. Jack in poverty
2. Mother smiles	2. Jack kills giant
3. Jack outside door	3. Jack rich

Figure 5.3 Jack's moments.

Step 1: Familiarise yourself with the story of 'Jack and the Beanstalk', which can be summarised as follows: a lazy boy, Jack, swaps his mother's cow for a magic bean, climbs a beanstalk, kills a giant and gains huge wealth.

Step 2: Consider Block A and Block B (Figure 5.3). Both blocks feature key moments from the 'Jack and the Beanstalk' story, but Block A features moments that are akin to snapshots (i.e. three visuals that each represent a scene) while Block B features more existential moments (i.e. the main character's experience of feeling variously poor, murderous, rich).

Step 3: Take the snapshot moments listed in Block A and rearrange them. The task is straightforward. You don't need to do anything to the three snapshot moments or change them in any way. Simply put them in different orders. Consider how the combined meaning changes depending on the order of the three elements.

Step 4: Take the existential moments listed in Block B and rearrange them. Again, consider how the combined meaning changes depending on the order of the three elements.

Step 5: Now, it's time to start writing. Take the three moments that make up Block A and expand them, writing them up as three short descriptions (just one or two sentences per element is plenty). Each description should be written with the aim that, when complete, it will be possible to rearrange the three descriptions in different orders and – in any order – the short scene they represent will still make sense. Ideally, more than that, whichever order the component parts are in, the scene should have clear visuals and good emotional impact.

Step 6: The task now is to test the Block A write-ups. Do the three component parts work in any order? If not, why not? What changes are needed?

Step 7: Now repeat Steps 5–6, but this time, take the three scenes that make up Block B and expand them, writing them up so that they can be rearranged and still form a coherent – though each time a different – story. These should be longer pieces of writing (aim for a paragraph each). Then, as for Block A, test the Block B write-ups. Do the three component parts work in any order?

Step 8: Consider the challenges presented by and insights gained from the activity.

Step 9: To extend this assignment, repeat Steps 1–7 using a different myth or fairytale. Or, you could choose 'snapshot' or 'existential' moments from one of your favourite video games and insert them into Figure 5.3, then record those moments using audio or video recording equipment. The idea here is to go through the steps of the assignment again, but this time using sound snippets instead of text to experiment with non-linear storytelling. To extend the assignment still further, generate a full-scale non-linear story in the form of a Web novel, for example, or using software such as Twine.

Discussion points: There is no one 'answer', of course, regarding what the various rearrangements of the story elements will yield. It is perfectly possible that different people will see different stories in different rearrangements. However, there are some resulting narrative upshots that can be outlined here to start reflection/discussion.

Block A discussion/reflection: If the Block A elements remain in their current 1→2→3 order (door slams → mother smiles → Jack outside door), then the moments can together form a point at the start of the story when the mother smiles relief that her lazy son has, of his own volition, left the house, slamming the door behind him as he goes to market. Rearrange the descriptions into 2→1→3 and the mother could have rather more forcefully told her son to leave: now, she is smiling satisfaction at her decisiveness in ousting her son (mother smiles → door slams → Jack outside door). Alternatively, if the Block A elements are rearranged 3→2→1 (Jack outside door → mother smiles → door slams) then the moments could together represent the point much later in the fairytale when Jack comes home after he has successfully killed the giant: here, the mother's smile becomes one of pride in her son's achievement and the door is slamming behind them both as they prepare to celebrate.

Block B discussion/reflection: If the Block B elements remain in their current 1→2→3 order, then the story is – as per the fairytale – one of Jack triumphing over the giant (Jack in poverty → Jack kills giant → Jack rich). However, if the elements are rearranged 3→2→1, then we get what could look like a story of a man ruined by hubris (Jack rich → Jack kills giant → Jack in poverty); or – if the order is 1→3→2 – the story could be one of a man who becomes so drunk on power that he commits a terrible act, and gets away with it (Jack in poverty → Jack rich → Jack kills giant).

Observations: Gaining a robust understanding of non-linear narratives (how they work, how to create them) is an important aspect of a multimodal writing practice. As indicated, websites and computer games are characterised by the offer to readers/viewers/players of multiple entry and exit points, whereby users can pursue different narrative paths. Writers of non-linear stories have to be able to anticipate and account for users reading story elements in different orders. They have to build skills in constructively fragmenting text. In addition, this assignment helps develop close reading and self-editing skills.

If getting to grips with this activity proves tricky, it can be helpful to consider one or two examples. This is the text-response to Block A of two students I worked with: '1. The front door slammed shut so roughly it shook the cottage to its bones.'/'2. Jack's mother stood at the stove stirring a pot of porridge. She smiled and tightened the threadbare shawl around her shoulders, shivering slightly.'/'3. Jack stood outside the door, pondering his next move. He kicked the dirt from his boots, stalling for time' (the three elements work effectively whether they are ordered 1→2→3, 3→2→1 or 2→1→3). This assignment was inspired by Marie-Laure Ryan's brief illustration of how non-linear narratives can work.[56] Ryan takes the basic framework of the Bible story of the virgin birth (Mary marries Joseph, Mary loses her virginity, Mary has a baby) and notes that, if the elements are switched around (Mary loses her virginity, Mary marries Joseph, Mary has a baby), then the story can become instead the story of a shotgun wedding. You could experiment with other versions of this Bible narrative. Alternatively, you could experiment with the film maker Sergei Eisenstein's well-known theory of montage and/or the

Beat poets' 'cut ups', which both involve repositioning story elements to see what new meanings arise. This could be done with random pictures cut from a magazine or sentences from newspaper articles. Or, it may be helpful to experiment with sections from Jennifer Egan's *Black Box*, a short story that was first published as separate tweets via the *New Yorker*'s Twitter account and so lends itself well to having component parts rearranged.[57]

Assignment 10: 'Make your own book'

Make a book on no budget.

Skills: Bold exploration | selecting, curating.

Individual/group: Solo or group exercise.

Equipment: Pen and paper plus 'found' materials.

Time: Between a few minutes and several weeks, it's your choice. A very simple 'book' can be assembled by just stapling a few sheets of paper together. If you want to do more than this, allow half an hour for Steps 1–3; after that, the amount of time it takes to make the book is entirely dependent on the particular project/s.

> **Practitioner note**: If self-publishing is a key aim, it's actually better for this assignment to choose one of your more experimental creative projects (something short is best), as this is likely to free you up to have fun and take some design risks. Then you can apply what you've learned to the project you plan to self-publish.

> **Tutor note**: For this assignment, it works well to invite the class to break into small groups, with each group producing a 'book' collaboratively. Steps 1–4 are best positioned early in a course. For Step 5, each group can be given about 5 minutes to present their finished publication to the class. Step 5 works well towards the end of a programme of study, when it can feel celebratory.

'Make your own book'

Make a book on no budget.

ACTION: This is a deceptively simple assignment. The task is to make a book, that's it. The content is up to you. There are just two rules: no budget; the book must be replicable.

Step 1: Consider the various stages in the production of a book and key tasks involved (e.g. in a commercial publishing house, an editor commissions the book; once the manuscript is delivered, it is copy-edited; production decisions are made about bindings, design decisions are made about fonts, for example).

Step 2: Consider the assignment's rules, i.e.:

Rule 1: No budget. The book must be made with found objects only. Paper, staples, needle and thread and so forth can be considered 'found objects', but no money should be spent on fancy bindings.

Rule 2: The book must be replicable. Even if the print run is just three books, it must be possible to make multiple copies.

Step 3: Decide what kind of book yours will be. If it is a collection of horror stories, this might lead to certain production decisions. If you're going to publish a collection of horror stories, it would probably look odd to have a lovely pink ribbon for the binding and/or an idyllic picture of a hayfield on the front cover, for example.

Step 4: Make the book.

Step 5: Consider the process and experience of making a book on no budget.

Step 6: To extend the assignment, a more technically advanced book can be made. This may involve using digital platforms such as Issuu along with software applications such as InDesign, in order to make the publication look more visually polished. Alternatively, a hard copy book can be made using self-publishing services such as Lulu or Amazon's KPD, with an ISBN applied for, a print run of twenty or fifty ordered and the resulting books made available for sale!

Discussion points: Areas for discussion/reflection might include: what were the biggest challenges, how were they overcome; what were the biggest surprises? The binding often provides the biggest challenge, and the associated solution often provides some surprises. Students in my classes have utilised a range of materials as bindings, from a single safety pin to a complex cardboard pattern that was cut out and glued to form a hinged box.

Observations: This assignment develops a number of skills that are key to a robust multimodal writing practice, including bold exploration. For pretty much any writer at any stage of his or her career, just the thought of publishing a piece of his or her creative work can feel bold. It's not necessary to use your own work, but whether you do or not, the assignment develops skills in selecting and curating, as it's necessary to make basic but important decisions about which section of text to put where. The logistics of book production can seem remote and/or unimportant to a writer. The absence of a budget forces close focus on how design and production details affect the experience of reading a book (choice of font, margin sizes, for example; whether the book's pages are bound with staples, thread or glue). The assignment can also prove empowering. For practitioners, it can seem as if the means of production are out of reach, with commercial publishers' editors impossible to contact. With this assignment, writer becomes editor and publisher rolled into one, gaining a sense of agency and facing down technical challenges that stand in the way of realising creative aims. Whether you make a pop-up book, or a stapled 'zine', or an entirely different kind of publication, all books are multimodal objects and the experience of producing one is highly likely to make other technologies seem less daunting.

CONCLUSION

This volume has considered how the rapid technological change that characterises the twenty-first century writing and publishing landscape affects writers, and it has presented a model of creativity designed to help writers develop the creative flexibility and resilience necessary to embrace the wealth of existing and emerging opportunities. In this final chapter, I review the context that makes such a model necessary, sum up the main accomplishments of *The Multimodal Writer* and consider areas for future research.

The distinction between book and computer has blurred, as has the distinction between producer and consumer of content.[1] On sites such as Wikipedia and Wattpad, we can read others' text and write new text; we have become 'prosumers' whereby the consumption and production of online content fuses into a single practice.[2] We can watch a video on a tablet while we embed a URL in a text on a smartphone and consider a draft document on our computer. Audio has gained new importance because it is so easy to combine listening to a podcast with activities such as exercising or travelling.[3] Visuals, too, have new centrality for writers, with photographs and gifs now a core part of social media 'language'.[4, 5] The top 'words' of 2014 and 2015 were digital pictograms: emojis of a love heart and 'Face with Tears of Joy' respectively.[6, 7] Writers are experimenting with emojis in fiction and also on Twitter 'bio's,[8, 9] where an emoji of a pile of books or a hand in the act of writing might support or even replace the word 'author' or 'novelist'.[10] Self-publishing, previously dismissed as 'vanity publishing', has become a potent force. The many people who possess computers and have internet connections can produce their own novels and disseminate them worldwide.[11, 12] Perceptions have changed so thoroughly that mainstream publishers such as Penguin and HarperCollins have experimented with providing self-publishing as a service and self-publishing is now sometimes the preferred choice of established writers.[13, 14]

Change can be difficult, it can be unnerving, certainly.[15] It can also be exciting and liberating, and it tends to come with costs. As technologies and genres continue to emerge and morph, there is an ever-increasing need for people who can, as the saying goes, 'think outside the box' – yet, as Huws notes, conditions resulting from such changes can be 'inimical to that very creativity'.[16]

In a digital age, the ability to move quickly between types of writing and technologies is increasingly essential for writers. Yet, it is simply not possible for any writer to be permanently up-to-date with every relevant development, there will always be a point at which a technology is new to someone and so may present difficulties.

New media technologies are changing the way we function as human beings, forcing us to move between the 'close reading' associated with novels and the fragmented, hyper-linked 'hyper reading' associated with online reading.[17] Self-identity has always been multifaceted, involving 'code-switching' both between private and public (home as opposed to work, for example) and between different public selves that each require different intonations and phrasings for different situations.[18] However, new media technologies bring new complexities and tensions to questions of self-identity. Via social media platforms, we can find that we are operating such a disparate range of voices and personas that we become 'transmediated', made up of multiple different parts, forming a browsable story-world that is integrated, dispersed, episodic, and interactive.[19] As discussed in Chapter 4, the idea that we are each a collection of 'I's, porous and permeated by other 'I's is perhaps particularly problematic for writers, who are now expected (by publishers, by readers) to maintain author platforms, posting regular updates via websites, blogs, Twitter that present a coherent author identity.[20, 21]

As discussed, it would be easy for a writer to become overwhelmed. It can feel as if digital technologies have 'magical qualities' and we must submit.[22] We can succumb to ideas of technological determinism, whereby we experience either 'false hope' that technical progress will provide all the answers or 'false hopelessness' due to an overwhelming sense of loss of human agency.[23] Rejecting such binary viewpoints, Andersen argues that we need a model for computer literacy that emphasises what Bruno Latour has called 'the actors in a technical project': then, notes Andersen, we see 'technologies as nodes on a network that also includes individuals and ideas, each element having an agency'.[24] A key aim of this book has been to give agency back to the writer. To achieve this, it has set out to provide a tried and tested toolkit.

Gibbons observes, 'One of the strongest criticisms of existing approaches to multimodality is the lack of empirical testing behind them.'[25] The findings that this book represents are drawn from an extensive programme of research that has empirical testing as its driving force.

The research embraces three decades' of practitioner experience, in-class trials of assignments spanning 6 years and in-depth interviews with a range of writers with a total of around 200 years' combined multimodal writing practice. However, as noted, each writer's experience of moving between different kinds of writing and technologies is unique. Every reader will develop a multimodal writing practice that is wholly individual, and which continues to change over time. That is, in an often tumultuous multimodal writing and publishing landscape (featuring a whole host of new genres and technologies that writers might engage with by choice or happenstance, now or in the future), there is an incalculably vast range of possible discrete practitioner experiences. Taking this vast range of variants into account, *The Multimodal Writer* provides a single toolkit.

The main accomplishments of this book are, I believe, fourfold. The auto-practitioner study set out in Chapter 2 demonstrates how a writer can remediate his or her own practice, thereby transferring existing skills in order to tackle new genres, technologies and writing and publishing situations effectively. Thus, the first main accomplishment of this book is to show that a significant proportion of the solutions available to a writer are internal and exist already (as discussed, importantly, they are in his or her control).

The second main accomplishment arises from the author interviews (Chapter 3). The author interviews provide a wide selection of sample resources and tactics which have proved effective for a selection of established authors when moving between genres and technologies. On a purely practical level, the sample resources and tactics that the interviews provide can be borrowed and experimented with. For this reason, they represent a wide range of potentially useful additions to a writer's toolkit as he or she works to develop a personalised model of creativity that is effective in a multimodal writing and publishing landscape. More significantly, since no one technology or set of technologies is central to the development of such a model, the authors' responses, in indicating how technologies that are new to an individual are approached, demonstrate how creative flexibility can be sustained. This represents the second main accomplishment.

As well as showing how a writer's own skills can be remediated and creative flexibility sustained, this book also provides a set of tried and tested assignments designed for use now. The pedagogical gap which the assignments address – as scholars including Kress, Yancey and Harper highlight – is significant.[26, 27, 28] As noted previously, to be 'deeply literate' in the digital world means being at home in a shifting mix of words, images and sounds.[29] How might a writer come to first feel and then remain at home in such a shifting mix? This book isolates the key skills needed and provides tried-and-tested assignments designed explicitly to develop them (Chapter 5). To do so is its third main accomplishment.

Yet, to recap briefly, writers must become at home in a *shifting mix* of morphing genres and technological change.[30] We must be able to negotiate an 'I' that is *porous, spilling and traversed*, we must get used to being a *dispersed, episodic* self.[31, 32] With new media technologies pulling us in different directions, the past to draw on, the future to look to and a set of prescribed skills to hone or develop from scratch, how can we retain the 'authentic' voice that has traditionally been the aim of creative writers? The model of creativity presented here shows that a writer can draw on internal and external writerly resources and utilise a range of writerly personas when moving between different types of writing. It shows too that, in order to orchestrate the huge number of possible permutations, a writer can utilise an 'inner auteur'. The inner auteur can be deployed to identify which resources and personas, in what combination, will be optimally effective for particular moves between different types of writing. That is, the model of creativity presented here accounts for the fact that a writer must be able to continue effectively with each separate type of writing *and* maintain an authorial voice that is at once appropriate for each separate genre and recognisable as the author's own, unique, authentic voice. In the face of the incalculably vast range of possible discrete practitioner experiences, the fourth main accomplishment of this book is to provide a model of creativity that is – as has been shown via empirical testing – replicable and, more significantly, effective.

Now, having reviewed the context that makes this volume prescient and summed up its main accomplishments, I will turn to areas for future research. The first relates to editing skills. As discussed in Chapter 1, in a writing and publishing environment in which a writer can publish text at the click of a button, the ability to self-edit has new significance. A number of the assignments in this volume (particularly 'Picture this', 'Proppian analysis' and 'Story mash-up', see Chapter 5) are designed to aid the development of skills including self-editing. The assignments can be repeated, to further develop self-editing skills. However, *The Multimodal Writer* is a single volume. Self-editing is a hard skill to learn. It tends to feel like a slog; it can be difficult to see the rewards. Regardless of the number of errors a social media post contains, interest in it might be signified by hundreds, thousands, even millions of 'likes' and/or repostings by readers all over the world. Such apparent global approval may feel like proof that there is no need to work at ensuring that sentences are grammatically correct. Editing skills can, in the current writing and publishing landscape, seem redundant. A future area of research is how to address this. This area is, of course, inconceivably vast, embracing as it does educational institutions from schools to universities as well as businesses and corporations that profit from extensive public engagement with social media platforms, regardless of content. It is nonetheless important that the widespread and apparently growing disinclination to develop self-editing skills is addressed, even if this can only be done through discrete and relatively small research projects. It is to be hoped that assignments provided here represent a useful contribution.

A second area for future research is how interactions between the material world, the body, the senses and the mind work together to enable effective negotiation of the twenty-first century digital and networked writing and publishing environment. Again, this is a vast area, and, as noted, scientific 'truths' of one generation have the unsettling tendency 'to be overturned or reversed in the next, especially in fields as rapidly developing as brain science and the science of consciousness'.[33] Nevertheless, within this vast area, research in one smaller area can be pointed to. We have become so used to working with linear narratives (starting a story at page one and continuing page by page to the conclusion) that the spatial way of thinking that is necessary when conceiving non-linear narratives (e.g. for video games and websites) can feel hard. Research into brain activity as it relates to the experience of working to compose non-linear narratives may prove particularly helpful for writers working to effectively and productively negotiate a digital writing and publishing landscape.

A third area for research is how metaphor is and can be used to aid negotiation of new media technologies. For example, 'cyberspace' is a metaphor drawn from William Gibson's 1984 novel *Neuromancer* and used to help us conceptualise the discrepancy between 'the miniscule size of the equipment required for computing' and 'the massive amount of tasks it can perform and the data it can store', as Cobley puts it.[34] Kate Pullinger, who has worked for many years on storytelling via new media technologies, refers to the importance of metaphor in conceptualising innovative storytelling practices (see Chapter 3). This research area is likely to enable identification of additional strategies that can be deployed as part of a robust and sustainable multimodal writing practice.

Finally, as this volume draws to a close, I will return briefly to the idea of *trespassing* as a valuable and important method of enquiry. Trespassing involves going somewhere that you are not meant to be. If you feel you are trespassing, this tends to come with a sense of trepidation which serves to keep the senses alert. If you feel that you are outside your area of expertise, this can enable a fresh perspective. A key characteristic of technostress is that (as we try to familiarise ourselves with new technologies and genres in fast-paced publishing contexts that are often live and public) we feel that we are in places where we shouldn't be. We can easily feel ill-equipped and/or under-qualified. Yet, writing has always been a mix of premeditated searching and undisciplined, perhaps only partly conscious rambling, over fences, through gaps in walls.[35] As Turchi frames it, writing is 'an act of *exploration*', that is: 'assertive action in the face of uncertain assumptions, often involving false starts, missteps, and surprises'.[36] Webb and Brien talk of creative writers as practitioners who take a *bricoleur*-bowerbird approach.[37] Seen in this frame, when a writer is working on fiction or creative non-fiction, he or she is a cross between a bowerbird, which seeks out all the blue things with which to make its nest, and a '*bricoleur*', or, jack of all trades, who makes do with what's available.[38] This inclination towards taking things from here and there (an enjoyment of appropriation and repurposing and piracy) fits very well with social media and cyber-environments characterised by prosumer engagement, where cutting and pasting and curation and content management (plundering and pilfering) play significant parts. Turchi talks of artistic creation as 'a voyage into the unknown', and, such voyages can be exciting.[39] If we recalibrate trepidation as excitement, then the experience of exploring our online, networked environment can become part of a bigger – more productive – picture of artistic endeavour.

Practices of tinkering, recycling and repurposing that are inherent to digital storytelling can be viewed as disruptive provocations, or, alternatively, as a strategy for engagement.[40] Technologies can viewed as tools, or writing partners.[41] The interactions of writing and programme, language and other media, the screen and the page can, as Smith[42] puts it, generate 'fruitful tensions'. Harper talks of how digital developments 'produce and support opportunities for human interaction and interconnection, well beyond the local or regional geography of direct physical contact, at a pace of experience and level of convenience never before accomplished'.[43] Ongoing, vibrant interactive discourses between readers and writers are an integral part of the literary landscape. Citing Henry Jenkins's suggestion that fanfiction is powerful precisely because it is often 'unpublishable', Krauth celebrates the fact that fanfiction is not bound by the constraints that govern commercial media production.[44]

Many authors of fanfiction publish anonymously; fanfiction sites are places where writers can cut their teeth, gaining feedback from readers to inform rewrites and revisions. Such sites are places where established writers can test new approaches. Poets including George Szirtzes experiment on platforms such as Twitter, novelists such as Margaret Atwood have presences on Wattpad.[45, 46] Harper talks of how the twenty-first century writing and publishing landscape enable 'extrinsic goals' of creative writing (such as books and publication) to recede and 'intrinsic goals' (the sheer joy of inventing) to come to the fore;[47] new media, or, 'synaptic' technologies, as he terms them, free us to immerse ourselves in enjoying the process of creation.

We are at a nexus that is imbued with unknowns and contradictions. The practice and pedagogy of creative writing could appear to be in crisis. Practitioners can, as discussed in Chapter 1, find the digital writing and publishing landscape destructive. Novelist Jonathan Franzen famously said, 'It's doubtful that anyone with an internet connection at his workplace is writing good fiction.'[48] Some writers find digital tools and networked environments so unnerving that they fear, as Deborah Moggach phrases it, 'if we venture into the new technology, will we somehow lose our voice?'[49] Similar responses abound in pedagogical contexts too. As discussed in the Introduction, wariness of new media technologies is widespread in higher education.[50] Yet even in that context, the Creative Writing classroom stands out for remaining strikingly and stubbornly 'low tech'.[51] However, it is not just that 'creative writing instruction needs to change'.[52] Action on this front is long overdue.[53]

It could seem, then, that Creative Writing is so behind that it will have trouble even catching up, since new media technologies continue to emerge and morph apace. However, I believe that the discipline of Creative Writing holds important answers. As MP Sharon Hodgson highlighted during a Westminster Hall debate, 'Students who are taught creative writing are taught creative thinking'.[54] Research by the Creative Industries Policy and Evidence Centre led by Nesta shows that creativity is increasingly valued by employers across jobs, across sectors.[55] According to the World Economic Forum, 'Creativity will become one of the top three skills workers will need' – alongside 'Complex Problem Solving' and 'Critical Thinking', skills that are also core aspects of creative writing practice.[56] In a world in which multimodality is an everyday reality, creative flexibility has gained new importance.

Murray observes that from Gutenberg's invention of the printing press in 1455, 'It took fifty years of experimentation and more to establish such conventions as legible typefaces and proof sheet corrections; page numbering and paragraphing; and title pages, prefaces, and chapter divisions, which together made the published book a coherent means of communication.'[57] Those working in the pedagogy of Creative Writing may have been slow to recognise the 'profound impact digital technology has on our discipline',[58] some or many writers may continue to find this profound impact unnerving, but, the changes being wrought by new media technologies on the writing and publishing landscape are still in their infancy.

There is pressure on us all today – in the work place, in leisure time, in creative writing practice – to be proficient and resourceful communicators, adept at shifting quickly and effectively between genres and technologies. As I have discussed, it is important that users of new media technologies are able to assimilate messages from multiple sources and (swiftly and effectively) turn such inputs into meaningful outputs, remaining adaptable as new technologies emerge.[59] This book – the auto-practitioner study, author interviews and assignments in combination – provides a toolkit that enables development of the creative flexibility that is necessary to thrive in a writing and publishing landscape characterised by multimodality.

Creative writing already contributes significantly beyond its own borders by 'defamiliarising the familiar' and thus inviting a reflective engagement with the world around us, a move that Webb and Brien argue 'has the potential to recast social and global relationships, and contribute to changing attitudes, practices and policies'.[60] Genres will emerge that haven't been conceived yet, so, too, means of production and dissemination. Practitioners who are ready and equipped with the creative flexibility necessary to experiment effectively with platforms and technologies can be at the vanguard of conceiving new genres and pioneering new means of creating and disseminating stories. Murray notes, 'When we expand the meaning-making conventions that make up human culture, we expand our ability to understand the world and connect with one another.'[61] What might begin here as development of individual creative practice could have more far-reaching implications. As we journey deeper into an era in which technology can feel alien and alienating, by reclaiming agency as writers – by trespassing when necessary, by embracing exploration – we may play parts in a bigger venture, invigorating human connectedness.

APPENDICES

Appendix I: Selected stories

'William and the Pious Bull'
by Thomas Hardy[1]
(Story in *Tess of the d'Urbervilles*, first published in 1891.)
521 words

ONCE there was a old aged man over at Mellstock – William Dewy by name – one of the family that used to do a good deal of business as tranters over there, Jonathan, do ye mind? – I knowed the man by sight as well as I know my own brother, in a manner of speaking. Well, this man was a coming home-along from a wedding where he had been playing his fiddle, one fine moonlight night, and for shortness' sake he took a cut across Forty-acres, a field lying that way, where a bull was out to grass. The bull seed William, and took after him, horns aground, begad; and though William runned his best and hadn't *much* drink in him (considering 'twas a wedding, and the folks well off), he found he'd never reach the fence and get over in time to save himself. Well, as a last thought, he pulled out his fiddle as he runned, and struck up a jig, turning to the bull, and backing towards the comer. The bull softened down, and stood still, looking hard at William Dewy, who fiddled on and on; till a sort of a smile stole over the bull's face. But no sooner did William stop his playing and turn to get over hedge than the bull would stop his smiling and lower his horns towards the seat of William's breeches. Well, William had to turn about and play on, willy-nilly; and 'twas only three o'clock in the world, and a' knowed that nobody would come that way for hours, and he so leery and tired that 'a didn't know what to do. When he had scraped till about four o'clock he felt that he verily would have to give over soon, and he said to himself. 'There's only this last tune between me and eternal welfare! Heaven save me, or I'm a done man.' Well, then he called to mind how he'd seen the cattle kneel o' Christmas Eves in the dead o' night. It was not Christmas Eve then, but it came into his head to play a trick upon the bull. So he broke into the Tivity Hymn, just as at

Christmas carol-singing; when, lo and behold, down went the bull on his bended knees, in his ignorance, just as if 'twere the true Tivity night and hour. As soon as his horned friend were down, William turned, clinked off like a long-dog, and jumped safe over hedge, before the praying bull had got on his feet again to take after him. William used to say that he's seen a man look a fool a good many times, but never such a fool as that bull looked when he found his pious feelings had been played upon, and 'twas not Christmas Eve. Yes, William Dewy, that was the man's name; and I can tell you to a foot where's be a-lying in Mellstock Churchyard at this very moment – just between the second yew-tree and the north aisle.

'Legend'
by Suniti Namjoshi
202 words

ONCE upon a time there was a she-monster. She lived submerged 20,000 feet under the sea, and was only a legend, until one day the scientists got together to fish her out. They hauled her ashore and loaded her on trucks and finally set her down in a vast amphitheatre where they began their dissection. It soon became evident that the creature was pregnant. They alerted security and sealed all the doors, being responsible men and unwilling to take chances with the monster's whelps, for who could know what damage they might do if unleashed on the world. But the she-monster died with her litter of monsters buried inside her. They opened the doors. The flesh of the monster was beginning to smell. Several scientists succumbed to the fumes. They did not give up. They worked in relays and issued gas masks. At last the bones of the creature were scraped quite clean, and they had before them a shining skeleton. The skeleton may be seen at the National Museum. It bears the legend: 'The Dreaded She-Monster. The fumes of this creature are noxious to men.'

Inscribed underneath are the names of the scientists who gave their lives to find this out.

'That Small Small Inch'
by Tania Hershman
234 words

YOU thought it was the oddest setting. You thought it was the strangest place to meet: a phone box. I said, I am very fond of this one. You looked at me like that again. Don't look at me like that, I said back to you, my nose an inch from yours inside this joyful phone box. I did grin then, to demonstrate that this was fun, a date. You didn't grin right back, as if you thought, Oh no, one of these spirits has gone inside her, what will she do now and next and after that and me here just a small small inch away? I heard you think that, really I did, we were pressing stomach to stomach. Feel it! I said to you then, and then my hunger made itself too clear. You did smile then and reached your hand across that inch and put it on my tummy. Does your phone box have coffee or cake? you said then, but your fingers on my cardigan which was only millimetres from the skin below had sent me flapping, all of me, and every warmth a spark a burst of red delight that I could no longer talk. I looked it into you instead, looked my words into your eyes and then, oh then, you heard it clear and, crossed that small small inch once more, this time with your mouth.

Appendix II: Tutor guidance (general)

The assignments in Chapter 5 can be introduced to a teaching setting easily and quickly with little if any preparation necessary.

While new media technologies and social media can of course be utilised for the assignments, it is important to note that they are not *required* for any of the assignments. As the Carnegie UK Trust's *Not Without Me: A digital world for all?*[2] notes, 'offline' is not just an acceptable place to start learning digital skills: 'Digital skills development starts offline and "offline" continues to be an important delivery method'.[3]

If you feel wariness of teaching digital skills to a classful of young people, keep two things in mind. First, the students may feel as uncomfortable as you about the prospect of using technology in the classroom. Even young people who are 'power users' or 'digital addicts'[4] can find it hard to transfer digital skills gained in a leisure context into a more formal setting. 'Young people are not digital natives, indeed not all young people possess even basic digital skills' say Wilson and Grant[5]; moreover, 'Advanced skills in one digital area can mask low skills in other digital competencies'.[6] Helping the students build confidence in negotiating the digital sphere is often much more important than teaching any particular technical skills.

A second thing to bear in mind is this: the notion that all tutors should have full and complete expertise at the outset and throughout can also prove to be a barrier to teaching digital skills. As indicated, in the case of new media technologies, it is simply not possible for *anyone* to be permanently abreast of everything. As I have discussed (Barnard, 2019), it is not only the case that tutors don't need to be technological experts; it may actively help students if they feel that they and the tutor are 'in it together', with students in a position to contribute knowledge and experience.

Andersen, quoting Feenberg, writes of the importance of looking beyond the technical aspects of software and hardware components.[7] We must, he argues, beware technological determinism, 'which yields either false hope based on inevitable technical progress or false hopelessness based on the loss of human agency in a world determined by technologies. The trick is to engage technologies while avoiding lenses through which "both utopian and dystopian visions [of technologies] are exaggerated"'.

It is often helpful for students to have choice regarding which technology or platform each uses to pursue his or her assignment. However, this reduces the chance still further of a single tutor having expertise that is directly relevant for all students.

There are more important issues at stake than the tutor not knowing InDesign or Photoshop, for example. Letter[8] argues that the educator should focus on what will be – regardless of the individual technologies – overarching problems for all the students. Often, for example, in the face of technical difficulties, 'the train of thought carrying [a student's] great ideas seems to have derailed', says Letter[9], asserting: 'The role of the instructor here is clear. It is most explicitly *not* to solve the problem for the student ... it is essential that the students learn to research and solve their own problems and that they become accustomed to the task-switching that creative work in new media requires'. Further, Letter[10] suggests, tutors should help students 'see 'their "technical difficulties" as a form of artistic constraint, the possible spark of a new stage in their creative process, rather than a wall that stymies progress.' New media technologies can become collaborators.

Finally, do not be shy of asking for help. One of the first things Leahy and Dechow[11] did when considering how to embed technology in the classroom was contact their university's Office of Academic Technology with 'a lot of questions', and: 'The university provided training for the students which made it possible for major assignments to be embedded promptly in the course.'

Appendix III: Methodology

The Multimodal Writer results from a programme of research comprising three main areas: an auto-practitioner study (Barnard, 2015), which underpins this volume; in-class trials of assignments (conducted

2012–2019); interviews with selected authors who have long-standing experience of moving between different types of writing (conducted 2016–2017). These three areas of research required separate research methods, which, together, comprise the methodology used to develop the model of creativity presented here (see Chapter 4).

The below provides further information on the methodology used.

Auto-practitioner study: The data for this section of the research is derived from a practitioner study of my own Creative Writing in the public sphere. My practice is characterised by an occupational eclecticism; from the outset, it has involved moving between different types of writing for different modes of dissemination. My public works include five books (Barnard 1993, 1994, 1996, 2000, 2011) and a selection of print and broadcast journalism (e.g. Barnard, 1999, 2008a; Barnard, 1997, 2008) which was submitted to a critical exegesis (Barnard, 2015) guided by consideration of how such moves were effected.

Author interviews: To gain broad-based insights drawn from empirical data, eight interviews were conducted with writers of international standing who each have 20 years or more experience of multimodal writing practice (Simon Armitage, Robert Coover, Jim Crace, Juliet Gardiner, Charlie Higson, Rhianna Pratchett, Kate Pullinger and Michèle Roberts). The writers interviewed represent a wide range of types of movements between different types of writing for different platforms. The interviews were conducted between June 2016 and May 2017. They were all face-to-face and digitally recorded and transcribed. A topic guide was used to ensure consistency of subject matter covered during the interviews. All transcripts were sent to the participants in order to confirm that they accurately reflected their views and amendments were inserted where requested.

In-class trials of assignments: To develop the assignments, a set of in-class trials accompanied by student evaluation sheets was conducted between October 2012 and January 2019.

The in-class trials were informed by my experience teaching Creative Writing in a wide range of institutions since 2000, including in UK universities at undergraduate and postgraduate level, in further education colleges and for industry initiatives such as Faber and Faber publisher's creative writing programme, The Faber Academy. Thus, early iterations of some of the assignments date back to 2000. Additionally, each assignment featured in this volume was trialled with writing students (undergraduate and postgraduate) in a classroom setting at a UK university, with student feedback gained for each trial using evaluation sheets which utilised the learning outcomes particular to the module in which the trial was being conducted and/or benchmarks adapted from The Quality Assurance Agency (QAA) (2016) *Subject Benchmark Statement: Creative Writing*. Students were invited to indicate whether the assignment had helped with a particular learning outcome/benchmark, and if so, how; additional space was provided for general comments on each exercise. This enabled a quantitative and qualitative assessment of the effectiveness of the assignments. (For further detail of sample trials see Barnard [2016], Barnard [2017] and Barnard [2019], which consider in-class trials utilising evaluation sheets of social media and data visualisation assignments.)

As well as being trialled during the in-class pilots with students and with other writing tutors, some of the assignments in this chapter featured as part of conference presentations and during a Focus Group at a UK further education college in May 2016 where useful feedback was gained from teachers of creative writing and other disciplines and from writing students representing a range of institutions.[12, 13]

The precise composition and construction of this selection of assignments is further informed by the author interviews (see Chapter 3) and by Kress, Yancey and Harper.[14, 15, 16] Addressing in broad terms the challenges faced by writers in a postdigital age, Kress, Yancey and Harper stress the need for a creative flexibility that enables swift and effective movement between genres and technologies. They all note the gap in existing pedagogies as regards the task of developing this creative flexibility, and they all set out calls to action, itemising skills that must now be taught if writers, aspiring writers and those who work with text are to effectively and productively negotiate a postdigital age. All highlight the pressing need to teach adaptability and, as Kress phrases it, 'reflective risk-taking and exploration of the unknown'; all point to the need to enable the ability to creatively transform templates; all write of the need to help develop skills associated with becoming 'members of a writing public' who engage in real-time discourse via 'non-linear and connective' new media technologies that blur the boundaries between professional and personal life.[17, 18, 19]

In summary, then, the assignments featured in this volume are informed by: classroom applications of the assignments dating back to 2000; the programme of academic research that this book represents which is itself informed by practitioner experience dating back over three decades; and, Kress, Yancey and Harper's indicative mapping of the pedagogical gap that needs to be filled.

Thus, the auto-practitioner study, the in-class pilots and the author interviews were used in combination to help identify the key resources (internal and external) and skills needed for a multimodal writing practice. Using these findings, the model of creativity (see Chapter 4) presented here was then developed, trialled as a class assignment itself and found to be effective as a template to help a writer identify the appropriate resources, develop the set of necessary skills and then orchestrate those components parts effectively in order to enable him or her to work productively and creatively as a multimodal writer.

Appendix IV: Note on interviewees

Simon Armitage is Professor of Poetry at the University of Leeds and was elected to serve as Professor of Poetry at the University of Oxford for 2015–2019. He is the author of numerous collections of poetry, including *The Shout: Selected Poems* (2005), which was short-listed for the National Book Critics Circle Award; *Kid* (1992), which won the Forward Prize; and his first collection, *Zoom!* (1989), a Poetry Society Book Choice. He has won an Eric Gregory Award and a Lannan Award, and was chosen as a *Sunday Times* Author of the Year. His translation of *Sir Gawain and the Green Night* (2007) from Middle English was selected as a Book of the Year by both the *New York Times* and the *Los Angeles Times*. Armitage has also published fiction, including the novels *The White Stuff* (2004) and *Little Green Man* (2001), and the memoir *All Points North* (1998). He has written extensively for radio, television, film and theatre, including the libretto for the opera *The Assassin Tree* (2006), the play *Mister Heracles* (2000), based on Euripedes's *The Madness of Heracles,* and the film *Xanadu* (1992). In 2010, for services to poetry, Armitage was awarded the CBE. He won the 2017 PEN America Award for Poetry in Translation and was awarded The Queens Gold Medal for Poetry 2018. www.simonarmitage.com/.

Robert Coover is the T. B. Stowell Professor Emeritus in Literary Arts at Brown University, Rhode Island. His first novel, *The Origin of the Brunists* (1966), won the William Faulkner Award. His other works include the collection of short fiction, *Pricksongs and Descants (1969)*, a collection of plays, *A Theological Position* (1975), such novels as *The Public Burning (1977), Spanking the Maid (1982), Gerald's Party (1986), Briar Rose (1997) and The Brunist Day of Wrath* (2014). Among other courses, as a Professor at Brown University, he teaches experimental narrative and literary hypermedia workshops. Non-teaching activities have included the creation and coordination of Brown's 'Freedom to Write' programme, and the organisation of several literary festivals and conferences. He is the recipient of many awards, including the Brandeis University, American Academy of Arts and Letters, National Endowment of the Arts, Rhode Island Governor's Arts, Pell, and Clifton Fadiman Awards. He was also awarded the Dugannon Foundation's REA award for his lifetime contribution to the short story, and the Rockefeller, Guggenheim, Lannan Foundation, and DAAD fellowships.

Jim Crace is a novelist and short story writer whose first book, *Continent* (1986), won the Whitbread First Novel Award, *The Guardian* Fiction Prize and the David Higham Prize for Fiction. His other books include *Signals of Distress* (1994), which won the Winifred Holtby Memorial Prize; *Quarantine* (1997), which was shortlisted for the Booker Prize for Fiction; *Being Dead* (1999), which won the Whitbread Novel Award, the National Book Critics' Circle Fiction Award (USA) and was shortlisted for both the Booker Prize for Fiction and the International IMPAC Dublin Literary Award; *Harvest* (2013), which was shortlisted for the 2013 Man Booker Prize, the Goldsmiths Prize and the Walter Scott Prize, and won the 2013 James Tait Black Memorial Prize and the International IMPAC Dublin Literary Award in 2015. His latest novel is *The Melody* (2018). He has also worked as a journalist and written radio plays and, as Writer in Residence at the Midlands Arts Centre, he directed the first Birmingham Festival of Readers and Writers. Jim Crace was awarded the E. M. Forster Award by the American Academy of Arts and Letters in 1992 and became a Fellow of the Royal Society of Literature in 1999. He is recipient of three Honorary Doctorates including from the University of Central England for Distinguished Literary Achievements.

Juliet Gardiner is a historian whose books include *The Penguin Dictionary of British History (2000)*; *Wartime: Britain 1939–1945* (2004); *The Children's War* (2006); *The Thirties: an Intimate History* (2010); and the autobiographical *Joining the Dots* (2017). She was the historical consultant and on-screen member of the 'war cabinet' in the *The 1940s House* for Channel 4 television, and wrote the accompanying book. In 2006 she acted as historical advisor for Working Title's film of Ian McEwan's novel, *Atonement*. She is a frequent broadcaster both on radio and television and has written and reviewed for various publications including *The Times, The Guardian, Financial Times, Daily Telegraph Magazine, Evening Standard, Daily Mail* and *BBC History magazine*. She is a former editor of *History Today* magazine, a Research Fellow at the Institute of

Historical Research of the School of Advanced Study at the University of London and an Honorary Fellow at the University of Edinburgh.

Charlie Higson is an author, actor, comedian and scriptwriter for television, film and radio. His *Young Bond* book series – *SilverFin* (2005), *Blood Fever* (2006), *Double or Die* (2007), *Hurricane Gold* (2007) and *By Royal Command* (2008) – sold over a million copies in the UK and has been translated into over 24 different languages; all five novels entered the children's bestseller charts in the top five. His other books include the adult thrillers – *King of the Ants* (1992), *Happy Now* (1993), *Full Whack* (1995) and *Getting Rid of Mr Kitchen* (1996) – and the bestselling zombie-adventure series for teenagers which began with *The Enemy* (2009). For television he co-created and starred in the sketch series *The Fast Show* (1994–2000), the spin-off sitcome *Swiss Toni* (2003/4) and dramas including *Randall & Hopkirk (Deceased)* (2000/01) and *Jekyll and Hyde* (2015). Film scripts include *Suite 16* (1994) and *King of the Ants* (2003). Twitter @monstroso, www.charliehigson.co.uk/.

Rhianna Pratchett is an award-winning, 18-year veteran of the games industry. She is co-director of the Narrativia multimedia production company. Her long-term love affair with games started when she was six and played Mazogs on the Sinclair ZX81. It later evolved through her work as a journalist for *PC Zone* magazine and *The Guardian*. But it was her passion for storytelling which won through when she moved into games development in 2003, eventually becoming one of the industry's most respected writers and narrative designers. During her time in the industry, Rhianna has wrestled the wild beasts of narrative for companies such as: Sony, EA, SEGA, 2K Games, Ubisoft, Codemasters and Square Enix. The titles she's helped bring to life include: Heavenly Sword, Mirror's Edge, the entire Overlord series, Tomb Raider and Rise of the Tomb Raider. Her work has received awards from the Writers' Guild of America award, the Writers' Guild of Great Britain, DICE, SXSW, and a BAFTA nomination. Rhianna is regularly named as one of the most influential and recognised women in games and has spoken on numerous panels, podcasts, conferences and documentaries. She also has the rare honour of having been interviewed by both *Vogue* and *Playboy*. In the world of comics, she's worked for DC, Dark Horse and Marvel (notably Mirror's Edge and Tomb Raider) and is currently writing film and TV projects with the Jim Henson Company, Film4 and O3 Productions. You can find Rhianna's latest short story in the *Press Start to Play* (2015) anthology by Penguin Random House. Like most writers, she likes hard liquor and soft cats. http://rhiannapratchett.com/.

Kate Pullinger is Professor of Creative Writing and Digital Media at Bath Spa University where she is also Director of the Centre for Research in the Cultural and Creative Industries. Her novel *The Mistress of Nothing*, won Canada's 2009 Governor General's Literary Award for Fiction. In 2014, she adapted her collaborative work of digital multimedia, *Flight Paths: A Networked Novel* (2007), co-created with Chris Joseph, as the novel *Landing Gear*, which was longlisted for Canada Reads. Also in 2014, she created the digital war memorial, *Letter to an Unknown Soldier*, with Neil Bartlett; 22,000 members of the public wrote letters to the soldier. Her project *Inanimate Alice* has also won numerous prizes. 2017 saw the publication of her novel for smartphones, *Jellybone,* and in 2018 *Breathe,* a ghost story for phones that personalises itself to every reader. www.katepullinger.com/.

Michèle Roberts is Emeritus Professor of Creative Writing at the University of East Anglia. Her fourteen novels include *Daughters of the House* which won the WH Smith Literary Award and was shortlisted for the Booker Prize; *Impossible Saints* (1997); *Ignorance* (2012); *The Walworth Beauty* (2017). Her memoir *Paper Houses* (2007) was BBC Radio 4's Book of the Week in June 2007. She has also published poetry and short stories, most recently collected in *Mud-stories of sex and love (2010).* She has also written food reviews for the *New Statesman*, essays including *Silly Lady Novelists?* (2017), plays including *Child Lover* (premiered Tramway Theatre, Glasgow, 1993) and a film for Channel 4 television, *Ma Semblable Ma Soeur* (1990), and she has co-authored artist's books. She has presented radio arts programmes such as the BBC's *Night Waves.* She was made a Chevalier de l'Ordre des Arts et des Lettres by the French Government and is a Fellow of the Royal Society of Literature. www. micheleroberts.co.uk/.

ACKNOWLEDGEMENTS

Grateful acknowledgement is made to the following authors and publishers for permission to reproduce copyright text material within this book: Tania Hershman and Tangent Books for 'That Small Small Inch', first published in PANK magazine and included in *My Mother Was An Upright Piano: Fictions*, by Tania Hershman (Tangent Books, 2012); Suniti Namjoshi and Spinifex Press for 'Legend', first published in *Feminist Fables* (Sheba Feminist Publisher, 1981; Spinifex Press, 1998). Thanks to Nova Science Publishers for permission to print a developed version of the assignment that first appeared in 'Twitter and Creative Writing: generating an "authentic" online self' (in *Twitter: Global Perspectives, Uses and Research Techniques*, Nova Science Publishers, 2019), an assignment that features in this book as 'Me, myself, I'.

My single biggest debt of gratitude is owed to Professor Paul Cobley, whose ongoing help and support has been imaginative and insightful.

Thanks are due to all at Red Globe Press: Jenna Steventon for her work as my editor, Rachel Bridgewater for her work at early stages, and Emily Lovelock; Georgia Park, Stanly Emelson and Angela Valente; Annie Stedman and Eleanor Wilson. Thanks to the reviewers, whose comments helped shape this volume.

I am grateful to Professor Simon Armitage, Professor Robert Coover, Jim Crace, Juliet Gardiner, Charlie Higson, Rhianna Pratchett, Professor Kate Pullinger and Professor Michèle Roberts for contributing time, reflections and conversation so generously. Special thanks to Dr Maggie Butt and Dr Sylvia Shaw, who, as Director of Studies and supervisor through my postdoctoral research, provided stimulating discussion and stringent readings of work that has contributed to this volume. Thanks, too, to the External Examiners of my PhD by Public Work: Professor Tessa McWatt and Dr Jonathan Taylor.

To my students, thank you, both for engaging so enthusiastically with class assignments and, more generally, for uplifting, surprising and stimulating fresh thoughts.

I am grateful to many people for conversations, advice, inspiration, practical support, encouragement, and readings of early drafts, in particular to: Richard Beswick; Helen Chadwick; Professor Billy Clark;

Deborah Curtis and Gavin Turk; colleagues in the DCMS Research Working Group on Digital Skills and Inclusion; Dr Jim Graham; Emma Hotopf; Professor Ursula Huws; Dr Paul Kerr; Dr Adam Lively; Dr Magnus Moar; Dr Irida Ntalla; Bill Parry Davis; Philippa Perry; Professor Andrea Phillips; Dr Kate Potts; David Prest, Deborah Dudgeon, Emma Barnaby, and all at Whistledown Productions; Lily Riddett; Dr Ian Roper; Lisa Shell; Caroline Stacey.

Particular thanks to: Professor John Barnard and Professor Hermione Lee; Clio Barnard and Jason Barnard; Dr Patsy Hickman; and, Susan Mitchell.

Eternal gratitude to my husband and children, for so much.

NOTES

Introduction

1. Schwab, Klaus (2016) *The Fourth Industrial Revolution*. (Geneva: World Economic Forum).
2. World Economic Forum (2016) *The Future of Jobs: Employment, Skills and Workforce Strategy for the Fourth Industrial Revolution*, Global Challenge Insight Report, January. Available at www3.weforum.org/docs/WEF_Future_of_Jobs.pdf [accessed 6 January 2019] p. 3.
3. Quoted in Handa, Carolyn (2004) 'Introduction' in Carolyn Handa (ed.), *Visual Rhetoric in a Digital World* (Boston, New York: Bedford/St Martin's) p. 1.
4. Gibbons, Alison (2011) *Multimodality, Cognition, and Experimental Literature*, ebook (London, New York: Routledge) [accessed 29 May 2017] p. 8.
5. Department for Digital, Culture, Media and Sport (DCMS) (2017) Policy paper, Digital skills and inclusion – Giving everyone access to the digital skills they need, 1 March (London: DCMS). Available at www.gov.uk/government/publications/uk-digital-strategy/2-digital-skills-and-inclusion-giving-everyone-access-to-the-digital-skills-they-need [accessed 17 April 2017] n.p.
6. Ibid.
7. Barnard in Parliament, Commons Select Committee, Culture Media and Support (DCMS) (2013) Written evidence submitted by Josie Barnard [SCE 088]. *HC 743 Support for the Creative Economy* (London: DCSS) November 2012. www.publications.parliament.uk/pa/cm201213/cmselect/cmcumeds/writev/suppcrec/m088.htm.
8. Barnard, Josie (2017) 'Testing possibilities: On negotiating writing practices in a "postdigital" age (tools and methods)'. *New Writing: The International Journal for the Practice and Theory of Creative Writing, 14*(2): 275–276. DOI: 10.1080/14790726.2016.127802.
9. See as examples: 'Eight tiny stories, translated from the emoji: James Hannaham and John W. Bateman turn random emoji into microfiction'. Available at https://electricliterature.com/eight-tiny-stories-translated-from-the-emoji-40d43d4b3d86 and artist Xu Bing's 2013 *Book from the Ground*.
10. Twine can be found at http://twinery.org/ [accessed 3 July 2017].
11. For sample discussion of 'BookTubing', see this July 2018 *New York Times* article by Conceppción de Leon, 'Meet the YouTube Stars Turning Viewers Into Readers'. Available at www.nytimes.com/2018/07/31/books/booktubers-youtube.html [accessed 29 January 2019].

12. Davis, Robert L. and Shadle, Mark F. (2007) *Teaching Multiwriting: Researching and Composing with Multiple Genres, Media, Disciplines and Cultures* (Carbondale: Southern Illinois Press) p. 9.

13. Nietzsche, Friedrich (tr. R. J. Hollingdale; Introduction by Richard Schacht) (1996) *Human, all too human* (Cambridge: Cambridge University Press) p. 143.

14. Olson, David R. (1994) *The World on Paper* (Cambridge: Cambridge University Press) p. xvi.

15. Webb, Jen and Brien, Donna Lee. (2012) 'Addressing the "Ancient Quarrel": Creative writing as research' in Michael Biggs and Henrik Karlsson (eds), *The Routledge Companion to Research in the Arts* (London: Routledge) pp. 186–203.

16. Ibid., p. 198.

17. Ibid., p. 197.

18. Kroll, Jeri and Harper, Graeme (2013) 'Introduction' in Jeri Kroll and Graeme Harper (eds), *Research Methods in Creative Writing* (Basingstoke: Palgrave Macmillan) p. 1.

19. Peary, Alexandria and Hunley, Tom C. (2015) 'Introduction' in Alexandria Peary and Tom C. Hunley (eds), *Creative Writing Pedagogies for the Twenty-First Century* (Carbondale: Southern Illinois Press) p. 2.

20. Jewitt, Carey, Bezemer, Jeff and O'Halloran, Kay (2016) *Introducing Multimodality* (London and New York: Routledge) p. 1.

21. Gibbons, Alison (2011) *Multimodality, Cognition, and Experimental Literature*, ebook (London, New York: Routledge) [accessed 29 May 2017] p. 23.

22. Oxford English Dictionary (1998) (Oxford: Oxford University Press).

23. Krauth, Nigel (2014) 'Multigraph, not monograph: Creative writing and new technologies' in John Potts (ed.), *The Future of Writing* (Basingstoke: Palgrave Macmillan) p. 59.

24. Koehler, Adam (2017) *Composition, Creative Writing Studies, and the Digital Humanities* (London: Bloomsbury Academic) p. 58.

25. Kress, Gunther (2010) *Multimodality: A Social Semiotic Approach to Contemporary Communication* (London: Routledge) p. 28.

26. Page, Ruth (2009) 'Introduction' in Ruth Page (ed.), *New Perspectives on Narrative and Multimodality* (London, New York: Routledge) p. 3.

27. Ibid., p. 6.

28. Ibid., p. 3.

29. Bowen, Tracey and Whithaus, Carl (2013) 'Introduction' in Tracey Bowen and Carl Whithaus (eds), *Multimodal Literacies and Emerging Genres* (Pittsburgh: University of Pittsburgh) p. 7.

30. Kress (2010), p. 7.

31. Bowen and Whithaus (2013).

32. Palmeri, Jason (2012) *Remixing Composition: A History Multimodal Writing Pedagogy* (Carbondale and Edwardsville: Southern Illinois Press).

33. Millard, Kathryn (2013) 'A screenwriter's *Reality* hunger'. *TEXT Journal*. Available at www.textjournal.com.au/speciss/issue18/Millard.pdf [accessed 22 August 2014].

34. Krauth, Nigel (2014) 'Multigraph, not monograph: Creative writing and new technologies' in John Potts (ed.), *The Future of Writing* (Basingstoke: Palgrave Macmillan).

35. Bowen and Whithaus (2013), p. 7.

36. For discussion see, for example: Gibbons, Alison (2012) *Multimodality, Cognition, and Experimental Literature*, ebook, (London, New York: Routledge) [accessed 29 May 2017] p. 1; Krauth, Nigel (2015) 'The radical future of teaching creative writing', Chapter 12 in Graeme Harper (ed.), *New Writing Viewpoints 11: Creative Writing and Education* (Bristol, Buffalo, Toronto: Multilingual Matters) p. 188–189.

37. Page, Ruth (2009) 'Introduction' in Ruth Page (ed.), *New Perspectives on Narrative and Multimodality* (London, New York: Routledge) p. 6.

38. Gibbons, Alison (2011) *Multimodality, Cognition, and Experimental Literature*, ebook (London, New York: Routledge) [accessed 29 May 2017] p. 219.

39. Ibid.

40. Bateman, John A. (2008) *Multimodality and Genre: A Foundation for the Systematic Analysis of Multimodal Documents* (Basingstoke: Palgrave Macmillan).

41. Page, Ruth (2009) 'Introduction' in Ruth Page (ed.), *New Perspectives on Narrative and Multimodality* (London, New York: Routledge) p. 8.

42. Moggach, Deborah (2000) 'Foreword' in author Jane Dorner's *The Internet: A Writer's Guide* (London: A&C Black) p. vi.

43. Wilkins, Kim (2014) 'Writing resilience in the digital age'. *New Writing: The International Journal for the Practice and Theory of Creative Writing*, *11*(1): 67–76. DOI:10.1080/14790726.2013.870579.

44. Wilkinson, Carl (2012) 'Shutting out a world of digital distraction'. *Telegraph*, 6 September. www.telegraph.co.uk/culture/books/9522845/Shutting-out-a-world-of-digital-distraction.html n.p.

45. Taylor Suchy, Susan (2013) 'The social media marketplace in the "Quaint" creative writing classroom: Our terms for engagement'. *TEXT, 17*(2): n.p. www.textjournal.com.au/oct13/suchy.htm/.

46. Barnard, Josie (2016) 'Tweets as microfiction: On Twitter's live nature and 140 character limit as tools for developing storytelling skills' in *New Writing: The International Journal for the Practice and Theory of Creative Writing*, pp. 3–16. DOI:10.1080/14790726.2015.1127975.

47. Chawinga, Winner Dominic (2017) 'Taking social media to a university classroom: Teaching and learning using Twitter and blogs'. *International Journal of Educational Technology in Higher Education, 14*(3): 1. DOI:10.1186/s41239-017-0041-6.

48. Sheppard, Jennifer (2009) 'The rhetorical work of multimedia production practices: It's more than Just technical skill' in *Computers and Composition, 26*: 123.

49. Dean Clark, Michael, Hergenrader, Trent, and Rein, Joseph (2015) 'Introduction' in Michael Dean Clark, Trent Hergenrader and Joseph Rein (eds), *Creative Writing in the Digital Age: Theory, Practice and Pedagogy* (London: Bloomsbury Academic) p. 2.

50. Ibid., p. 2.

51. Millard, Kathryn, and Munt, Alex (2014) 'The design of writing: 29 observations' in John Potts (ed.), *The Future of Writing*, edited by John Potts (Basingstoke: Palgrave Macmillan) p. 91.

52. Krauth, Nigel (2015) 'The radical future of teaching creative writing', in Graeme Harper (ed.), *New Writing Viewpoints 11: Creative Writing and Education* (Bristol, Buffalo, Toronto: Multilingual Matters) p. 184.

53. The Quality Assurance Agency (QAA) (2016) *Subject Benchmark Statement: Creative Writing* (Gloucester: The Quality Assurance Agency for Higher Education). Available at www.qaa.ac.uk/en/Publications/Documents/SBS-Creative-Writing-16.pdf [accessed 3 January 2018] p.15.

54. Dean Clark, Michael (2015) 'The marketable creative: Using technology and broader notions of skill in the fiction course' in Michael Dean Clark, Trent Hergenrader and Joseph Rein (eds), *Creative Writing in the Digital Age: Theory, Practice and Pedagogy* (London: Bloomsbury Academic) p. 61.

55. Peary, Alexandria and Hunley, Tom C. (2015) 'Introduction' in Alexandria Peary and Tom C. Hunley (eds), *Creative Writing Pedagogies for the Twenty-First Century* (Carbondale: Southern Illinois Press) pp. 2–3.

56. Myers, D. G. (1996) *The Elephants Teach: Creative Writing Since 1880* (Chicago: Prentice Hall) p. 73.

57. Wandor, Micheline (2012) 'Can Creative Writing Really be Taught in British Universities?'. *The Fortnightly Review*, April 22. Available at http://fortnightlyreview.co.uk/2012/04/uk-creative-writing/ [accessed 29 January 2015] n.p.

58. Krauth, Nigel (2016) *Creative Writing and the Radical: Teaching and Learning the Fiction of the Future New Writing Viewpoints 13* (Bristol: Multilingual Matters) p. 16.

59. Ibid., pp. 50–51.

60. Smith, Hazel (2005) *The Writing Experiment: Strategies for Innovative Creative Writing* (Crows Nest, NSW: Allen and Unwin) p. iv.

61. Krauth (2016), p. 19.

62. Ibid.

63. See as examples of books on how to write fiction, screenplays, creative nonfiction or video games Brande (1981), Lavandier (2005), Gutkind (1997) and Despain (2008).

64. Barnard, Josie (2015a) 'The Multimodal Writer: One Practitioner's Experience of Moving Between Different Types of Writing for Different Modes of Dissemination' (unpublished PhD thesis), Middlesex University, London.

65. Kress, Gunther (2010) *Multimodality: A Social Semiotic Approach to Contemporary Communication* (London: Routledge) pp. 196–197.

66. Yancey, Kathleen Blake (2014) 'Made not only in words: Composition in a new key' in Claire Lutkewitte (ed.), *Multimodal Composition: A Critical Sourcebook* (Boston, New York: Bedford Books) pp. 74–75.

67. Harper, Graeme (2015) 'Creative writing in the age of synapses' in Michael Dean Clark, Trent Hergenrader and Joseph Rein (eds), *Creative Writing in the Digital Age: Theory, Practice and Pedagogy* (London: Bloomsbury Academic) pp. 13–15.

68. Kress (2010), p. 196.

69. Yancey (2014), p. 75.

70. Harper (2015), p. 14.

71. Page, Ruth (2009) 'Introduction' in Ruth Page (ed.), *New Perspectives on Narrative and Multimodality* (London, New York: Routledge) p. 8.

72. Jenkins, Henry, with Katie Clinton, Ravi Purushotma, Alice J. Robison, Margaret Weigel (2006) *Confronting the Challenges of Participatory Culture: Media Education for the 21st Century* (Chicago: The MacArthur Foundation) p. 10. Available at www.macfound.org/media/article_pdfs/JENKINS_WHITE_PAPER.PDF.

73. Leahy, Anna and Dechow, Douglas (2015) 'Concentration, form, and ways of (digitally) seeing' in Michael Dean Clark, Trent Hergenrader and Joseph Rein (eds), *Creative Writing in the Digital Age: Theory, Practice and Pedagogy* (London: Bloomsbury Academic) p. 33.

74. Pittaway, Gail (2015) 'Movement, maps, mnemonics and music: Teaching fiction and poetry using sight and sound' in Graeme Harper (ed.), *New Writing Viewpoints 11: Creative Writing and Education* (Bristol, Buffalo, Toronto: Multilingual Matters) p. 120.

1. Twenty-First Century Writing and Publishing: a wider context

1. James, E. L. (2011) *Fifty Shades of Grey* (New York: Knopf Doubleday Publishing Group).

2. Todd, Anna (2014) *After* (New York: Gallery Books).

3. Walker, Rob (2017) 'The young "Instapoet" Rupi Kaur: From social media star to bestselling writer'. *The Guardian,* 28 May. Available at www.theguardian. com/books/2017/may/27/rupi-kaur-i-dont-fit-age-race-class-of-bestselling-poet-milk-and-honey [accessed 7 September 2017].

4. Kaur, Rupi (2015) *Milk and Honey* (London: Simon & Schuster).

5. Sinclair, Iain (2017) *The Last London: True Fictions from an Unreal City* (London: Oneworld Publications).

6. Sinclair, Iain (2018) 'Under offer (Last London) – A CD of music and spoken word with Bill Parry-Davies', *Iain Sinclair.* www.iainsinclair.org. uk/?s=soundcloud [accessed 9 January 2018].

7. Feather, John (1998) *A History of British Publishing* (London and New York: Routledge) p. 9.

8. Ibid., p. 89.

9. Trevelyan, G. M. (1986) *English Social History: A Survey of Six Centuries* (Harmondsworth: Penguin) pp. 589–594.

10. Squires, Claire and Padmina Ray Murray (2013) 'The digital publishing communications circuit'. *Book 2.0, 3*(1): 3–23. DOI:10.1386/btwo.3.1.3_1.
11. Squires and Murray (2013), p. 3.
12. Feather (1998), p. 1.
13. Williams, Kevin (2010) *Get Me a Murder a Day! A History of Media and Communication in Britain* (London: Bloomsbury Academic) p. 38.
14. Hayward, Max (1983) (edited and with an introduction by Patricia Blake; preface by Leonard Schapiro; bibliography by Valerie Jensen) *Writers in Russia: 1917–1978* (London: Harvill Press) pp. 81–82.
15. Squires and Murray (2013), p. 3.
16. Krauth, Nigel (2014) 'Multigraph, not monograph: Creative writing and new technologies' in John Potts (ed.), *The Future of Writing* (Basingstoke: Palgrave Macmillan) p. 59.
17. Baron, Dennis (2013) *A Better Pencil: Readers, Writers, and the Digital Revolution* (Oxford, New York: Oxford University Press) p. 157.
18. For discussion see Hayles (2008), Page and Bronwen (2011), Krauth (2014) and Corrigan-Kavanagh (2019).
19. For discussion of 'a-books' see Corrigan-Kavanagh (2019).
20. Weiler, Lance (2017) '30+ Immersive storytelling platforms, apps, resources & tools'. *Medium*, 23 July. Available at https://medium.com/columbia-dsl/ 30-immersive-storytelling-platforms-apps-resources-tools-e428309574be [accessed 3 January 2019] n.p.
21. Ashwini, Amit (2017) 'Everything You Need to Know About IoT Prototyping'. *Medium,* 11 December. Available at https://medium.com/swlh/everything-you-need-to-know-about-iot-prototyping-e4ad2739bc6a [accessed 3 January 2019] n.p.
22. Henke, Harold (2001) 'The Global Impact of eBooks on ePublishing'. *SIGDOC'01*, October 21–24: 175. Santa Fe, New Mexico, USA, ACM 1-5813-295-6/01/0010.
23. Young, Sherman (2014) 'Me myself I: Revaluing self-publishing in the electronic age' in Potts, John (ed.), *The Future of Writing* (Basingstoke: Palgrave Macmillan) p. 37.
24. Tapscott, Don, and Williams, Anthony D. (2006) *Wikinomics: How Mass Collaboration Changes Everything* (London: Atlantic Books).
25. Ibid., p. 52.
26. Davies, Rosamund (2017) 'Collaborative production and the transformation of publishing: The case of Wattpad' in James Graham and Alessandro Gandini (eds), *Collaborative Production in the Creative Industries* (London: University of Westminster Press) p. 58.
27. Ibid., p. 58.
28. Ibid., p. 59.
29. Roth, Philip (1989) *The Facts: A Novelist's Autobiography* (London: Jonathan Cape) p. 4.

30. Smyth, Sara (2016) 'The new breed of celebrity authors...Miranda and Monty's dogs! Comedian and celebrity garden will go head to head as they publish books about their pets'. *Daily Mail*, 28 August. Available at www.dailymail.co.uk/news/article-3762719/The-new-breed-celebrity-authors-Miranda-Monty-s-dogs-Comedian-celebrity-garden-head-head-publish-books-pets.html [accessed 10 April 2017].

31. Cowdrey, Katherine (2016) 'Miranda Hart's fans' stories to feature in promotional e-book'. *The Bookseller*, 9 July. Available at www.thebookseller.com/news/hodder-launch-andme-e-book-competition-promote-miranda-harts-new-book-363081 [accessed 10 April 2017].

32. Coelho, Paulo (2014b) 'Interview with Ellen Gamerman: Paulo Coelho on Reaching Out to Fans on Social Media'. *Wall Street Journal blogspot*, 15 August. Available at www.wsj.com/video/paulo-coelho-on-reaching-out-to-fans-on-social-media/E1261501-BBF0-47FC-913A-7CCE90BCA204.html [accessed 10 April 2017].

33. Quoted in Blackwell, Laura (2013) 'Neil Gaiman sets Twitter ablaze with fan collaboration'. *PC World*, March 2018. Available at www.pcworld.com/article/2030776/neil-gaiman-sets-twitter-ablaze-with-fan-collaboration.html [accessed 10 April 2017].

34. Gaiman, Neil (2013) *A Calendar of Tales*, Blackberry. Available at www.acalendaroftales.com/ [accessed 10 April 2017].

35. Dalrymple, William (2011) 'My favourite travel book, by the world's greatest travel writers'. *The Guardian*, 16 September. Available at www.theguardian.com/travel/2011/sep/16/travel-writers-favourite-books [accessed 18 March 2018].

36. *Open Book*, 15.30 p. m., 22.10.2017, radio programme (London: BBC Radio 4).

37. Lerner, Betsy (2000), *An Editor's Advice to Writers: The Forest for the Trees* (London: Macmillan) p. 5.

38. Ibid., p. 4.

39. Hayles, N. Katherine (2012) *How We Think: Digital Media and Contemporary Technogenesis* (Chicago, London: The University of Chicago Press) p. 99.

40. Ibid., p. 99.

41. Prose, Francine (2006) *Reading Like a Writer: A Guide for People Who Love Books and for Those Who Want to Write Them* (New York: Harper Collins) pp. 2–3.

42. Tivnan, Tom and Richards, Laura (2011) 'Business focus: literary festivals'. *The Bookseller*, 18 March. Available at www.thebookseller.com/feature/business-focus-literary-festivals.html [accessed 21 October 2013].

43. Available at www.literaryfestivals.co.uk/ [accessed 6 January 2019].

44. Wagner, Erica (2017) '7 of the best literary festivals'. *Harper's Bazaar* 24 April. Available at www.harpersbazaar.com/uk/culture/news/a41116/our-literary-editor-on-the-rise-of-the-literary-festivals/ [accessed 3 January 2019].

45. Meehan, Michael (2005) 'The Word Made Flesh: Festival, Carnality and Literary Consumption'. *TEXT*, Special Issue No 4, October. Available at www.textjournal.com.au/speciss/issue4/meehan.htm [accessed 21 October 2013].

46. Author of *The number one ladies' detective agency* series. For more information see www.alexandermccallsmith.co.uk/ [accessed 1 February 2019].

47. Barnard, Josie (2015b) 'Pedagogical benefits for creative writing students of running a literary festival, a practitioner-teacher's observations' in *The Festival and Events Experience* (Eastbourne: Leisure Studies Association Publications, University of Brighton) p. 48.

48. Gere, Charlie (2012) *Community Without Community in Digital Culture* (Basingstoke: Palgrave Macmillan).

49. Llewellyn, Caro (2005) 'The Hunger for Ideas'. *TEXT*, Special Issue No 4, October. Available at www.textjournal.com.au/speciss/issue4/llewellyn.htm [accessed 21 October 2013].

50. Wagner (2017), n.p.

51. Taylor, Jonathan P. (2014) 'Guest post: Managing A Writing Life by Jonathan P Taylor'. *MorgEn Bailey – Editor, Com Columnist / Judge, Tutor & Writing Guru*, 22 April. Available at https://morgenbailey.wordpress.com/2014/04/22/guest-post-managing-a-writing-life-by-jonathan-p-taylor/ [accessed 20 April 2018].

52. Hall, Frania (2013) *The Business of Digital Publishing: An Introduction to the Digital Book and Journal Industries* (London: Routledge) p. 11.

53. Baron, Dennis (2013) *A Better Pencil: Readers, Writers, and the Digital Revolution* (Oxford, New York: Oxford University Press).

54. Moggach, Deborah (2000) 'Foreword' in author Jane Dorner's *The Internet: A Writer's Guide* (London: A&C Black) p. vi.

55. Mangen, Anne, and Adrian van der Weel. (2017) 'Why don't we read hypertext novels?'. *Convergence: The International Journal of Research Into New Media Technologies, 23*(2): 166–181 (Sage) DOI:10.1177/1354856515586042.

56. Krauth, Nigel (2014) 'Multigraph, not monograph: Creative writing and new technologies' in John Potts (ed.), *The Future of Writing* (Basingstoke: Palgrave Macmillan) pp. 71–72.

57. Hergenrader, Trent (2015) 'Game spaces: Videogames as story-generating systems for creative writers' in Michael Dean Clark, Trent Hergenrader and Joseph Rein (eds), *Creative Writing in the Digital Age: Theory, Practice and Pedagogy* (London: Bloomsbury Academic) p. 47.

58. Mangan, Lucy (2019) 'Black Mirror: Bandersnatch review – The TV of tomorrow is now here'. *The Guardian*, 1 January. Available at www.theguardian.com/tv-and-radio/2019/jan/01/black-mirror-bandersnatch-review-charlie-brooker-netflix-tv-of-tomorrow-is-now-here [accessed 3 January 2019].

59. Tapscott, Don, and Williams, Anthony D. (2006) *Wikinomics: How Mass Collaboration Changes Everything* (London: Atlantic Books) p. 125.

60. Wendig, Chuck (2013) *The Kick-Ass Writer* (Cincinnatti, Ohio: Writer's Digest Books) p. 267.

61. Lauer, Claire (2014) 'Contending with terms: "Multimodal" and "Multimedia" in the academic and public spheres' in Claire Lutkewitte, (ed.), *Multimodal Composition: A Critical Sourcebook* (Boston, New York: Bedford Books) p. 24.

62. Takolander, Maria (2017) 'Grounding the "auto-intoxicated" Romantic poet: A socio-material theory of poetic praxis'. *TEXT* Special Issue 41: 9, Romanticism and Contemporary Writing: Legacies and Resistances 1 (eds), Stephanie Green and Paul Hetherington, October. Available at www.textjournal.com.au/speciss/issue41/Takolander.pdf [accessed 15 January 2019].

63. Newman, Nic (2018) 'Journalism, Media, and Technology Trends and Predictions 2018' in *Digital News Publications*, published by the Reuters Institute for the Study of Journalism with the support of Google's Digital News Initiative. Available at www.digitalnewsreport.org/publications/2018/journalism-media-technology-trends-predictions-2018/ [accessed 15 January 2019].

64. Bing, Xu (2013) *Book from the Ground: From Point to Point* (North Adams, MA: MASS MoCA).

65. Andersen, Tore Rye (2017) 'Staggered transmissions: Twitter and the return of serialized literature'. *Convergence: The International Journal of Research into New Media Technologies, 23*(1): 9.

66. Egan, Jennifer (2012) 'Black box'. *The New Yorker*, 4 & 11 June. Available at www.newyorker.com/magazine/2012/06/04/black-box-2 [accessed 22 April 2018].

67. Yancey, Kathleen Blake (2014) 'Made not only in words: Composition in a new key' in Claire Lutkewitte (ed.), *Multimodal Composition: A Critical Sourcebook* (Boston, New York: Bedford Books) p. 80.

68. Kress, Gunther (2010) *Multimodality: A Social Semiotic Approach to Contemporary Communication* (London: Routledge) p. 193.

69. Wilkins, Kim (2014) 'Writing resilience in the digital age'. *New Writing: The International Journal for the Practice and Theory of Creative Writing, 11*(1): 67–76. DOI:10.1080/14790726.2013.870579, p. 68.

70. Carr, Nicholas (2010) 'Author Nicholas Carr: the web shatters focus, rewires brains'. *Wired,* 24 May. www.wired.com/magazine/2010/05/ff_nicholas_carr [accessed 10 April 2017].

71. Pilkington, Ed (2012) 'Amanda Hocking, the writer who made millions by self-publishing online'. *The Guardian*, 12 January. Available at www.theguardian.com/books/2012/jan/12/amanda-hocking-self-publishing [accessed 10 April 2017].

72. Letter, Amy (2015) 'Creative writing for new media' in Michael Dean Clark, Trent Hergenrader and Joseph Rein (eds), *Creative Writing in the Digital Age: Theory, Practice and Pedagogy* (London: Bloomsbury Academic) pp. 178–179.

73. Wilson, Gina and Grant, Anna (2017) *Not Without Me: A Digital World for All?: Findings from a Programme of Digital Inclusion for Vulnerable Young People Across the UK* (Dunfermline: Carnegie United Kingdom Trust).

74. Koehler, Adam (2015) 'Screening subjects: Workshop pedagogy, media ecologies, and (new) student' in Michael Dean Clark, Trent Hergenrader and Joseph Rein (eds), *Creative Writing in the Digital Age: Theory, Practice and Pedagogy* (London: Bloomsbury Academic) p. 23; Koehler, Adam (2017) *Composition, Creative Writing Studies, and the Digital Humanities* (London: Bloomsbury Academic) pp. 75–77.

75. Adsit, Janelle (2015) 'Giving an account of oneself: Teaching identity construction and authorship in creative nonfiction and social in Michael Dean Clark, Trent Hergenrader and Joseph Rein (eds), *Creative Writing in the Digital Age: Theory, Practice and Pedagogy* (London: Bloomsbury Academic) p. 106.

76. Koehler (2015), p. 23.

77. Baym, Nancy K (2015) *Personal Connections in the Digital Age* (Cambridge: Polity) p. 118.

78. Wilson and Grant (2017), p. 3.

79. Koehler (2015), p. 25.

80. Barnard (2017, 2019).

81. Takolander (2017).

82. Adsit (2015), p. 107.

83. Ackroyd, Peter (1990) *Dickens* (London: Sinclair-Stevenson).

84. Baym (2015), p. 119.

85. Elwell, J. Sage (2014) 'The transmediated self: Life between the digital and the analog'. *Convergence: The International Journal of Research into New Media Technologies, 20*(2): 233–234.

86. Ackroyd (1990), p. 836.

87. Barnard (2019).

88. Ibid., p. 205.

89. Boyd, D., Golder, S. & Lotan, G. (2010) 'Tweet, tweet, retweet: Conversational aspects of retweeting on Twitter'. HICSS-43, IEEE: Kauai, HI, 6 January.

90. Kwan, L. (2018) *#AmWriting: How authors negotiate their individual creative labour on social media* (Thesis). Royal Roads University Victoria, British Columbia, Canada. Available at www.viurrspace.ca/bitstream/handle/10613/5448/Kwan_ royalroads_1313O_10502.pdf?sequence=1&isAllowed=y [accessed 28 November 2018], p. 32.

91. Pope, Rob (1998) *The English Studies Book* (London and New York: Routledge) p. 199.

92. Cobley, Paul (2001) *Narrative* (London, New York: Routledge) pp. 211–212.

93. Bowen, Tracey and Whithaus, Carl (2013) 'Introduction' in Tracey Bowen and Carl Whithaus (eds), *Multimodal Literacies and Emerging Genres* (Pittsburgh: University of Pittsburgh) p. 2.

94. Pope (1998), p. 199.

95. Cobley (2001), p. 214.

96. Bruce Sterling and William Gibson's *The difference engine*, widely considered to be the first Steampunk novel, was first published in 1990.

97. Yancey (2014), p. 63.
98. Wolfe, Tom (1975) *The New Journalism* (London: Picador) p. 11.
99. Hendrix, J. (2012) 'Odd Corners Round About Brooklyn'. *The Paris Review*, 2 April. Available at www.theparisreview.org/blog/2012/04/02/odd-corners-round-about-brooklyn/ [accessed 25 August 2014].
100. Barnes, Djuna (1990) *Djuna Barnes's New York*, Barry, A. (ed.); foreword by Messerli, Douglas (London: Virago) pp. 174–179.
101. Koehler (2015), p. 26.
102. Adsit (2015), p. 106.
103. Ibid., p. 106.
104. Baverstock, Alison (2012) 'Why self-publishing needs to be taken seriously'. *LOGOS, 23/4*: 43 DOI: 10.1163/1878-4712-11112005.
105. For discussion, see Perez, Sarah (2014) 'Twitter Is Experimenting With a New Way to Retweet'. *TechCrunch*, 24 June. Available at https://techcrunch.com/2014/06/24/twitter-is-experimenting-with-a-new-way-to-retweet/ [accessed 23 November 2018].
106. For discussion, see Perez, Sarah (2017) 'Twitter officially expands its character count to 280 starting today'. *TechCrunch*, 7 November. Available at https://techcrunch.com/2017/11/07/twitter-officially-expands-its-character-count-to-280-starting-today/ [accessed 23 November 2018].
107. See Snapchat Support. Available at https://support.snapchat.com/en-US/article/when-are-snaps-chats-deleted [accessed 1 February 2019].
108. FP Staff (2018) 'Snapchat announces slate of new scripted webseries, documentaries called Snap Originals'. *Firstpost*, 10 October. Available at www.firstpost.com/entertainment/snapchat-announces-slate-of-new-scripted-webseries-documentaries-called-snap-originals-5354001.html [accessed 3 January 2019].
109. Bowen and Whittaus (2013), p. 2.
110. Lahire, Bernard (tr. Gwendolyn, Wells) (2010) 'The double life of writers'. *New Literary History, 41*(2): 443–465. Spring, John Hopkins University Press, DOI: 10.1353/nlh.2010.0001.
111. Stach, Reiner (tr. Shelley Frisch) (2013) *Kafka: The Years of Insight* (Princeton and Oxford: Princeton University Press) p. 2.
112. Lycett, Andrew (2007) *Conan Doyle: The Man who Created Sherlock Holmes* (London: Weidenfeld & Nicolson) p. 163.
113. Wakefield, Dan (2013) in Vonnegut, Kurt (edited and with an introduction by Dan Wakefield) (2013) *Kurt Vonnegut: Letters* (London: Vintage) pp. 28–29.
114. Harper (2015), p. 13.
115. Cramer, Florian (2014) 'What is "Post-Digital"?'. *APRA, A Peer Reviewed Journal About Post-Digital Research, 3*(1), Available at www.aprja.net/?p=1318 [accessed 22 April 2016].
116. Harper (2015), p. 8.

2. Negotiating the Starting Block: auto-practitioner study

1. Barnard, Josie (2017) 'Testing possibilities: On negotiating writing practices in a "postdigital" age (tools and methods)'. *New Writing: The International Journal for the Practice and Theory of Creative Writing 14*(2): 275–289. DOI: 10.1080/14790726.2016.127802, p. 275.

2. Millard, Kathryn, and Munt, Alex (2014) 'The design of writing: 29 observations' in John Potts (ed.), *The Future of Writing*, edited by John Potts (Basingstoke: Palgrave Macmillan) p. 91.

3. As examples of fiction and creative non-fiction books see Barnard 1993, 1996, 2000, 2011; as examples of journalism/scripts see Barnard 1997, 2002, 2003, 2008, 2009.

4. Wolf, Christa (trans. Jan van Heurck) (1991) 'The sense and nonsense of being naive' in Philomena Mariani (ed.), *Critical Fictions: The Politics of Imaginative Writing* (Seattle: Bay Press) p. 230.

5. Woolf, Virginia (1945) *A room of one's own* (New York: Harmondsworth).

6. Connolly, Cyril (1949) *Enemies of Promise* (London: Routledge & Kegan Paul).

7. Lahire, Bernard (tr. Wells, Gwendolyn) (2010) 'The double life of writers'. *New Literary History, 41*(2): 443–465. Spring, John Hopkins University Press, DOI: 10.1353/nlh.2010.0001.

8. Ibid., p. 446.

9. Prose, Francine (2006) *Reading Like a Writer: A Guide for People Who Love Books and for Those Who Want to Write Them* (New York: Harper Collins) p. 2.

10. Gere, Charlie (2002) *Digital Culture* (London: Reaktion) p. 15.

11. Hayles, N. Katherine (2008) *Electronic Literature: New Horizons for the Literary* (Notre Dame: University of Notre Dame) p. 88.

12. Angel, Maria, and Anna Gibbs (2013) 'At the Time of Writing: Digital Media, Gesture and Handwriting'. *Electronic Book Review* 2013, August. Available at http://electronicbookreview.com/thread/electropoetics/gesture, n.p.

13. Barnard, Josie (2017) 'Testing possibilities: On negotiating writing practices in a "postdigital" age (tools and methods)'. *New Writing: The International Journal for the Practice and Theory of Creative Writing, 14*(2): 281. DOI:10.108 0/14790726.2016.127802.

14. Hayles, N. Katherine (2012) *How We Think: Digital Media and Contemporary Technogenesis* (Chicago, London: The University of Chicago Press) p. 95.

15. Goldberg, Natalie (1986) *Writing Down the Bones: Freeing the Writer Within.* Foreword Judith Guest (Boston; London: Shambahla) p. 9.

16. In Knowles, Elizabeth (2004) *Oxford Dictionary of Quotations* (Oxford: Oxford University Press) p. 296.

17. Bowen, Elizabeth (1986b) *The Mulberry Tree: Writings of Elizabeth Bowen: Selected and Introduced by Hermione Lee* (San Diego; New York; London: Harcourt Brace Jovanovich) p. 226.

18. Bowen, Elizabeth (1986a) 'Notes on writing a novel', in Hermione Lee (ed.), *The Mulberry Tree: Writings of Elizabeth Bowen: Selected and Introduced by Hermione Lee* (San Diego; New York; London: Harcourt Brace Jovanovich) pp. 35–48.

19. Forster, E. M. (1961) 'The Plot' in R. Shcoles (ed.), *Approaches to the Novel: Materials for a Poetics: Collected and Edited by Robert Scholes, University of Virgini* (San Francisco: Chandler Publishing Company) pp. 155–158.

20. Ibid., p. 157.

21. Author foreword (pp. 331–333) in Borges, Jorges Luis (1998) *Collected Fictions.* trans. Hurley, A. (London: Allen Lane) p. 331.

22. Dawson, Marie (1997) 'An interview with Eudora Welty'. *Poets and Writers Magazine, 25*(5): 27, Sept–Oct.

23. Goldberg (1986) p. 157.

24. Alter, Robert (1981) *The Art of Biblical Narrative* (New York: Basic Books) pp. 88–113.

25. For discussion see Campbell, Gordon (2010) *Bible: The Story of the King James Version, 1611–2011* (Oxford: Oxford University Press).

26. Yancey, Kathleen Blake (2014) 'Made not only in words: Composition in a new key' in Claire Lutkewitte (ed.), *Multimodal Composition: A Critical Sourcebook* (Boston, New York: Bedford Books) p. 63.

27. Barnard, Josie, and Haskel, Lisa (1985) *The Friday Buzz*, radio series, BBC Radio Merseyside, 19.00 hours, weekly, 22 February–12 April.

28. Eisenstein, Sergei (2010) *Sergei Eisenstein, Selected Works, Volume III, Writings, 1937–47*, (ed.) Taylor, R. (trans. W. Powell) (London; New York: I. B Tauris).

29. Faulkner, William (1963) *As I Lay Dying* (Harmondsworth: Penguin Books in association with Chatto & Windus).

30. Faulkner, William (1964) *The Sound and the Fury* (Harmondsworth: Penguin Books in association with Chatto & Windus).

31. BBC (2008) *Glossary of common media terms*, online. Available at http://news.bbc.co.uk/1/hi/school_report/4791411.stm [accessed 22 August 2014].

32. Oz, Amos (1999) *The Story Begins: Essays on Literature,* trans. Maurie Goldberg-Bartura (London: Chatto and Windus) p. 2.

33. Rombauer, Irma von Starkloff, and Becker, Marion Rombauer (1963) *The Joy of Cooking*, illustrated by Ginnie Hofmann & Beverley Warner (London; Haarlem printed: J. M. Dent & Sons).

34. Parker, Peter (ed.) (1994) *The Reader's Companion to the Twentieth Century Novel,* (London: Fourth Estate).

35. Parker, Peter (ed.) (1995) *The Reader's Companion to Twentieth Century Writers* (London: Fourth Estate).

36. Barnard, Josie (1996) *Poker Face* (London: Virago).

37. Barnard, Josie (1993) *The Virago Women's Guide to New York* (London: Virago).

38. Although Chatwin 'disliked an early-1970s stint in journalism', it was probably an assignment for the *Sunday Times* to write a profile of Irish designer and architect Eileen Gray that led to his 1977 creative non-fiction work *In Patagonia*, notes Thomas Mallon (2011) The wanderer. *The New York Times*, 25 February. Available at www.nytimes.com/2011/02/27/books/review/Mallon-t.html?pagewanted=all&_r=0 [accessed 23 August 2014].

39. Barnard, Josie (1996) *Poker Face* (London: Virago).
40. Barnard, Josie (2000) *The Pleasure Dome* (London: Virago).
41. Barnard, Josie (2003a) (programme, producer) *Heroes of Telemark*, radio, BBC Radio 4, 15 May, 20.00 hrs.
42. Barnard, Josie (2003b) 'Heroes? Not us'. *The Guardian*, 12 May, pp. 6–7.
43. *The Urban Programme* (1985), Film festival, Unity Theatre, Hope Street, Liverpool, 9–10 November.
44. *North London Literary Festival* (2013), Literary festival, Middlesex University, Hendon, London, 26–27 March.
45. Barnard, Josie (2015b) 'Pedagogical benefits for creative writing students of running a literary festival, a practitioner-teacher's observations,'. *The Festival and Events Experience*, *127*: 60–61. (Eastbourne: Leisure Studies Association Publications, University of Brighton).
46. Ong, Walter J. (1982) *Orality and Literacy: The Technologizing of the Word* (London: Methuen).
47. McLuhan, Marshall (1962) *The Gutenberg Galaxy: The Making of Typographic Man* (Toronto: University of Toronto Press) p. 3.
48. The British Library is the national library of the United Kingdom; it is based on London's Euston Road in London (for more information see www.bl.uk/).
49. Barnard (2017), p. 285.
50. Ozick, Cynthia (1996) *Portrait of the Artist as a Bad Character and Other Essays on Writing* (London: Pimlico) p. 136.

3. Paradigmatic Aspects: author interviews

1. Wiseman, S. J. (1996) *Aphra Benn* (Plymouth: Northcote House in association with the British Council) p. 66.
2. Ibid., p. 1.
3. Powers, Ron (2005) *Mark Twain: A Life* (New York, London, Toronto, Sydney: Free Press) p. 363.
4. Massumi, Brian (2015) *The Politics of Affect* (Cambridge, UK; Malden, MA: Polity Press) p. 48.
5. For discussion of video game writing terminology see Despain (2008).
6. Pullinger, Kate (2017) *Jelly Bone*, mobile app (oolipo). Available at www.oolipo.com/stories/jellybone [accessed 2 February 2019].

4. Creative Writing and Multimodality: assembling a toolkit, component parts

1. Bateman, John A. (2008) *Multimodality and Genre: A Foundation for the Systematic Analysis of Multimodal Documents* (Basingstoke: Palgrave Macmillan).
2. Page, Ruth (2009) 'Introduction' in Ruth Page (ed.), *New Perspectives on Narrative and Multimodality* (London, New York: Routledge) pp. 1–13.

3. Gibbons, Alison (2011) *Multimodality, Cognition, and Experimental Literature*, ebook (London, New York: Routledge) [accessed 29 May 2017].

4. Page (2009), p. 80.

5. Coe, Jonathan (2016) 'My Writing Day'. *The Guardian*, 4 June. Available at www.theguardian.com/books/2016/jun/04/jonathan-coe-my-writing-day [accessed 10 April 2017] n.p.

6. Palmeri, Jason (2012) *Remixing Composition: A History Multimodal Writing Pedagogy* (Carbondale and Edwardsville: Southern Illinois Press).

7. Ibid., p. 26.

8. Ibid., pp. 35–36.

9. Welty, Eudora (1984) *One Writer's Beginnings* (Cambridge, MA; London, England: Harvard University Press).

10. Ibid., p. 3.

11. Ibid., pp. 5–6.

12. Ibid., p. 9.

13. Mikhail Bulgakov in J. A. E. Curtis (1991) *Manuscripts don't Burn: Mikhail Bulgakov, a Life in Letters and Diaries* (London: Bloomsbury) p. 79.

14. Hemingway, Ernest (1964) *A Moveable Feast* (London: Jonathan Cape) pp. 12–14.

15. Ibid., p. 12.

16. Page (2009), p. 7.

17. Palmeri (2012), p. 150.

18. Wilson, Gina and Anna Grant (2017) *Not Without Me: A Digital World for All?: Findings from a Programme of Digital Inclusion for Vulnerable Young People across the UK* (Dunfermline: Carnegie United Kingdom Trust) p. 62.

19. Baron, Dennis (2013) *A Better Pencil: Readers, Writers, and the Digital Revolution* (Oxford, New York: Oxford University Press).

20. Ong, Walter J. (1982) *Orality and Literacy: The Technologizing of the Word* (London: Methuen) p. 81.

21. Bolter, David Jay and Grusin, Richard (2000) *Remediation: Understanding New Media* (Cambridge, MA; London: The MIT Press) p. 15.

22. Cranny-Francis, Anne (2005) *Multimedia Texts and Contexts* (London: Sage) p. 5.

23. Palmeri (2012), p. 89.

24. Hayles, N. Katherine (2012) *How We Think: Digital Media and Contemporary Technogenesis* (Chicago, London: The University of Chicago Press) p. 68.

25. Piper, Andrew (2012) *Book Was There: Reading in Electronic Times* (Chicago, London: The University of Chicago Press) p. x.

26. Mikhail Bulgakov in Curtis (1991), p. 79.

27. Hemingway (1964), p. 12.

28. Brande, Dorothea and Gardner, John (Foreword) (1981) *Becoming a Writer* (Los Angeles: J. P. Tarcher, Inc).

29. Ibid., pp. 48–49.

30. Ibid., p. 155.

31. Weldon, Fay (1993) 'Harnessed to the Harpy' in Boylan, Clare (ed.), *The Agony and the Ego: The Art and Strategy of Fiction Writing Explored* (Harmondsworth: Penguin) p. 185.

32. Stein, Gertrude (1974) 'How writing is written' (1935) in Robert Bartlett Hass (ed.), *How Writing is Written: Volume II of the Previously Uncollected Writings of Gertrude Stein* (Los Angeles: Black Sparrow Press) p. 154.

33. Tillman, Lynne (1991) 'Critical Fiction/Critical Self' in Philomena Mariani (ed.), *Critical Fictions: The Politics of Imaginative Writing* (Seattle: Bay Press) p. 103.

34. Bolter and Grusin (2000), p. 233.

35. Rotman, Brian (2008) *Becoming Beside Ourselves: The Alphabet, Ghosts and Distributed Human Being* (Durham and London: Duke University Press) p. 99.

36. Elwell, J. Sage (2014) 'The transmediated self: Life between the digital and the analog'. *Convergence: The International Journal of Research into New Media Technologies, 20*(2): 233. Sage.

37. Deleuze, G. and Guattari, F. (1999) *A Thousand Plateaus: Capitalism and Schizophrenia* (London: The Athlone Press) p. 7.

38. Ibid., p. 8.

39. Bakhtin, Mikhail Mikhailovich (1990) 'Author and hero in aesthetic activity' in Michael Holquist and Vadim Lyapunov (eds), *Art and Answerability: Early Philosophical Essay.* trans. and notes Vadim Lyapunov (supplementary trans. Kenneth Bostrom) (Austin: University of Texas Press) p. 23.

40. Ibid., p. 23.

41. Eudora Welty in Dawson, Marie (1997) 'An interview with Eudora Welty'. *Poets and Writers Magazine, 25*(5): September–October, p. 27.

42. Coe (2016), n.p.

43. Brande (1981), p. 155.

44. Melrose, Susan (2006) 'Bodies without bodies' in Susan Broadhurst and Josephine Machon, (eds), *Performance and Technology: Practices of Virtual Embodiment and Interactivity* (Basingstoke: Palgrave Macmillan) pp. 1–17.

45. Cokely, Edward T. and Feltz, Adam (2014) 'Expert intuition' in Lisa M. Osbeck, Barbara S. Held (eds), *Rational Intuition: Philosophical Roots, Scientific Investigations* (New York, Cambridge: Cambridge University Press) p. 213.

46. Melrose (2006), p. 13.

47. Oz, Amos (1999) *The Story Begins: Essays on Literature.* trans. Bar-Tura, M., (London: Chatto and Windus) p. 2.

48. Hayles (2012), p. 95.

49. McLuhan, Marshall (1962) *The Gutenberg Galaxy: The Making of Typographic Man* (Toronto: University of Toronto Press) pp. 278–279.

50. Hayles (2012), pp. 20–21.

51. Clark, Andy (2008) *Supersizing the Mind: Embodiment, Action and Cognitive Extension* (Oxford, New York: Oxford University Press) p. 219.

52. Hayles (2012), p. 96.

53. Ibid.

54. Hurley, S. L. (1998) *Consciousness in Action* (Cambridge MA: Harvard University Press) p. 2.

55. Rotman (2008), p. 104.

56. Weldon (1993), p. 185.

57. Brande (1981), pp. 48–49.

5. Developing a Multimodal Writing Practice: assignments

1. See the 'Tutor guidance (general)' in the appendices and the individual 'Tutor note' attached to each assignment for tips and guidance.

2. For further information on the pedagogical pilots, see 'Methodology'.

3. Palmeri, Jason (2012) *Remixing Composition: A History Multimodal Writing Pedagogy* (Carbondale and Edwardsville: Southern Illinois Press) p. 150.

4. Wilson, Gina and Grant, Anna (2017) *Not Without Me: A Digital World for All?: Findings from a Programme of Digital Inclusion for Vulnerable Young People across the UK* (Dunfermline: Carnegie United Kingdom Trust) p. 62.

5. Powers, Ron (2005) *Mark Twain: A Life* (New York, London, Toronto, Sydney: Free Press) p. 363.

6. Ibid., p. 363.

7. Leahy and Dechow (2015), p. 33.

8. Kress, Gunther (2010) *Multimodality: A Social Semiotic Approach to Contemporary Communication* (London: Routledge) pp. 196–197.

9. Yancey, Kathleen Blake (2014) 'Made not only in words: Composition in a new key' in Claire Lutkewitte (ed.), *Multimodal Composition: A Critical Sourcebook* (Boston, New York: Bedford Books) pp. 74–75.

10. Harper, Graeme (2015) 'Creative writing in the age of synapses' in Michael Dean Clark, Trent Hergenrader and Joseph Rein (eds), *Creative Writing in the Digital Age: Theory, Practice and Pedagogy* (London: Bloomsbury Academic) pp. 13–15.

11. Weldon, Fay (1993) 'Harnessed to the Harpy' in Clare Boylan (ed.), *The Agony and the Ego: The Art and Strategy of Fiction Writing Explored* (Harmondsworth: Penguin) p. 185.

12. Morrison, Toni (2008) Carolyn C. Denard (ed.), *Toni Morrison: Conversations* (Jackson, Miss: University Press of Mississippi) p. 142.

13. Berger, John (1972) *Ways of Seeing* (London: British Broadcasting Corporation; Harmondsworth: Penguin).

14. Gunaratnam, Yasmin and Bell, Vikki (2017) 'How John Berger changed our way of seeing art'. *The Conversation,* 5 January. Available at http://theconversation.com/how-john-berger-changed-our-way-of-seeing-art-70831 [accessed 15 January 2019].

15. Simanowski quoted in Takolander, Maria (2017) 'Grounding the "auto-intoxicated" Romantic poet: A socio-material theory of poetic praxis'. *TEXT* Special Issue 41: Romanticism and Contemporary Writing: Legacies and Resistances 1 (eds) Stephanie Green and Paul Hetherington, October. Available at www.textjournal.com.au/speciss/issue41/Takolander.pdf [accessed 15 January 2019] p. 9.

16. Takolander (2017), p. 1.

17. Goldsmith quoted in Koehler, Adam (2017) *Composition, Creative Writing Studies, and the Digital Humanities* (London: Bloomsbury Academic) p. 76.

18. Koehler (2017), p. 76.

19. Adobe's Premiere Rush is available at www.adobe.com/uk/products/premiere-rush.html?sdid=2XBSC55C&mv=search&ef_id=CjwKCAiAv9riBRANE iwA9DqvlYSZzY7V4SzAvjtD6Q9SZ4oXsozrez6RqhD2q79q2uyP3e9lEt So9xoCQ-wQAvD_BwE:G:s&s_kwcid=AL!3085!3!301513456527!e!!g!!free% 20video% 20editing%20software [accessed 3 January 2019].

20. Audacity, a free and open-source digital audio editor and recording application software, is widely considered good for 'beginners'. It is available at www.audacityteam.org/ [accessed 3 January 2019].

21. Wakelet, available at https://wakelet.com/findoutmore.html [accessed 30 October 2018].

22. 'Hashtags' are a convention on social media platforms whereby users attach a hash sign (#) to the beginning of a particular word or phrase to help other users easily and quickly find posts on that topic.

23. For discussion of 'free writing' see Andersen, Linda (2006) 'The Creative Process' in Linda Andersen (ed.) written and produced by The Open University, *Creative Writing: A Workbook with Readings* (Abingdon, Oxfordshire: Routledge) p. 23.

24. Bell, Alice, Ensslin Astrid, Ciccoricco David, et al. (2010) 'A [s]creed for digital fiction'. *Electronic Book Review*, 7 March. Available at: www.electronicbookreview. com/thread/electropoetics/DFINative [accessed 20 January 2019] n.p.

25. For more detailed discussion of a similar exercise, including consideration of the pedagogical benefits, see Barnard 2016.

26. Wilson and Grant (2017).

27. Andersen, Tore Rye (2017) 'Staggered transmissions: Twitter and the return of serialized literature'. *Convergence: The International Journal of Research into New Media Technologies, 23*(1): 34–48.

28. Egan, Jennifer (2012) 'Black Box' in *The New Yorker*, 4 & 11 June. Available at www.newyorker.com/magazine/2012/06/04/black-box-2 [accessed 22 April 2018].

29. Mitchell, David (2015) @I_Bombadil, *Twitter* @I_Bombadil, 7 September–31 October.

30. Andersen, Tore Rye (2017) 'Staggered transmissions: Twitter and the return of serialized literature'. *Convergence: The International Journal of Research into New Media Technologies, 23*(1): 46.

31. Elwell, J. Sage (2014) 'The transmediated self: Life between the digital and the analog'. *Convergence: The International Journal of Research into New Media Technologies, 20*(2): 233–249, Sage.

32. For discussion see Barnard, Josie (2015) 'Live and public: One practitioner's experience and assessment of Twitter as a tool for archiving creative process'. *Journal of Writing in Creative Practice, Writing-PAD, 7*(3): 493–503.

33. Pells, Rachael (2015) 'Joanne Harris interview: The Chocolat author is in militant mood when it comes to writers' rights'. *Independent*, 22 August. Availableatwww.independent.co.uk/arts-entertainment/books/features/joanne-harris-interview-the-chocolat-author-is-in-militant-mood-when-it-comes-to-writers-rights-10462112.html [accessed 30 December 2018].

34. Cripps, Charlotte (2013) 'Twihaiku? Micropoetry? The rise of Twitter poetry. *Independent*, 16 July. Available at www.independent.co.uk/arts-entertainment/books/features/twihaiku-micropoetry-the-rise-of-twitter-poetry-8711637.html [accessed 30 December 2018].

35. Laing, Audrey (2017) 'Authors using social media: Layers of identity and the online author community'. *Publishing Research Quarterly, 33*: 260. DOI 10.1007/s12109-017-9524-5

36. For sample consideration of use of 'lol' see O'Carroll, Lisa (2012) 'Rebekah Brooks: David Cameron signed off texts 'LOL''. *The Guardian*, 11 May. Available at www.theguardian.com/media/2012/may/11/rebekah-brooks-david-cameron-texts-lol [accessed 30 December 2018].

37. For sample consideration of use of full stops in social media see Golby, J. (2015) 'Science has spoken: Ending a text with a full stop makes you a monster'. *The Guardian*, 9 December. Available at www.theguardian.com/technology/shortcuts/2015/dec/09/science-has-spoken-ending-a-text-with-a-full-stop-makes-you-a-monster [accessed 30 December 2018].

38. Neurath, Otto (1936) *International Picture Language* (London: Kegan Paul) p. 30.

39. Manovich, Lev (2011) 'What is visualization?'. *Visual Studies, 26*(1): 36–49. DOI:10.1080/1472586X.2011.548488.

40. For discussion see Chapter 4 and Barnard (2017).

41. Propp, Vladimir (2005) (First Edition Translated by Laurence Scott with an Introduction by Svatava Pirkova-Jakobson; Second Edition Revised and Edited with a Preface by Louis A. Wagner / New Introduction by Alan Dundes) *Morphology of the Folktale* (Austin: University of Texas Press).

42. Ibid., pp. 26–55.

43. Ibid., p. 25.

44. Ibid., p. 39.

45. Ibid., p. 29.

46. Ibid., p. 39.

47. Ibid., p. 60.

48. Ibid., p. 53.

49. Ibid., p. 64.

50. See, for example, the Brothers Grimm version of 'Hansel and Gretel' on Project Gutenberg (2008), e-book #2591, 14 December. Available at www. gutenberg.org/files/2591/2591-h/2591-h.htm#link2H_4_0020 [accessed, 4 January 2019].

51. Adsit, Janelle (2015) 'Giving an account of oneself: Teaching identity construction and authorship in creative nonfiction and social in Michael Dean Clark, Trent Hergenrader and Joseph Rein (eds), *Creative Writing in the Digital Age: Theory, Practice and Pedagogy* (London: Bloomsbury Academic) p. 106.

52. Booker, Christopher (2005) *The Seven Basic Plots: Why We Tell Stories* (London: Continuum).

53. Tobias, Ronald B. (2012) *20 Master Plots: And How to Build Them* (Cincinnati, Ohio: Writer's Digest Books).

54. Ozick, Cynthia (1996) *Portrait of the Artist as a Bad Character and Other Essays on Writing* (London: Pimlico) p. 136.

55. A version of 'Jack and the Beanstalk' as told by Flora Annie Steel can be found on Project Gutenberg (2005), e-book #17034, 9 November. Available at www. gutenberg.org/files/17034/17034-h/17034-h.htm [accessed 4 February 2019].

56. Ryan, Marie-Laure (2011) The Interactive Onion: Layers of User Participation in Digital Narrative Texts in Ruth Page and Bronwen Thomas (eds.), *New Narratives: Stories and Storytelling in the Digital Age* (Lincoln; London: University of Nebraska Press) p. 42.

57. Egan (2012).

Conclusion

1. Krauth, Nigel (2014) 'Multigraph, not monograph: Creative writing and new technologies' in John Potts (ed.), *The Future of Writing* (Basingstoke: Palgrave Macmillan) p. 74.

2. Graham, Elyse (2015) 'The past and futures of annotation: How reading communities drive media change'. *Book 2.0, 5*(1 & 2): 62–63, *Intellect*, DOI: 10.1386/btwo.5.1-2.59_1.

3. Walkley, George (2017) 'Surfing the second wave'. *The Author* (London: The Society of Authors) p. 44.

4. Takolander, Maria (2017) 'Grounding the "auto-intoxicated" Romantic poet: A socio-material theory of poetic praxis'. *TEXT,* Special Issue 41: Romanticism and Contemporary Writing: Legacies and Resistances 1 eds Stephanie Green and Paul Hetherington, October. Available at www.textjournal.com.au/speciss/issue41/Takolander.pdf [accessed 15 January 2019] p. 9.

5. Newman, Nic (2018) 'Journalism, Media, and Technology Trends and Predictions 2018'. *Digital News Publications*, published by the Reuters Institute for the Study of Journalism with the support of Google's Digital News Initiative. Available at: www.digitalnewsreport.org/publications/2018/journalism-media-technology-trends-predictions-2018/ [accessed 15 January 2019].

6. Takolander (2017), p. 9.

7. Peters, Tim (2016) 'Emojis, Comics, and the Novel of the Future'. *Los Angeles Review of Books*, 26 April. Available at https://lareviewofbooks.org/article/emojis-comics-novel-future/ [accessed 15 January 2019] n.p.

8. See as example Hannaham, James and Bateman, John W. (2017) 'Eight Tiny Stories, Translated from the Emoji'. Electric Lit. Available at https://electricliterature.com/eight-tiny-stories-translated-from-the-emoji-40d43d4b3d86 [accessed 15 January 2019] n.p.

9. See as example Bing, Xu (2013) *Book from the Ground: from Point to Point* (North Adams, MA: MASS MoCA).

10. In early 2019, for example, John-Paul Flintoff https://twitter.com/jpflintoff?lang=en and Jill Mansell https://twitter.com/JillMansell featured emojis of a pile of books and a hand holding a pen respectively in their Twitter biographies [accessed 24 January 2019].

11. Cobley, Paul (2001) *Narrative* (London, New York: Routledge) p. 206.

12. Henke, Harold (2001) 'The Global Impact of eBooks on ePublishing'. *SIGDOC'01*, October 21–24: 175. Santa Fe, New Mexico, USA, ACM 1-5813-295-6/01/0010.

13. Squires, Claire, and Padmina, Ray Murray (2013) 'The digital publishing communications circuit'. *Book 2.0, 3*(1): 3–23. DOI:10.1386/btwo.3.1.3_1.

14. Baverstock, Alison (2012) 'Why self-publishing needs to be taken seriously'. *LOGOS, 23/4*: 45. DOI: 10.1163/1878-4712-11112005.

15. Yancey, Kathleen Blake (2014) 'Made not only in words: Composition in a new key' in Claire Lutkewitte (ed.), *Multimodal Composition: A Critical Sourcebook* (Boston, New York: Bedford Books) p. 84.

16. Huws, Ursula (2014) *Labor in the Global Digital Economy: The Cybertariat Comes of Age* (New York: The Monthly Review Press) pp. 83–84.

17. Hayles, N. Katherine (2012) *How We Think: Digital Media and Contemporary Technogenesis* (Chicago, London: The University of Chicago Press).

18. Baym, Nancy K (2015) *Personal Connections in the Digital Age* (Cambridge: Polity).

19. Elwell, J. Sage (2014) 'The transmediated self: Life between the digital and the analog'. *Convergence: The International Journal of Research into New Media Technologies, 20*(2): 233. Sage.

20. Rotman, Brian (2008) *Becoming Beside Ourselves: The Alphabet, Ghosts and Distributed Human Being* (Durham and London: Duke University Press) p. 8.

21. Krauth, Nigel (2014) 'Multigraph, not monograph: Creative writing and new technologies' in John Potts (ed.), *The Future of Writing* (Basingstoke: Palgrave Macmillan) p. 59.

22. Gere, Charlie (2002) *Digital Culture* (London: Reaktion) p. 15.

23. Andersen, Daniel (2008). 'The low bridge to high benefits: Entry-level multimedia, literacies and motivation'. *Computers and Composition, 25*: 41.

24. Ibid., p. 41.

25. Gibbons, Alison (2012) *Multimodality, Cognition, and Experimental Literature*, ebook (London, New York: Routledge) [accessed 29 May 2017] p. 219.

26. Kress, Gunther (2010) *Multimodality: A Social Semiotic Approach to Contemporary Communication* (London: Routledge) pp. 196–197.

27. Yancey (2014), pp. 74–75.

28. Harper, Graeme (2015) 'Creative writing in the age of synapses' in Michael Dean Clark, Trent Hergenrader and Joseph Rein (eds), *Creative Writing in the Digital Age: Theory, Practice and Pedagogy* (London: Bloomsbury Academic) pp. 13–15.

29. Lanham quoted in Handa, Carolyn (2004) 'Introduction' in Carolyn Handa (ed.), *Visual Rhetoric in a Digital World* (Boston, New York: Bedford/St Martin's) p. 1.

30. Ibid., p. 1.

31. Rotman, Brian (2008) *Becoming Beside Ourselves: The Alphabet, Ghosts and Distributed Human Being* (Durham and London: Duke University Press) p. 8.

32. Elwell, J. Sage (2014) 'The transmediated self: Life between the digital and the analog'. *Convergence: The International Journal of Research into New Media Technologies, 20*(2): 233. Sage.

33. Hayles (2012), pp. 20–21.

34. Cobley, Paul (2001) *Narrative* (London, New York: Routledge) p. 203.

35. Turchi, Peter (2004) *Maps of the Imagination: The Writer as Cartographer* (San Antonio, Texas: Trinity University Press) p. 12.

36. Ibid., p. 12.

37. Webb, Jen and Brien, Donna Lee (2012) 'Addressing the "Ancient Quarrel": Creative writing as research', in Michael Biggs and Henrik Karlsson (eds), *The Routledge Companion to Research in the Arts* (London: Routledge) pp. 186–203.

38. Ibid., pp. 198–201.

39. Turchi (2004), p. 13.

40. Arrigoni, Gabriella and Zics, Brigitta (2016) 'Fiction and curatorial practice: developing alternative experiences for digital artistic prototypes'. *International Journal of Performance Arts and Digital Media, 12*(1): 82–94. DOI: 10.1080/14794713.2015.1133960, p. 85.

41. Brown Jr., James J. (2015) 'Writing with machines: Data and process in Taroko Gorge' in Michael Dean Clark, Trent Hergenrader and Joseph Rein (eds), *Creative Writing in the Digital Age: Theory, Practice and Pedagogy* (London: Bloomsbury Academic) p. 131.

42. Smith, Hazel (2004) 'Cursors and crystal balls: Digital technologies and the futures of writing'. *TEXT, 8*(2): n.p. www.textjournal.com.au/oct04/smith.htm.

43. Harper (2015), p. 8.

44. Krauth (2014), p. 69.

45. Cripps, Charlotte (2013) 'Twihaiku? Micropoetry? The rise of Twitter poetry'. *Independent*, 16 July. Available at www.independent.co.uk/arts-entertainment/books/features/twihaiku-micropoetry-the-rise-of-twitter-poetry-8711637.html [accessed 30 December 2018] n.p.

46. Davies, Rosamund (2017) 'Collaborative production and the transformation of publishing: The case of Wattpad' in James Graham and Alessandro Gandini (eds), *Collaborative Production in the Creative Industries* (London: University of Westminster Press) p. 60.

47. Harper (2015), p. 9.

48. Quoted in Wilkinson, Carl (2012) 'Shutting out a world of digital distraction'. *Telegraph*, 6 September. Available at www.telegraph.co.uk/culture/books/9522845/Shutting-out-a-world-of-digital-distraction.html [accessed 10 April 2017] n.p.

49. Moggach, Deborah (2000) 'Foreword' in Jane Dorner's *The Internet: A Writer's Guide* (London: A&C Black) p. vi.

50. For discussion, see Barnard (2016, 2017).

51. Taylor Suchy, Susan (2013) 'The social media marketplace in the "Quaint" creative writing classroom: Our terms for engagement'. *TEXT, 17*(2): n.p. www.textjournal.com.au/oct13/suchy.html/.

52. Dean Clark, Michael (2015) 'The marketable creative: Using technology and broader notions of skill in the fiction course' in Michael Dean Clark, Trent Hergenrader and Joseph Rein (eds), *Creative Writing in the Digital Age: Theory, Practice and Pedagogy* (London: Bloomsbury Academic) p. 61.

53. See for example, Wandor (2012), n.p.; Harper (2015), p. 7; Peary and Hunley (2017), p. 1; Koehler (2017), p. 1.

54. Hodgson quoting Barnard in HCDeb (13 February 2014) Column 335WH. Available at https://publications.parliament.uk/pa/cm201314/cmhansrd/cm140213/halltext/140213h0001.htm [accessed 22 April 2018].

55. Easton, Eliza (2018) *Creativity and the Future of Skills* (London: Nesta).

56. Gray, Alex (2016) 'The 10 skills you need to thrive in the Fourth Industrial Revolution'. *World Economic Forum*, 19 January. Available at www.weforum.org/agenda/2016/01/the-10-skills-you-need-to-thrive-in-the-fourth-industrial-revolution/ [accessed 12 January 2017] n.p.

57. Murray, Janet (2012) *Inventing the Medium: Principles of Interaction Design as a Cultural Practice* (Cambridge, MA; London, England: MIT) p. 28.

58. Dean Clark, Michael; Hergenrader, Trent; and Rein, Joseph (2015) 'Introduction' in Michael Dean Clark, Trent Hergenrader and Joseph Rein (eds), *Creative Writing in the Digital Age: Theory, Practice and Pedagogy* (London: Bloomsbury Academic) p. 2.

59. Barnard in Parliament, Commons Select Committee, Culture Media and Support (DCMS) (2013) 'Written evidence submitted by Josie Barnard [SCE 088]'. *HC 743 Support for the creative economy* (London: DCSS), November 2012. www.publications.parliament.uk/pa/cm201213/cmselect/cmcumeds/writev/suppcrec/m088.htm.

60. Webb and Brien (2012), p. 203.

61. Murray (2012), p. 2.

Appendices

1. Hardy, Thomas (1912) extract from *Tess of the d'Urbervilles* (London: Macmillan) pp. 142–143.

2. Wilson, Gina and Grant, Anna (2017) *Not Without Me: A digital world for all?: Findings from a programme of digital inclusion for vulnerable young people across the UK* (Dunfermline: Carnegie United Kingdom Trust).

3. Wilson and Grant (2017) p. 62.

4. Letter (2015) pp. 178–179.

5. Wilson and Grant (2017), p. 6.

6. Ibid., p. 4.

7. Quoting Feenberg, Andersen, Daniel (2008) 'The Low Bridge to High Benefits: Entry-level Multimedia, Literacies and Motivation' in *Computers and Composition* 25, p. 41.

8. Letter (2015).

9. Ibid., p. 185.

10. Ibid., p. 184.

11. Leahy and Dechow (2015) p. 33.

12. Conferences including:

    Barnard, Josie and Vodanovic, Lucia (2015) 'Social media in the classroom'. Paper presented to *Mix.03 Digital*, Bath Spa University, Bath (UK), 2–4 July.

    Barnard, Josie (2013a) 'Tweeting to meet learning objectives'. Paper presented to HEA (Higher Education Academy) *Storyville: Exploring narratives of teaching and learning*, Brighton (UK), 29–30 May.

    Barnard, Josie (2014) 'Technology in Higher Education: Teaching, learning and responding to student demand'. Paper presented to Westminster Higher Education Forum Keynote Seminar, *MOOCs and technology enhanced learning*, London (UK), 21 October.

    Barnard, J. (2017a) The "postdigital" creative writing classroom, an evidence-based response. Paper presented to *MIX 2017: Revolutions, Regenerations, Reflections*, Bath Spa University, Bath (UK), 10–12 July.

    Barnard, J. (2018) 'How mapping the task of creating an "authentic" online self can aid digital inclusion, a case study'. Paper presented to Liverpool University/DCMS Digital Inclusion Working Group's *Digital Inclusion: Policy and Research Conference*, Liverpool University in London, London (UK), 21–22 June.

    Barnard, J. (2018a) 'The multimodal writer: How affect can aid negotiation of the creation of multiple, transmediated selves'. Paper presented to *Affect and Social Media 4.0*, University of East London, London (UK), 7 November.

    Barnard, J. (2018b) 'The multimodal writer: A toolkit to enable effective and productive negotiation of new and emerging media technologies'. Paper presented to the *National Association of Writers in Education Conference (with Paper Nation)*, Park Inn, York (UK), 9–11 November.

13. Focus Group. (2016) 'Creative Writing workshop'. At Mary Ward Centre, London (UK), 21 May.

14. Kress, Gunther (2010) *Multimodality: A Social Semiotic Approach to Contemporary Communication* (London: Routledge), pp. 196–197.

15. Yancey, Kathleen Blake (2014) 'Made not only in words: Composition in a new key' in Claire Lutkewitte (ed.), *Multimodal Composition: A Critical Sourcebook* (Boston, New York: Bedford Books) pp. 74–75.

16. Harper, Graeme (2015) 'Creative writing in the age of synapses' in Michael Dean Clark, Trent Hergenrader and Joseph Rein (eds), *Creative Writing in the Digital Age: Theory, Practice and Pedagogy* (London: Bloomsbury Academic) pp. 13–15.

17. Kress (2010), p. 196.

18. Yancey (2014), p. 75.

19. Harper (2015), p. 14.

WORKS CITED

Ackroyd, P. (1990) *Dickens* (London: Sinclair-Stevenson).

Adsit, J. (2015) 'Giving an account of oneself: Teaching identity construction and authorship in creative nonfiction and social' in M. Dean Clark, T. Hergenrader & J. Rein (eds), *Creative writing in the digital age: Theory, practice and pedagogy* (London: Bloomsbury Academic) pp. 105–120.

Alter, R. (1981) *The art of Biblical narrative* (New York: Basic Books).

Amato, J. & Fleisher, K. (2015) 'Two creative writers look askance at digital composition (crayon on paper)' in M. Dean Clark, T. Hergenrader & J. Rein (eds), *Creative writing in the digital age: Theory, practice and pedagogy* (London: Bloomsbury Academic) pp. 73–87.

Andersen, D. (2008) 'The low bridge to high benefits: Entry-level multimedia, literacies and motivation'. *Computers and Composition, 25*(1): 40–60.

Andersen, L. (2006) 'The creative process' in L. Andersen (ed.) written and produced by The Open University, *Creative writing: A workbook with readings* (Abingdon, Oxfordshire: Routledge), pp. 17–32.

Andersen, T. R. (2017) 'Staggered transmissions: Twitter and the return of serialized literature'. *Convergence: The International Journal of Research into New Media Technologies, 23*(1): 34–48.

Angel, M. & Gibbs, A. (2013) 'At the time of writing: Digital media, gesture, and handwriting'. *Electronic Book Review*, August 2013. www.electronicbookreview.com/thread/electropoetics/gesture [accessed 10 June 2016].

Arrigoni, G. & Zics, B. (2016) 'Fiction and curatorial practice: Developing alternative experiences for digital artistic prototypes'. *International Journal of Performance Arts and Digital Media, 12*(1): 82–94. DOI: 10.1080/14794713.2015.1133960.

Ashwini, A. (2017) 'Everything you need to know about IoT prototyping'. *Medium*, 11 December. Available at: www.medium.com/swlh/everything-you-need-to-know-about-iot-prototyping-e4ad2739bc6a [accessed 3 January 2019].

Baker, K. (2016) 'Social media law: An essential guide'. *The Guardian*, 12 August. Available at www.theguardian.com/law/2016/aug/12/social-media-law-an-essential-guide [accessed 23 September 2018].

Bakhtin, M. M. (1990) 'Author and hero in aesthetic activity' in M. Holquist & V. Liapunov (eds.), *Art and answerability: Early philosophical essay*. trans. and notes V. Liapunov; supplementary trans. K. Bostrom. (Austin: University of Texas Press) pp.4–256.

Barnard, J. & Haskel, L. (1985) *The Friday buzz*, radio series, BBC Radio Merseyside, 19.00 hrs, weekly, 22 February–12 April.

Barnard, J. (1993) *The Virago women's guide to New York* (London: Virago).

Barnard, J. (1994) *The Virago Women's Guide to London.* (London: Virago).

Barnard, J. (1996) *Poker face* (London: Virago).

Barnard, J. (1997) (programme, producer) 'Velcro'. *In Celebration*, radio, BBC Radio 4, 29 November, 17.40 hrs.

Barnard, J. (1999) Author interview, 'Everymum in designer wellies'. *Independent on Sunday,* 6 June, p. 11 ('Books' section). Available from www.independent.co.uk/ arts-entertainment/books/everymum-in-designer-wellies-1098487.html.

Barnard, J. (2000) *The pleasure dome* (London: Virago).

Barnard, J. (2002) (column, author) 'Shelving' in *Home Truths*, radio, BBC Radio 4, 27 January, 09.00 hrs.

Barnard, J. (2003a) (programme, producer) *Heroes of Telemark*, radio, BBC Radio 4, 15 May, 20.00 hrs.

Barnard, J. (2003b) 'Heroes? Not us'. *The Guardian,* 12 May, pp. 6–7. www. theguardian.com/media/2003/may/12/tvandradio.g2 [accessed 26 May 2019].

Barnard, J. (2008a) 'Transports of delight'. *Slightly Foxed: The Real Reader's Quarterly*, *15*, Autumn, pp. 90–93.

Barnard, J. (2008b) 'Southern comfort'. *Slightly Foxed: The Real Reader's Quarterly, 19*, Autumn 2008, pp. 40–45.

Barnard, J. (2009) (programme, producer), *M1 Magic*, Radio, BBC Radio 4, 28 October, 11.00 hrs.

Barnard, J. (2011) *The book of friendship* (London: Virago Press).

Barnard, J. (2015) 'Live and public: One practitioner's experience and assessment of Twitter as a tool for archiving creative process'. *Journal of Writing in Creative Practice, Writing-PAD, 7*(3): 493–503.

Barnard, J. (2015a) *The multimodal writer: One practitioner's experience of moving between different types of writing for different modes of dissemination (Unpublished PhD Thesis)* (London: Middlesex University).

Barnard, J. (2015b) 'Pedagogical benefits for creative writing students of running a literary festival, a practitioner-teacher's observations'. *The Festival and Events Experience, 127*: 47–69 (Eastbourne: Leisure Studies Association Publications, University of Brighton).

Barnard, J. (2016) 'Tweets as microfiction: On Twitter's live nature and 140 character limit as tools for developing storytelling skills'. *New Writing: The International Journal for the Practice and Theory of Creative Writing, 13*(1), 3–16. DOI:10.1080 /14790726.2015.1127975.

Barnard, J. (2017) 'Testing possibilities: On negotiating writing practices in a 'postdigital' age (tools and methods)'. *New Writing: the International Journal for the Practice and Theory of Creative Writing, 14*(2): 275–289. DOI: 10.1080/ 14790726.2016.1278025.

Barnard, J. (2019) 'Twitter and creative writing: Generating an "authentic" online self' in I. Chiluwa & G. Bouvier (eds.), *Twitter: Global perspectives, uses and research technique* (New York: Nova Science Publishers).

Barnes, D. (1990) *Djuna Barnes's New York,* A. Barry (ed.); foreword by D. Messerli. (London: Virago).

Baron, D. (2013) *A better pencil: Readers, writers, and the digital revolution* (Oxford, New York: Oxford University Press).

Bateman, J. A. (2008) *Multimodality and genre: A foundation for the systematic analysis of multimodal documents* (Basingstoke: Palgrave Macmillan).

Baverstock, A. (2012) 'Why self-publishing needs to be taken seriously'. *Logos, 23*(4): 41–46. DOI: 10.1163/1878-4712-11112005.

Baym, N. K. (2015) *Personal connections in the digital age* (Cambridge: Polity).

BBC. (2008) *Glossary of common media terms.* Available at http://news.bbc.co.uk/1/mobile/school_report/4791411.stm [accessed 22 August 2014].

Bell, A., Ensslin A., Ciccoricco D. et al. (2010) 'A [s]creed for digital fiction'. *Electronic book review*, 7 March. Available at: www.electronicbookreview.com/thread/electropoetics/DFINative [accessed 20 January 2019].

Berger, J. (1972) *Ways of seeing* (Harmondsworth: Penguin).

Biersdorfer, J. D. (2016) 'How to get Twitter's blue badge of authenticity'. *New York Times*, 24 August. Available at https://www.nytimes.com/2016/08/25/technology/personaltech/how-to-get-twitters-blue-badge-of-authenticity.html [accessed 23 September 2018].

Bing, X. (2013) *Book from the ground: From point to point* (North Adams, MA: MASS MoCA).

Blackwell, L. (2013) 'Neil Gaiman sets Twitter ablaze with fan collaboration'. *PC World,* March 18. Available at www.pcworld.com/article/2030776/neil-gaiman-sets-twitter-ablaze-with-fan-collaboration.html [accessed 10 April 2017].

Bolter, D. J. & Grusin, R. (2000) *Remediation: Understanding new media* (Cambridge, MA; London: The MIT Press).

Booker, C. (2005) *The seven basic plots: Why we tell stories* (London: Continuum).

Borges, J. L. (1998) *Collected fictions.* trans. A. Hurley (London: Allen Lane).

Bowen, E. (1986a) 'Notes on writing a novel' in H. Lee (ed.), *The mulberry tree: Writings of Elizabeth Bowen: Selected and introduced by Hermione Lee* (San Diego; New York; London: Harcourt Brace Jovanovich) pp. 35–48.

Bowen, E. (1986b) *The mulberry tree: Writings of Elizabeth Bowen: Selected and introduced by Hermione Lee* (San Diego; New York; London: Harcourt Brace Jovanovich).

Bowen, T. & Whithaus, C. (2013) 'Introduction' in T. Bowen & C. Whithaus (eds), *Multimodal literacies and emerging genres* (Pittsburgh: University of Pittsburgh) pp. 1–12.

Boyd, D., Golder, S. & Lotan, G. (2010) 'Tweet, tweet, retweet: Conversational aspects of retweeting on Twitter'. *HICSS-43*, IEEE: Kauai, HI, 6 January.

Brande, D. & Gardner, J. (Foreword) (1981) *Becoming a writer* (Los Angeles: J. P. Tarcher).

Brown Jr., J. J. (2015) 'Writing with machines: Data and process in Taroko Gorge' in M. Dean Clark, T. Hergenrader & J. Rein (eds), *Creative writing in the digital age: Theory, practice and pedagogy* (London: Bloomsbury Academic) pp. 129–140.

Cain, M. (2012) 'Forcing authors into the book-promoting limelight'. *Channel 4 News*, 15 August. Available at www.blogs.channel4.com/culture/book-festivals-force-writers-jekyll-hyde-lifestyle/3131#sthash.FmqxNDR1.dpuf [accessed 21 October 2013].

Campbell, G. (2010) *Bible: The story of the King James Version, 1611–2011* (Oxford: Oxford University Press).

Carr, N. (2010) 'Author Nicholas Carr: The web shatters focus, rewires brains' in *Wired*, 24 May. Available at www.wired.com/magazine/2010/05/ff_nicholas_carr [accessed 10 April 2017].

Capote, T. (1966) *In cold blood: A true account of a multiple murder and its consequences* (London: Hamish Hamilton).

Chawinga, W. D. (2017) 'Taking social media to a university classroom: Teaching and learning using Twitter and blogs'. *International Journal of Educational Technology in Higher Education, 14*(3): 1–19. DOI:10.1186/s41239-017-0041-6.

Clancy, C. (2015) 'The text is where it's at: Digital storytelling assignments that teach lessons in creative writing' in M. Dean Clark, T. Hergenrader & J. Rein (eds), *Creative writing in the digital age: Theory, practice and pedagogy* (London: Bloomsbury Academic) pp.165–176.

Clark, A. (2008) *Supersizing the Mind: Embodiment, Action and Cognitive Extension* (Oxford, New York: Oxford University Press).

Clark, A. (2011) Finding the mind. *Philosophical Studies, 152*(3): 447–461. DOI: 10.1007/s11098-010-9598-9.

Cobley, P. (2001) *Narrative* (London, New York: Routledge).

Coe, J. (2016) 'My writing day'. *The Guardian*, 4 June. Available at www.theguardian.com/books/2016/jun/04/jonathan-coe-my-writing-day [accessed 10 April 2017].

Coelho, P. (2014a) *Adultery* (London: Cornerstone Digital).

Coelho, P. (2014b) 'Interview with Ellen Gamerman: Paulo Coelho on reaching out to fans on social media'. *Wall Street Journal blogspot*, 15 August. Available at www.wsj.com/video/paulo-coelho-on-reaching-out-to-fans-on-social-media/E126150 1-BBF0-47FC-913A-7CCE90BCA204.html [accessed 10 April 2017].

Cokely, E. T. & Feltz, A. (2014) 'Expert intuition' in L. M. Osbeck, B. S. Held (eds), *Rational intuition: Philosophical roots, scientific investigations* (New York, Cambridge: Cambridge University Press) pp. 213–238.

Connolly, C. (1949) *Enemies of promise* (London: Routledge & Kegan Paul).

Corrigan-Kavanagh, E. (2019) Next Generation Paper. *The Writing Platform*, 7 March. Available at http://thewritingplatform.com/2019/03/next-generation-paper/ [accessed 17 May 2019].

Cowdrey, K. (2016) 'Miranda Hart's fans' stories to feature in promotional e-book'. *The Bookseller*, 9 July. Available at www.thebookseller.com/news/hodder-launch-and-me-e-book-competition-promote-miranda-harts-new-book-363081 [accessed 10 April 2017].

Cramer, F. (2014) What is 'postdigital'? *APRA, A Peer Reviewed Journal About Post-Digital Research, 3*(1). Available at www.aprja.net/?p=1318 [accessed 22 April 2016].

Cranny-Francis, A. (2005) *Multimedia texts and contexts* (London: Sage).

Cripps, C. (2013) 'Twihaiku? Micropoetry? The rise of Twitter poetry'. *Independent*, 16 July. Available at www.independent.co.uk/arts-entertainment/books/features/twihaiku-micropoetry-the-rise-of-twitter-poetry-8711637.html [accessed 30 December 2018].

Curtis, J. A. E. (1991) *Manuscripts don't burn: Mikhail Bulgakov, a life in letters and diaries* (London: Bloomsbury).

Dalrymple, W. (2011) 'My favourite travel book, by the world's greatest travel writers'. *The Guardian*, 16 Sept. Available at www.theguardian.com/travel/2011/sep/16/travel-writers-favourite-books [accessed 18 March 2018].

Davies, R. (2017) 'Collaborative production and the transformation of publishing: The case of Wattpad' in J. Graham & A. Gandini (eds), *Collaborative production in the creative industries* (London: University of Westminster Press) pp. 51–67.

Davis, R. L. & Shadle, M. F. (2007) *Teaching multiwriting: Researching and composing with multiple genres, media, disciplines and cultures* (Carbondale: Southern Illinois Press).

Dawson, M. (1997) 'An interview with Eudora Welty'. *Poets and Writers Magazine*, 25(5): 20–32. Sept–Oct.

Dean Clark, M. (2015) 'The marketable creative: Using technology and broader notions of skill in the fiction course' in M. Dean Clark, T. Hergenrader & J. Rein (eds), *Creative writing in the digital age: Theory, practice and pedagogy*, pp. 61–72 (London: Bloomsbury Academic).

Dean Clark M., Hergenrader, T. & Rein, J. (2015) 'Introduction' in M. Dean Clark, T. Hergenrader & J. Rein (eds), *Creative writing in the digital age: Theory, practice and pedagogy* (London: Bloomsbury Academic) pp. 1–5.

Deleuze, G. & Guattari, F. (1999) *A thousand plateaus: Capitalism and schizophrenia* (London: The Athlone Press).

Department for Digital, Culture, Media and Sport (DCMS). (2017), Policy paper, Digital skills and inclusion - Giving everyone access to the digital skills they need, 1 March (London: DCMS). Available at www.gov.uk/government/publications/uk-digital-strategy/2-digital-skills-and-inclusion-giving-everyone-access-to-the-digital-skills-they-need [accessed 17 April 2017].

Despain, W. (ed.) (2008) *Professional techniques for video game writing* (Welleseley, MA: A K Peters).

Easton, E. (2018) *Creativity and the future of skills* (London: Nesta).

Egan, J. (2012) 'Black Box'. *The New Yorker*, 4 & 11 June. Available at www.newyorker.com/magazine/2012/06/04/black-box-2 [accessed 22 April 2018].

Eisenstein, S. (2010) *Sergei Eisenstein, selected works, Volume III, Writings, 1937–47*, (ed.) R. Taylor; trans. W. Powell. (London; New York: I. B Tauris).

Elwell, J. S. (2014) 'The transmediated self: Life between the digital and the analog'. *Convergence: The International Journal of Research into New Media Technologies*, 20(2): 233–249.

Faulkner, W. (1963) *As I lay dying* (Harmondsworth: Penguin Books in association with Chatto & Windus).

Faulkner, W. (1964) *The sound and the fury* (Harmondsworth: Penguin Books in association with Chatto & Windus).

Feather, J. (1998) *A history of British publishing* (London and New York: Routledge).

Forster, E. M. (1961) 'The plot' in R. Shcoles (ed.) *Approaches to the novel: Materials for a poetics: Collected and edited by Robert Scholes, University of Virgini* (San Francisco: Chandler Publishing Company) pp. 155–158.

FP Staff. (2018) 'Snapchat announces slate of new scripted web series, documentaries called Snap Originals'. *Firstpost*, 10 October. Available at www.firstpost.com/entertainment/snapchat-announces-slate-of-new-scripted-webseries-documentaries-called-snap-originals-5354001.html [accessed 3 January 2019].

Gaiman, N. (2013) *A calendar of tales* (Blackberry). Available at www.acalendaroftales.com/ [date accessed 10 April 2017].

Gere, C. (2002) *Digital culture* (London: Reaktion).

Gere, C. (2012) *Community without community in digital culture* (Basingstoke: Palgrave Macmillan).

Gibbons, A. (2012) *Multimodality, cognition, and experimental literature, Ebook* (London, New York: Routledge) [accessed 29 May 2017].

Goffman, E. (1959) *The presentation of self in everyday life* (Garden City, NY: Doubleday & Co.).

Goldberg, N. (1986) *Writing down the bones: Freeing the writer within.* Foreword J. Guest (Boston; London: Shambahla).

Gray, A. (2016) 'The 10 skills you need to thrive in the Fourth Industrial Revolution'. *World Economic Forum*, 19 January. Available at www.weforum.org/agenda/2016/01/the-10-skills-you-need-to-thrive-in-the-fourth-industrial-revolution/ [accessed 12 January 2017].

Gunaratnam, Y. & Bell, V. (2017) 'How John Berger changed our way of seeing art'. *The Conversation,* 5 January. Available at www.theconversation.com/how-john-berger-changed-our-way-of-seeing-art-70831 [accessed 15 January 2019].

Gutkind, L. (1997) *Creative non-fiction: Writing and selling the literature of reality* (New York; Chichester: John Wiley & Sons).

Hall, F. (2013) *The business of digital publishing: An introduction to the digital book and journal industries* (London: Routledge).

Handa, C. (2004) 'Introduction' in C. Handa (ed.), *Visual rhetoric in a digital world* (Boston, New York: Bedford/St Martin's), pp. 1–5.

Hannaham, J. & Bateman, J. W. (2017) 'Eight tiny stories, translated from the emoji'. *Electric Lit.* Available at www.electricliterature.com/eight-tiny-stories-translated-from-the-emoji-40d43d4b3d86 [accessed 15 January 2019].

Hardy, T. (1912) *Extract from Tess of the d'Urbervilles* (London: Macmillan).

Harper, G. (2015) 'Creative writing in the age of synapses' in M. Dean Clark, T. Hergenrader & J. Rein (eds.), *Creative writing in the digital age: Theory, practice and pedagogy,* (London: Bloomsbury Academic), pp. 7–17.

Hart, M. (2016) *Peggy and me* (London: Hodder & Stoughton).

Hayles, N. K. (2008) *Electronic literature: New horizons for the literary* (Notre Dame: University of Notre Dame).

Hayles, N. K. (2012) *How we think: Digital media and contemporary technogenesis* (Chicago, London: The University of Chicago Press).

Hayward, M. (1983) (edited and with an introduction by P. Blake; preface by Leonard Schapiro; bibliography by Valerie Jensen) *Writers in Russia: 1917–1978* (London: Harvill Press).

HC Deb. (13 February 2014) *Column 335WH*. Available at www.publications. parliament.uk/pa/cm201314/cmhansrd/cm140213/halltext/140213h0001.htm [accessed 22 April 2018].

Hemingway, E. (1964) *A moveable feast* (London: Jonathan Cape).

Hendrix, J. (2012) 'Odd corners round about brooklyn'. *The Paris Review*, 2 April. Available at www.theparisreview.org/blog/2012/04/02/odd-corners-round-about-brooklyn/ [accessed 25 August 2014].

Henke, H. (2001) 'The global impact of ebooks on epublishing'. *SIGDOC'01*, October 21–24: 172–180. Santa Fe, New Mexico, USA, ACM 1-5813-295-6/01/001.

Hergenrader, T. (2015) 'Game spaces: Videogames as story-generating systems for creative writers' in M. Dean Clark, T. Hergenrader & J. Rein (eds), *Creative writing in the digital age: Theory, practice and pedagogy* (London: Bloomsbury Academic), pp. 45–59.

Hurley, S. L. (1998) *Consciousness in action* (Cambridge, MA: Harvard University Press).

Huws, U. (2014) *Labor in the global digital economy: The cybertariat comes of age* (New York: The Monthly Review Press).

James, E. L. (2011) *Fifty shades of grey* (New York: Knopf Doubleday Publishing Group).

Jenkins, H., with Clinton, K., Purushotma, R., Robison, A. J. & Weigel, M. (2006) *Confronting the challenges of participatory culture: Media education for the 21st century*. Available at www.macfound.org/media/article_pdfs/JENKINS_WHITE_PAPER. PDF.

Jewitt, C., Bezemer, J. & O'Halloran, K. (2016) *Introducing multimodality* (London and New York: Routledge).

Kaur, R. (2015) *Milk and honey* (Kansas City: Andrews McMeel Publishing).

Knowles, E. (2004) *Oxford dictionary of quotations* (Oxford: Oxford University Press), p. 296.

Koehler, A. (2015) 'Screening subjects: Workshop pedagogy, media ecologies, and (new) student' in M. Dean Clark, T. Hergenrader & J. Rein (eds), *Creative writing in the digital age: Theory, practice and pedagogy* (London: Bloomsbury Academic), pp. 17–28.

Koehler, A. (2017) *Composition, creative writing studies, and the digital humanities* (London: Bloomsbury Academic).

Krauth, N. (2014) 'Multigraph, not monograph: Creative writing and new technologies' in J. Potts (ed.), *The future of writing* (Basingstoke: Palgrave Macmillan), pp. 58–76.

Krauth, N. (2015) 'The radical future of teaching creative writing' in G. Harper (ed.), *New writing viewpoints 11: Creative writing and education* (Bristol, Buffalo, Toronto: Multilingual Matters), pp. 183–195.

Krauth, N. (2016) *Creative writing and the radical: Teaching and learning the fiction of the future (new writing viewpoints)* (Bristol: Multilingual Matters).

Kress, G. (2010) *Multimodality: A social semiotic approach to contemporary communication* (London: Routledge).

Kroll, J. & Harper, G. (2013) 'Introduction' in J. Kroll & G. Harper (eds), *Research methods in creative writing* (Basingstoke: Palgrave Macmillan), pp. 1–13.

Kwan, L. (2018) *#AmWriting: How authors negotiate their individual creative labour on social media* (Thesis). Royal Roads University Victoria, British Columbia, Canada. Available at www.viurrspace.ca/bitstream/handle/10613/5448/Kwan_royalroads_1313O_10502.pdf?sequence=1&isAllowed=y [accessed 28 November 2018].

Lahire, B. (tr. G. Wells) (2010) 'The double life of writers'. *New Literary History,* 41(2): 443–465.

Laing, A. (2017) 'Authors using social media: Layers of identity and the online author community'. *Publishing Research Quarterly, 33*(3): 254–267. DOI: 10.1007/s12109-017-9524-5

Lauer, C. (2014) 'Contending with terms: "multimodal" and "multimedia" in the academic and public spheres' in C. Lutkewitte (ed.), *Multimodal composition: A critical sourcebook* (Boston, New York: Bedford Books), pp. 22–41.

Lavandier, Y. (tr. B. Besserglik) (2005) *Writing drama: A comprehensive guide for playwrights and scriptwriters* (Cergy Cedex, France: Le Clown & l'Enfant).

Leahy, A. & Dechow, D. (2015) 'Concentration, form, and ways of (digitally) seeing' in M. Dean Clark, T. Hergenrader & J. Rein (eds), *Creative writing in the digital age: Theory, practice and pedagogy* (London: Bloomsbury Academic), pp. 30–44.

Lerner, B. (2000) *An editor's advice to writers: The forest for the trees* (London: Macmillan).

Letter, A. (2015) 'Creative writing for new media' in M. Dean Clark, T. Hergenrader & J. Rein (eds), *Creative writing in the digital age: Theory, practice and pedagogy* (London: Bloomsbury Academic), pp. 177–189.

Llewellyn, C. (2005) 'The hunger for ideas'. *TEXT,* 4(October). Available at www.textjournal.com.au/speciss/issue4/llewellyn.htm [accessed 21 October 2013].

Lutkewitte, C. (ed.) (2014) *Multimodal composition: A critical sourcebook* (Boston, New York: Bedford Books).

Lycett, A. (2007) *Conan Doyle: The man who created Sherlock Holmes* (London: Weidenfeld & Nicolson).

Madrigal, A. C. (2018) 'Retweets are trash: A modest proposal to improve Twitter – and perhaps the world'. *The Atlantic Magazine,* April Issue. Available at www.theatlantic.com/magazine/archive/2018/04/the-case-against-retweets/554078/?single_page=true [accessed 28 November 2018].

Mallon, T (2011) 'The wanderer'. *The New York Times,* 25 February. Available at www.nytimes.com/2011/02/27/books/review/Mallon-t.html?pagewanted=all&_r=0 [accessed 23 August 2014].

Mangan, L. (2019) 'Black mirror: Bandersnatch review – The TV of tomorrow is now here'. *The Guardian*, 1 January. Available at www.theguardian.com/tv-and-radio/2019/jan/01/black-mirror-bandersnatch-review-charlie-brooker-netflix-tv-of-tomorrow-is-now-here [accessed 3 January 2019].

Mangen, A. & van der Weel, A. (2017) 'Why don't we read hypertext novels?' *Convergence: The International Journal of Research Into New Media Technologies, 23*(2): 166–181. DOI:10.1177/135485651558604.

Manovich, L. (2011) 'What is visualization?'. *Visual Studies, 26*(1): 36–49. DOI:10.1080/1472586X.2011.548488.

Massumi, B. (2015) *The politics of affect* (Cambridge, UK; Malden, MA: Polity Press).

McLuhan, M. (1962) *The Gutenberg galaxy: The making of typographic man* (Toronto: University of Toronto Press).

Meehan, M. (2005) 'The word made flesh: Festival, carnality and literary consumption'. *TEXT, 4*(October). Available at www.textjournal.com.au/speciss/issue4/meehan.htm [date accessed 21 October 2013].

Melrose, S. (2006) 'Bodies without bodies' in S. Broadhurst & J. Machon (eds), *Performance and technology: Practices of virtual embodiment and interactivity* (Basingstoke: Palgrave Macmillan), pp. 1–17.

Millard, K. (2013) 'A screenwriter's *reality* hunger'. *TEXT Journal*. Available at www.textjournal.com.au/speciss/issue18/Millard.pdf [accessed 22 August 2014].

Millard, K. & Munt, A. (2014) 'The design of writing: 29 observations' in J. Potts (ed.), *The future of writing* (Basingstoke: Palgrave Macmillan), pp. 90–103.

Mitchell, D. (2015) @I_Bombadil, *Twitter* @I_Bombadil, 7 September–31 October.

Moggach, D. (2000) 'Foreword' in J. Dorner (ed.), *The internet: A writer's guide* (London: A&C Black), p. vi.

Morrison, T. (2008) In Zia Jaffrey 'Toni Morrison' pp. 139–154, in C. C. Denard (ed.), Toni Morrison: Conversations (Jackson, MS: University Press of Mississippi).

Murray, J. (2012) *Inventing the medium: Principles of interaction design as a cultural practice* (Cambridge, MA and London, England: MIT).

Myers, D. G. (1996) *The Elephants Teach: Creative Writing Since 1880* (Chicago: Prentice Hall).

Neurath, O. (1936) *International picture language* (London: Kegan Paul).

Newman, N. (2018) 'Journalism, media, and technology trends and predictions 2018'. *Digital News Publications*, published by the Reuters Institute for the Study of Journalism with the support of Google's Digital News Initiative. Available at www.digitalnewsreport.org/publications/2018/journalism-media-technology-trends-predictions-2018/ [accessed 15 January 2019].

Nietzsche, F. (tr. R. J. Hollingdate; Introduction by R. Schacht) (1996) *Human, all too human* (Cambridge: Cambridge University Press).

Olson, D. R. (1994) *The world on paper* (Cambridge: Cambridge University Press).

Ong, W. J. (1982) *Orality and literacy: The technologizing of the word* (London: Methuen).

Open Book, 15.30 p.m., 22.10.2017, radio programme (London: BBC Radio 4).

Oz, A. (tr. M. Bar-Tura) (1999) *The story begins: Essays on literature* (London: Chatto & Windus).

Ozick, C. (1996) *Portrait of the artist as a bad character and othereEssays on writing* (London: Pimlico).

Page, R. (2009) 'Introduction' in R. Page (ed.), *New perspectives on narrative and multimodality* (London, New York: Routledge), pp. 1–13.

Page, R. & Thomas B. (eds) (2011) *New narratives: Stories and storytelling in the digital age* (Lincoln: University of Nebraska Press).

Palmeri, J. (2012) *Remixing composition: A history multimodal writing pedagogy* (Carbondale and Edwardsville: Southern Illinois Press).

Parker, P. (ed.) (1994) *The reader's companion to the twentieth century novel* (London: Fourth Estate).

Parker, P. (ed.) (1995) *The reader's companion to twentieth century writers* (London: Fourth Estate).

Parliament, Commons Select Committee, Culture Media and Support (DCMS) (2013) 'Written evidence submitted by Josie Barnard [SCE 088]'. *HC 743 Support for the creative economy* (London: DCSS), November 2012. Available at www.publications.parliament.uk/pa/cm201213/cmselect/cmcumeds/writev/suppcrec/m088.htm.

Peary, A. & Hunley, T. C. (2015) 'Introduction' in A. Peary & T. C. Hunley (eds), *Creative writing pedagogies for the twenty-first century* (Carbondale: Southern Illinois Press), pp. 1–6.

Peary, Alexandria and Hunley, Tom C. (eds) (2015) *Creative Writing Pedagogies for the Twenty-First Century* (Carbondale: Southern Illinois Press).

Pedersen, A-M. & Skinner, C. (2007) 'Collaborating on multimodal projects' in C. Selfe (ed.), *Multimodal composition: Resources for teachers* (Cresskill, NJ: Hampton Press), pp. 39–47.

Pells, R. (2015) 'Joanne Harris interview: The Chocolat author is in militant mood when it comes to writers' rights'. *Independent*, 22 August. Available at www.independent.co.uk/arts-entertainment/books/features/joanne-harris-interview-the-chocolat-author-is-in-militant-mood-when-it-comes-to-writers-rights-10462112.html [accessed 30 December 2018].

Perez, S. (2014) 'Twitter is experimenting with a new way to retweet'. *TechCrunch*, 24 June. Available at https//techcrunch.com/2014/06/24/twitter-is-experimenting-with-a-new-way-to-retweet/ [accessed 23 November 2018].

Perez, S. (2017) 'Twitter officially expands its character count to 280 starting today'. *TechCrunch*, 7 November. Available at https://techcrunch.com/2017/11/07/twitter-officially-expands-its-character-count-to-280-starting-today/ [accessed 23 November 2018].

Peters, T. (2016) 'Emojis, comics, and the novel of the future'. *Los Angeles Review of Books*, 26 April. Available at lareviewofbooks.org/article/emojis-comics-novel-future/ [accessed 15 January 2019].

Pilkington, E. (ed.) (2012) 'Amanda Hocking, the writer who made millions by self-publishing online'. *The Guardian*, 12 January. Available at www.theguardian.com/books/2012/jan/12/amanda-hocking-self-publishing [accessed 10 April 2017].

Piper, A. (2012) *Book was there: Reading in electronic times* (Chicago, London: The University of Chicago Press).

Pittaway, G. (2015) 'Movement, maps, mnemonics and music: Teaching fiction and poetry using sight and sound' in G. Harper (ed.), *New writing viewpoints 11: Creative writing and education* (Bristol, Buffalo, Toronto: Multilingual Matters), pp. 120–132.

Pope, R. (1998) *The English studies book* (London and New York: Routledge).

Powers, R. (2005) *Mark Twain: A life* (New York, London, Toronto, Sydney: Free Press).

Propp, V. (2005) (First Edition Translated by Laurence Scott with an Introduction by Svatava Pirkova-Jakobson; Second Edition Revised and Edited with a Preface by Louis A. Wagner/New Introduction by Alan Dundes) *Morphology of the folktale* (Austin: University of Texas Press).

Prose, F. (2006) *Reading like a writer: A guide for people who love books and for those who want to write them* (New York: Harper Collins).

Pullinger, K. (2017) *Jelly bone*, mobile app (oolipo). Available at www.oolipo.com/stories/jellybone [accessed 2 February 2019].

The Quality Assurance Agency (QAA). (2016) *Subject benchmark statement: Creative writing* (Gloucester: The Quality Assurance Agency for Higher Education). Available at www.qaa.ac.uk/docs/qaa/subject-benchmark-statements/sbs-creative-writing-16.pdf?sfvrsn=d4e2f781_8 [accessed 3 January 2018].

Rombauer, I. S. & Becker, M. R. (1963) *The Joy of Cooking* illustrated by G. Hofmann & B. Warner (London; Haarlem printed: J. M. Dent & Sons).

Roth, P. (1989) *The facts: A novelist's autobiography* (London: Jonathan Cape).

Rotman, B. (2008) *Becoming beside ourselves: The alphabet, ghosts, and distributed human being* (Durham and London: Duke University Press).

Ryan, M-L. (2011) 'The interactive onion: Layers of user participation in digital narrative texts' in R. Page & B. Thomas (eds), *New narratives: Stories and storytelling in the digital age* (Lincoln; London: University of Nebraska Press).

Scheg, A. G. (2015) 'Reconsidering the online story with #25wordstory' in M. Dean Clark, T. Hergenrader & J. Rein (eds), *Creative writing in the digital age: Theory, practice and pedagogy* (London: Bloomsbury Academic), pp. 121–128.

Schwab, K. (2016) *The Fourth Industrial Revolution* (Geneva: World Economic Forum).

Selfe, C. (ed.) (2007) *Multimodal composition: Resources for teachers* (Cresskill, NJ: Hampton Press).

Sheppard, J. (2009) 'The rhetorical work of multimedia production practices: It's more than just technical skill'. *Computers and Composition, 26*: 122–131.

Sinclair, I. (2017) *The last London: True fictions from an unreal city* (London: Oneworld Publications).

Sinclair, I. (2018) 'Under offer (Last London) – a CD of music and spoken word with Bill Parry-Davies'. Available at www.iainsinclair.org.uk/?s=soundcloud [accessed 9 January 2018].

Smith, H. (2004) 'Cursors and crystal balls: Digital technologies and the futures of writing'. *TEXT,* 8(2). Available at www.textjournal.com.au/oct04/smith.htm

Smith, H. (2005) *The writing experiment: Strategies for innovative creative writing* (Crows Nest, NSW: Allen & Unwin).

Smyth, S. (2016) 'The new breed of celebrity authors…Miranda and Monty's dogs! Comedian and celebrity garden will go head to head as they publish books about their pets'. *Daily Mail,* 28 August. Available at www.dailymail.co.uk/news/article-3762719/The-new-breed-celebrity-authors-Miranda-Monty-s-dogs-Comedian-celebrity-garden-head-head-publish-books-pets.html [accessed 10 April 2017].

Stach, R. (tr. S. Frisch) (2013) *Kafka: The years of insight* (Princeton and Oxford: Princeton University Press).

Stein, G. (1974) 'How writing is written' (1935) in R. B. Hass (ed.), *How writing is written: Volume II of the previously uncollected writings of Gertrude Stein* (Los Angeles: Black Sparrow Press), pp. 151–160.

Squires, C. & Padmina, R. M. (2013) 'The digital publishing communications circuit'. *Book 2.0, 3*(1): 3–23. DOI:10.1386/btwo.3.1.3_1.

Takolander, M. (2017) 'Grounding the "auto-intoxicated" Romantic poet: A socio-material theory of poetic praxis'. *TEXT, 41*: 1–11. Available at www.textjournal.com.au/speciss/issue41/Takolander.pdf [accessed 15 January 2019].

Tapscott, D. & Williams, A. D. (2006) *Wikinomics: How mass collaboration changes everything* (London: Atlantic Books).

Taylor, J. P. (2014) 'Guest post: Managing a writing life by Jonathan P Taylor'. *Morgen 'with an E' Bailey – Editor, Com Columnist/Judge, Tutor & Writing Guru,* 22 April. Available at www.morgenbailey.wordpress.com/2014/04/22/guest-post-managing-a-writing-life-by-jonathan-p-taylor/ [accessed 20 April 2018].

Taylor Suchy, S. (2013) 'The social media marketplace in the 'quaint' creative writing classroom: Our terms for engagement'. *TEXT, 17*(2) http://www.textjournal.com.au/oct13/suchy.htm.

Tillman, L. (1991) 'Critical fiction/critical self' in P. Mariani (ed.), *Critical fictions: The politics of imaginative writing* (Seattle: Bay Press), pp. 97–103.

Tivnan, T. & Richards, L. (2011) 'Business focus: Literary festivals'. *The Bookseller,* 18 March. Available at www.thebookseller.com/feature/business-focus-literary-festivals.html [accessed 21 October 2013].

Tobias, R. B. (2012) *20 master plots: And how to build them* (Cincinnati, OH: Writer's Digest Books).

Todd, A. (2014) *After* (London: Simon & Schuster).

Trevelyan, G. M. (1986) *English social history: A survey of six centuries* (Harmondsworth: Penguin).

Turchi, P. (2004) *Maps of the imagination: The writer as cartographer* (San Antonio, TX: Trinity University Press).

Universities UK. (2018) *Solving Future Skills Challenges* (London: Universities UK). Available at www.universitiesuk.ac.uk/policy-and-analysis/reports/Documents/2018/solving-future-skills-challenges.pdf [accessed 14 November 2018].

Vonnegut, K. (edited and with an introduction by Dan Wakefield) (2013) *Kurt Vonnegut: Letters* (London: Vintage).

Wagner, E. (2017) '7 of the best literary festivals'. *Harper's Bazaar,* 24 April. Available at www.harpersbazaar.com/uk/culture/news/a41116/our-literary-editor-on-the-rise-of-the-literary-festivals [accessed 3 January 2019].

Wakefield, D. (2013) in K. Vonnegut (edited and with an introduction by D. Wakefield) *Kurt Vonnegut: Letters* (London: Vintage) pp. 28–29.

Walker, R. (2017) 'The young "Instapoet" Rupi Kaur: from social media star to bestselling writer'. *The Guardian,* 28 May. Available at www.theguardian.com/books/2017/may/27/rupi-kaur-i-dont-fit-age-race-class-of-bestselling-poet-milk-and-honey [accessed 7 September 2017].

Walkley, G. (2017) 'Surfing the second wave'. *The Author* (London: The Society of Authors), pp. 44–45.

Wandor, M. (2012) 'Can Creative Writing Really be Taught in British Universities?' *The Fortnightly Review,* 22 April. Available at www.fortnightlyreview.co.uk/2012/04/uk-creative-writing/ [accessed 29 January 2015].

Ward, S. J. A. (2014) 'Radical media ethics'. *Digital Journalism, 2*(4): 455–471. DOI: 10.1080/21670811.2014.952985.

Webb, J. and Brien, D. L., (2012) 'Addressing the "Ancient quarrel": Creative writing as research' in M. Biggs and H. Karlsson (eds), *The Routledge Companion to Research in the Arts* (London: Routledge), pp. 186–203.

Weiler, L. (2017) '30+ Immersive Storytelling platforms, apps, resources & tools'. *Medium,* 23 July. Available at: www.medium.com/columbia-dsl/30-immersive-story-telling-platforms-apps-resources-tools-e428309574be [accessed 3 January 2019].

Weldon, F. (1993) 'Harnessed to the Harpy' in Clare Boylan (ed.), *The Agony and the Ego: The Art and Strategy of Fiction Writing Explored* (Harmondsworth: Penguin), pp. 179–193.

Welty, E. (1984) *One Writer's Beginnings* (Cambridge, MA; London, England: Harvard University Press).

Wendig, C. (2013) *The Kick-ass Writer* (Cincinnatti, OH: Writer's Digest Books).

Williams, K. (2010) *Get Me A Murder A Day! A History of Media and Communication in Britain* (London: Bloomsbury Academic).

Wilkins, K. (2014) 'Writing resilience in the digital age'. *New Writing: The International Journal for the Practice and Theory of Creative Writing, 11*(1): 67–76. DOI:1 0.1080/14790726.2013.870579.

Wilkinson, C. (2012) 'Shutting out a world of digital distraction'. *Telegraph,* 6 September. Available at www.telegraph.co.uk/culture/books/9522845/Shutting-out-a-world-of-digital-distraction.html [accessed 10 April 2017].

Wilson, G. and Grant, A. (2017) *Not without Me: A Digital World for All?: Findings from A Programme of Digital Inclusion for Vulnerable Young People across the UK* (Dunfermline: Carnegie United Kingdom Trust).

Wiseman, S. J. (1996) *Aphra Benn* (Plymouth: Northcote House in association with the British Council).

Wolf, C. (trans. Heurck, J.) (1991) 'The sense and nonsense of being Naive' in P. Mariani (ed.), *Critical Fictions: The Politics of Imaginative Writing* (Seattle: Bay Press), pp. 230–238.

Wolfe, T. (1975) *The New Journalism* (London: Picador).

Woolf, V. (1945) *A room of one's own* (New York: Harmondsworth).

World Economic Forum (2016) *The Future of Jobs: Employment, Skills and Workforce Strategy for the Fourth Industrial Revolution*, Global Challenge Insight Report, January. Available at www3.weforum.org/docs/WEF_Future_of_Jobs.pdf [accessed 6 January 2019].

Wysocki, A. F., Johnson-Eilola, J., Selfe, C., Sirc, G. (eds) (2004) *Writing New Media: Theory and Applications for Expanding the Teaching of Composition* (Logan: Utah State University Press).

Yancey, K. B. (2014) 'Made not only in words: Composition in a new key' in Claire Lutkewitte (ed.), *Multimodal Composition: A Critical Sourcebook* (Boston, New York: Bedford Books), pp. 62–88.

Young, S. (2014) 'Me myself I: revaluing self-publishing in the electronic age' in Potts, John (ed.), *The Future of Writing* (Basingstoke: Palgrave Macmillan), pp. 33–43.

INDEX

Printed in Poland
by Amazon Fulfillment
Poland Sp. z o.o., Wrocław